COMPETING WITH HIGH QUALITY DATA

COMPETING WITH HIGH QUALITY DATA:

CONCEPTS, TOOLS, AND TECHNIQUES FOR BUILDING A SUCCESSFUL APPROACH TO DATA QUALITY

Rajesh Jugulum

WILEY

Cover Design: C. Wallace
Cover Illustration: Abstract Background © iStockphoto/ aleksandarvelasevic

This book is printed on acid-free paper. ∞

Copyright © 2014 by John Wiley & Sons, Inc. All rights reserved

Published by John Wiley & Sons, Inc., Hoboken, New Jersey
Published simultaneously in Canada

For general information about our other products and services, please contact our Customer Care Department within the United States at (800) 762-2974, outside the United States at (317) 572-3993 or fax (317) 572-4002.

Wiley publishes in a variety of print and electronic formats and by print-on-demand. Some material included with standard print versions of this book may not be included in e-books or in print-on-demand. If this book refers to media such as a CD or DVD that is not included in the version you purchased, you may download this material at http://booksupport.wiley .com. For more information about Wiley products, visit www.wiley.com.

Library of Congress Cataloging-in-Publication Data:

Jugulum, Rajesh.
    Competing with high quality data: concepts, tools, and techniques for building a successful approach to data quality / Rajesh Jugulum.
        pages cm
    Includes index.
        ISBN 978-1-118-34232-9 (hardback); ISBN: 978-1-118-41649-5 (ebk.);
ISBN: 978-1-118-42013-3 (ebk.); ISBN 978-1-118-84096-2 (ebk.).
1. Electronic data processing—Quality control.   2. Management.   I. Title.

    QA76.9.E95J84   2014
    004—dc23

                                                                    2013038107

Printed in the United States of America

10 9 8 7 6 5 4 3 2 1

Contents

Foreword

Over the past few years, there has been a dramatic shift in focus in infor
mation technology from the technology to the information. Inexpensive,
large-scale storage and high-performance computing systems, easy access
to cloud computing; and the widespread use of software-as-a-service, are
all contributing to the commoditization of technology. Organizations are
now beginning to realize that their competitiveness will be based on their
data, not on their technology, and that their data and information are
among their most important assets.

In this new data-driven environment, companies are increasingly utilizing analytical techniques to draw meaningful conclusions from data.
However, the garbage-in-garbage-out rule still applies. Analytics can only
be effective when the data being analyzed is of high quality. Decisions
made based on conclusions drawn from poor quality data can result in
equally poor outcomes resulting in significant losses and strategic mis-
steps for the company. At the same time, the seemingly countless numbers
of data elements that manifest themselves in the daily processes of a modern enterprise make the task of ensuring high data quality both difficult
and complex. A well-ground data quality program must understand the
complete environment of systems, architectures, people, and processes. It
must also be aligned with business goals and strategy and understand the
intended purposes associated with specific data elements in order to prioritize them, build business rules, calculate data quality scores, and then
take appropriate actions. To accomplish all of these things, companies
need to have a mature data quality capability that provides the services,
tools and governance to deliver tangible insights and business value from
the data. Firms with this capability will be able to make sounder decisions based on high quality data. Consistently applied, this discipline can
produce a competitive advantage for serious practitioners.

Those embarking on their journey to data quality will find this book to
be a most useful companion. The data quality concepts and approaches

are presented in a simple and straightforward manner. The relevant materials are organized into two sections- Section I focuses on building an effective data quality program, while Section II concentrates on the tools and techniques essential to the program's implementation and execution. In addition, this book explores the relationship between data analytics and high-quality data in the context of big data as well as providing other important data quality insights.

The application of the approaches and frameworks described in this book will help improve the level of data quality effectiveness and efficiency in any organization. One of the book's more salient features is the inclusion of case examples. These case studies clearly illustrate how the application of these methods has proven successful in actual instances.

This book is unique in the field of data quality as it comprehensively explains the creation of a data quality program from its initial planning to its complete implementation. I recommend this book as a valuable addition to the library of every data quality professional and business leader searching for a data quality framework that will, at journey's end, produce and ensure high quality data!

John R. Talburt
Professor of Information Science and Acxiom Chair of Information
Quality at the University of Arkansas at Little Rock (UALR)

Prelude

When I begin to invest my time reading a professional text, I wonder to what degree I can trust the material. I question whether it will be relevant for my challenge. And I hope that the author or authors have applied expertise that makes the pages in front of me worthy of my personal commitment. In a short number of short paragraphs I will address these questions, and describe how this book can best be leveraged.

I am a practicing data management executive, and I had the honor and privilege of leading the author and the contributors to this book through a very large-scale, extremely successful global data quality program design, implementation, and operation for one of the world's great financial services companies. The progressive topics of this book have been born from a powerful combination of academic/intellectual expertise and learning from applied business experience.

I have since moved from financial services to healthcare and am currently responsible for building an enterprise-wide data management program and capability for a global industry leader. I am benefiting greatly from the application of the techniques outlined in this book to positively affect the reliability, usability, accessibility, and relevance for my company's most important enterprise data assets. The foundation for this journey must be formed around a robust and appropriately pervasive data quality program.

Competing with High Quality Data chapter topics, such as how to construct a Data Quality Operating Model, can be raised to fully global levels, but can also provide meaningful lift at a departmental or data domain scale. The same holds true for utilizing Statistical Process Controls, Critical Data Element Identification and Prioritization, and the other valuable capability areas discussed in the book.

The subject areas also lead the reader from the basics of organizing an effort and creating relevance, all the way to utilizing sophisticated advanced techniques such as Data Quality Scorecards, Information System

Testing, Statistical Data Tracing, and Developing Multivariate Diagnostic Systems. Experiencing this range of capability is not only important to accommodate readers with different levels of experience, but also because the data quality improvement journey will often need to start with rudimentary base level improvements that later need to be pressed forward into finer levels of tuning and precision.

You can have confidence in the author and the contributors. You can trust the techniques, the approaches, and the systematic design brought forth throughout this book. They work. And they can carry you from data quality program inception to pervasive and highly precise levels of execution.

Don Gray
Head of Global Enterprise Data Management at Cigna

Preface

According to Dr. Genichi Taguchi's quality loss function (QLF), there is an associated loss when a quality characteristic deviates from its target value. The loss function concept can easily be extended to the data quality (DQ) world. If the quality levels associated with the data elements used in various decision-making activities are not at the desired levels (also known as *specifications* or *thresholds*), then calculations or decisions made based on this data will not be accurate, resulting in huge losses to the organization. The overall loss (referred to as "loss to society" by Dr. Taguchi) includes direct costs, indirect costs, warranty costs, reputation costs, loss due to lost customers, and costs associated with rework and rejection. The results of this loss include system breakdowns, company failures, and company bankruptcies. In this context, everything is considered part of society (customers, organizations, government, etc.). The effect of poor data quality during the global crisis that began in 2007 cannot be ignored because inadequate information technology and data architectures to support the management of risk were considered as one of the key factors.

Because of the adverse impacts that poor-quality data can have, organizations have begun to increase the focus on data quality in business in general, and they are viewing data as a critical resource like others such as people, capital, raw materials, and facilities. Many companies have started to establish a dedicated data management function in the form of the chief data office (CDO). An important component of the CDO is the data quality team, which is responsible for ensuring high quality levels for the underlying data and ensuring that the data is fit for its intended purpose. The responsibilities of the DQ constituent should include building an end-to-end DQ program and executing it with appropriate concepts, methods, tools, and techniques.

Much of this book is concerned with describing how to build a DQ program with an operating model that has a four-phase DAIC (Define, Assess, Improve, and Control) approach and showing how various concepts, tools, and techniques can be modified and tailored to solve DQ problems. In addition, discussions on data analytics (including the big data context) and establishing a data quality practices center (DQPC) are also provided.

This book is divided into two sections—Section I: Building a Data Quality program and Section II: Executing a Data Quality program—with 14 chapters covering various aspects of the DQ function. In the first section, the DQ operating model (DQOM) and the four-phase DAIC approach are described. The second section focuses on a wide range of concepts, methodologies, approaches, frameworks, tools, and techniques, all of which are required for successful execution of a DQ program. Wherever possible, case studies or illustrative examples are provided to make the discussion more interesting and provide a practical context. In Chapter 13, which focuses on data analytics, emphasis is given to having good quality data for analytics (even in the big data context) so that benefits can be maximized. The concluding chapter highlights the importance of building an enterprise-wide data quality practices center. This center helps organizations identify common enterprise problems and solve them through a systematic and standardized approach.

I believe that the application of approaches or frameworks provided in this book will help achieve the desired levels of data quality and that such data can be successfully used in the various decision-making activities of an enterprise. I also think that the topics covered in this book strike a balance between rigor and creativity. In many cases, there may be other methods for solving DQ problems. The methods in this book present some perspectives for designing a DQ problem-solving approach. In the coming years, the methods provided in this book may become elementary, with the introduction of newer methods. Before that happens, if the contents of this book help industries solve some important DQ problems, while minimizing the losses to society, then it will have served a fruitful purpose.

I would like to conclude this section with the following quote from Arthur Conan Doyle's *The Adventure of the Copper Beeches*:

"Data! Data!" I cried impatiently, "I cannot make bricks without clay."

I venture to modify this quote as follows:

"Good data! Good data!" I cried impatiently, "I cannot make usable bricks without good clay."

Rajesh Jugulum

Acknowledgments

Writing this book was a great learning experience. The project would not have been completed without help and support from many talented and outstanding individuals.

I would like to thank Joe Smialowski for his support and guidance provided by reviewing this manuscript and offering valuable suggestions. Joe was very patient in reviewing three versions of the manuscript, and he helped me to make sure that the contents are appropriate and made sense. I wish to thank Don Gray for the support he provided from the beginning of this project and writing the Prelude to the book. I also thank Professor John R Talburt for writing the Foreword and his helpful remarks to improve the contents of the book. Thanks are also due to Brian Bramson, Bob Granese, Chuan Shi, Chris Heien, Raji Ramachandran, Ian Joyce, Greg Somerville, and Jagmeet Singh for their help during this project. Bob and Brian contributed to two chapters in this book. Chuan deserves special credit for his efforts in the CDE-related chapters (Chapters 6 and 7), and sampling discussion in data tracing chapter (Chapter 11), and thanks to Ian for editing these chapters.

I would like to express my gratitude to Professor Nam P. Suh, and Dr. Desh Deshpande for the support provided by giving the quotes for the book.

I am also thankful to Ken Brzozowski and Jennifer Courant for the help provided in data tracing–related activities. Thanks are due to Shannon Bell for help in getting the required approvals for this book project.

I will always be indebted to late Dr. Genichi Taguchi for what he did for me. I believe his philosophy is helpful not only in industry-related activities, but also in day-to-day human activities. My thanks are always due to Professor K. Narayana Reddy, Professor A.K. Choudhury, Professor B.K. Pal, Mr. Shin Taguchi, Mr. R.C. Sarangi, and Professor Ken Chelst for their help and guidance in my activities.

I am very grateful to John Wiley & Sons for giving me an opportunity to publish this book. I am particularly thankful to Amanda Shettleton and Nancy Cintron for their continued cooperation and support for this project. They were quite patient and flexible in accommodating my requests. I would also like to thank Bob Argentieri, Margaret Cummins, and Daniel Magers for their cooperation and support in this effort.

Finally, I would like to thank my family for their help and support throughout this effort.

COMPETING WITH HIGH QUALITY DATA

Chapter 1

The Importance of Data Quality

1.0 INTRODUCTION

In this introductory chapter, we discuss the importance of data quality (DQ), understanding DQ implications, and the requirements for managing the DQ function. This chapter also sets the stage for the discussions in the other chapters of this book that focus on the building and execution of the DQ program. At the end, this chapter provides a guide to this book, with descriptions of the chapters and how they interrelate.

1.1 UNDERSTANDING THE IMPLICATIONS OF DATA QUALITY

Dr. Genichi Taguchi, who was a world-renowned quality engineering expert from Japan, emphasized and established the relationship between poor quality and overall loss. Dr. Taguchi (1987) used a quality loss function (QLF) to measure the loss associated with quality characteristics or parameters. The QLF describes the losses that a system suffers from an adjustable characteristic. According to the QLF, the loss increases as the characteristic y (such as thickness or strength) gets further from the target value (m). In other words, there is a loss associated if the quality characteristic diverges from the target. Taguchi regards this loss as a loss to society, and somebody must pay for this loss. The results of such losses include system breakdowns, company failures, company bankruptcies, and so forth. In this context, everything is considered part of society (customers, organizations, government, etc.).

Figure 1.1 shows how the loss arising from varying (on either side) from the target by Δ_0 increases and is given by $L(y)$. When y is equal to m,

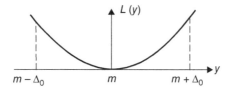

Figure 1.1   Quality Loss Function (QLF)

the loss is zero, or at the minimum. The equation for the loss function can be expressed as follows:

$$L(y) = k(y - m)^2 \tag{1.1}$$

where k is a factor that is expressed in dollars, based on direct costs, indirect costs, warranty costs, reputational costs, loss due to lost customers, and costs associated with rework and rejection. There are prescribed ways to determine the value of k.

The loss function is usually not symmetrical—sometimes it is steep on one side or on both sides. Deming (1960) says that the loss function need not be exact and that it is difficult to obtain the exact function. As most cost calculations are based on estimations or predictions, an approximate function is sufficient—that is, close approximation is good enough.

The concept of the loss function aptly applies in the DQ context, especially when we are measuring data quality associated with various data elements such as customer IDs, social security numbers, and account balances. Usually, the data elements are prioritized based on certain criteria, and the quality levels for data elements are measured in terms of percentages (of accuracy, completeness, etc.). The prioritized data elements are referred to as critical data elements (CDEs).

If the quality levels associated with these CDEs are not at the desired levels, then there is a greater chance of making wrong decisions, which might have adverse impacts on organizations. The adverse impacts may be in the form of losses, as previously described. Since the data quality levels are a "higher-the-better" type of characteristic (because we want to increase the percent levels), only half of Figure 1.1 is applicable when measuring loss due to poor data quality. Figure 1.2 is a better representation of this situation, showing how the loss due to variance from the target by Δ_0 increases when the quality levels are lower than m and is given

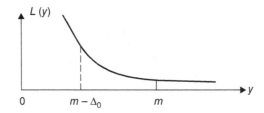

Figure 1.2   Loss Function for Data Quality Levels (Higher-the-Better
Type of Characteristic)

by $L(y)$. In this book, the target value is also referred to as the *business specification* or *threshold*.

As shown in Figure 1.2, the loss will be at minimum when y attains a level equal to m. This loss will remain at the same level even if the quality levels are greater than m. Therefore, it may be not be necessary to improve the CDE quality levels beyond m, as this improvement will not have any impact on the loss.

Losses due to poor quality can take a variety of forms (English, 2009), such as denying students entry to colleges, customer loan denial, incorrect prescription of medicines, crashing submarines, and inaccurate nutrition labeling on food products. In the financial industry context, consider a situation where a customer is denied a loan on the basis of a bad credit history because the loan application was processed using the wrong social security number. This is a good example of a data quality issue, and we can imagine how such issues can compound, resulting in huge losses to the organizations involved. The Institute of International Finance and McKinsey & Company (2011) cite one of the key factors in the global financial crisis that began in 2007 as inadequate information technology (IT) and data architecture to support the management of financial risk. This highlights the importance of data quality and leads us to conclude that the effect of poor data quality on the financial crisis cannot be ignored. During this crisis, many banks, investment companies, and insurance companies lost billions of dollars, causing some to go bankrupt. The impacts of these events were significant and included economic recession, millions of foreclosures, lost jobs, depletion of retirement funds, and loss of confidence in the industry and in the government.

All the aforementioned impacts can be classified into two categories, as described in Taguchi (1987): losses due to the functional variability of the

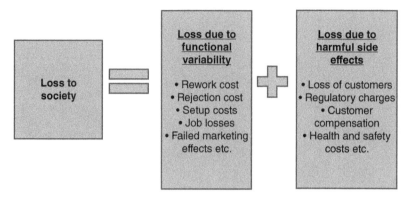

Figure 1.3   Sources of Societal Losses

process and losses due to harmful side effects. Figure 1.3 shows how all the costs in these categories add up.

In this section, we discussed the importance of data quality and the implications of bad data. It is clear that the impact of bad data is quite significant and that it is important to manage key data resources effectively to minimize overall loss. For this reason, there is a need to establish a dedicated data management function that is responsible for ensuring high data quality levels. Section 1.2 briefly describes the establishment of such a function and its various associated roles.

1.2   THE DATA MANAGEMENT FUNCTION

In some organizations, the data management function is referred to as the *chief data office* (CDO), and it is responsible for the oversight of various data-related activities. One way of overseeing data-related activities is to separate them into different components such as data governance, data strategies, data standards, and data quality. The *data governance* component is important because it navigates subsequent data-related activities. This includes drivers such as steering committees, program management aspects, project and change management aspects, compliance with organization requirements, and similar functions. The *data strategy* component is useful for understanding the data and planning how to use it effectively. The *data standards* component is responsible for ensuring that the various parties using the data share the same understanding across the organization. This is accomplished by developing standards around various data elements and data models. The *data quality* component is responsible for cleaning the data and making sure that it is fit for the intended purpose, so it can be used in various decision-making activities. This group should work closely with the data strategy component.

Please note that we are presenting one of the several possible ways of overseeing the data management function, or CDO. The CDO function should work closely with various functions, business units, and technology groups across the organization to ensure that data is interpreted consistently in all functions of the organization and is fit for the intended purposes. An effective CDO function should demonstrate several key attributes, including the following:

- Clear leadership and senior management support
- Key data-driven objectives
- A visual depiction of target areas for prioritization
- A tight integration of CDO objectives with company priorities and objectives
- A clear benefit to the company upon execution

As this book focuses on data quality, various chapters provide descriptions of the approaches, frameworks, methods, concepts, tools, and techniques that can be used to satisfy the various DQ requirements, including the following:

- Developing a DQ standard operating model (DQOM) so that it can be adopted by all DQ projects
- Identifying and prioritizing critical data elements
- Establishing a DQ monitoring and controlling scheme
- Solving DQ issues and performing root-cause analyses (RCAs)
- Defining and deploying data tracing and achieving better data lineage
- Quantifying the impact of poor data quality

All of these requirements are necessary to ensure that data is fit for its purpose with a high degree of confidence.

Sections 1.3 and 1.4 explain the solution strategy for DQ problems, as well as the organization of this book, with descriptions of the chapters. The main objective of these chapters is that readers should be able to use the concepts, procedures, and tools discussed in them to meet DQ requirements and solve various DQ problems.

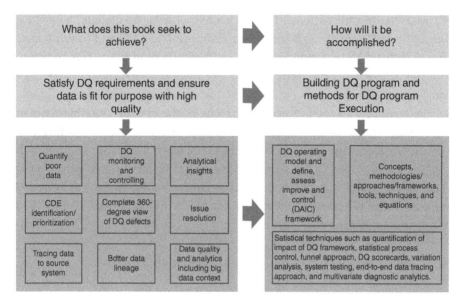

Figure 1.4   DQ Solution Strategy

1.3   THE SOLUTION STRATEGY

Given the preference for satisfying DQ-related requirements while ensuring fitness of the data with high quality levels, the top-level solution strategy focuses on building the DQ program and designing the methods for executing it. Having chosen a top-level solution strategy, the subrequirements can be defined as shown in Figure 1.4.

Much of this book is concerned with expanding the solution strategy shown in Figure 1.4 with the help of a set of equations, concepts, and methods. In addition, discussions on data analytics (including the big data context) and establishing a data quality practices center (DQPC) are also provided.

1.4   GUIDE TO THIS BOOK

The chapters of this book are divided into two sections. Section I describes how to build a data quality program and Section II describes how to execute the data quality program.

Section I: Building a Data Quality Program. The first section includes two chapters that describe the DQ operating model and DQ methodology. Chapter 2 emphasizes the importance of the data quality program structure, objectives, and management routines, and the portfolio of projects that need to be focused on to build and institutionalize processes that drive business value. Chapter 3 provides a description of the DQ methodology with the four-phase Define, Assess, Improve, and Control (DAIC) approach. The emphasis here is on ensuring that every DQ project follows these phases to reduce costs, reduce manual processing or rework, improve reporting, or enhance the revenue opportunity.

Section II: Executing a Data Quality Program. The second section includes the remaining chapters of the book, which cover a wide range of concepts, methods, approaches, frameworks, tools, and techniques that are required for successful execution of a DQ program. Chapter 4 focuses on the quantification of the impacts of poor data quality. Chapter 5 describes statistical process control (SPC) techniques and their relevance in DQ monitoring and reporting. Chapters 6 and 7 describe the CDE identification, validation, and prioritization process, and Chapter 8 describes the importance of designing DQ scorecards and how they can be used for monitoring and reporting purposes. Chapter 9 provides an approach to resolve various issues affecting data quality. These issues can be related directly to the data or the processes providing the data.

Chapter 10 provides a methodology to identify issues or problems in source systems or operational data sources with an experimental design based approach. Chapter 11 discusses an end-to-end approach for performing data tracing so that prioritized CDEs can be traced back to the source system and proper corrective actions can be taken. Chapter 12 focuses on effective use of information to design multivariate diagnostic systems so that we can make appropriate business decisions. Chapter 13 highlights the importance of data quality to perform high-quality analytics including the big data context. This chapter also discusses the role of data innovation and its relevance in modern industry. Chapter 14, which is the concluding chapter, focuses on building a data quality practices center that has the operational capabilities to provide DQ services and satisfy all DQ requirements.

Table 1.1 shows a summary of all the chapters of this book.

Table 1.1   Guide to This Book—Descriptions of Chapters

Section/Chapter		Description
Chapter 1		This introductory chapter discusses the importance of data quality (DQ), understanding DQ implications, and the requirements for managing the data quality function.
Section I	Chapter 2	This chapter describes the building of a comprehensive approach and methodology (referred to as the data quality operating model) that allows us to understand the current state of data quality, organize around information critical to the enterprise and the business, and implement practices and processes for data quality measurement.
	Chapter 3	This chapter discusses the four-phased Define, Assess, Improve, and Control approach that can be used to execute DQ projects. This comprehensive approach helps readers understand several aspects of the DQ project life cycle.
Section II	Chapter 4	This chapter focuses on the methodology that can be used to quantify the impact of poor-quality data with an illustrative example.
	Chapter 5	Chapter 5 describes the importance of statistical process control (SPC) along with descriptions of various control charts and the relevance of SPC in DQ monitoring and control.
	Chapter 6	This chapter discusses how to identify CDEs, validate CDEs, and conduct CDE assessment with the help of data quality rules and data quality scores.
	Chapter 7	This chapter discusses how to prioritize these CDEs and reduce the number of CDEs to be measured using the funnel approach. It also demonstrates the applicability of this approach using a case study.

Table 1.1 *(continued)*

Section/Chapter		Description
Section II	Chapter 8	The purpose of this chapter is to describe a means to construct and implement effective DQ scorecards. Using the proposed approach, users can store, sort, and retrieve DQ defect information and perform remediation through statistical analysis.
	Chapter 9	This chapter explains the linkage between data quality and process quality by providing an approach to resolve various issues affecting data quality. These issues can be related directly to the data or the processes providing the data
	Chapter 10	This chapter describes a methodology that can be used to test the performance of a given system and identify failing factors that are responsible for poor information/data quality.
	Chapter 11	This chapter describes the end-to-end data tracing methodology, its important aspects, and how it can be linked to data lineage to improve data quality accuracy.
	Chapter 12	This chapter describes the Mahalanobis-Taguchi Strategy (MTS) and its applicability to developing a multivariate diagnostic system with a measurement scale. This type of diagnostic system is helpful in utilizing high-quality data in an effective way to come to meaningful conclusions.
	Chapter 13	This chapter briefly discusses the importance of data quality to performing high-quality analytics (including the big data context) and making appropriate decisions based on the analytics. It also discusses the role of data innovation and its relevance in modern industry.
	Chapter 14	This chapter focuses on building a data quality practices center (DQPC) and its fundamental building blocks. Such a center will have the operational capability to provide services, tools, governance, and outputs to deliver tangible insights and business value from the data.

Section I

Building a Data Quality Program

Chapter 2

The Data Quality Operating Model[1]

2.0 INTRODUCTION

As mentioned in Chapter 1, the core purpose of the DQ program is to satisfy various requirements that ensure the data is fit for its intended purpose and that it is of high quality. In order to satisfy these requirements, we must have a systematic DQ program that can be applied to various DQ-related projects. The data quality program structure, objectives, management routines, and portfolio of projects need to be focused on building and institutionalizing processes and project results that drive business value. This chapter describes the building of such a comprehensive approach and methodology (referred to as the data quality operating model, or DQOM), which allows us to understand the current state of data quality, organize around information critical to the enterprise and the business, and implement practices and processes for data quality measurement.

2.1 DATA QUALITY FOUNDATIONAL CAPABILITIES

The process of building and strengthening the data quality program requires a concerted effort across business, technology, operations, and executive teams. The focus throughout is to continuously build, enhance, and extend the DQ capabilities across the organization. Once implemented, these capabilities constitute a steady-state operating environment that actively defines, manages, measures, and improves the quality of the data that is critical to key business processes throughout the enterprise. In the process of doing this, the business can achieve

[1] **Brian Bramson** is thanked for generously contributing this chapter.

more comprehensive, complete, valid, accurate, and timely informa-tion, enabling better decision making and faster and more accurate responses to customers and regulators. Additional benefits, including cost and resource efficiencies, enhanced decision making, and reve-nue-generating opportunities, can be derived by implementing the data quality operating model. The model described in this chapter is designed to establish data quality capabilities while building robust program structures and executing data quality improvement projects. As project teams work on the various aspects of the program planning and execution, they should find that each and every task contributes to such benefits. Stronger data quality capabilities increase confidence in the data that supports products, services, analytics, and reporting. These capabilities also increase the effectiveness and efficiency of the company's operations. The following is a list of various DQ capabilities, along with brief descriptions.

2.1.1   Program Strategy and Governance

Strategy and governance include a plan for understanding the current state of data quality for critical data and how to improve DQ to meet the strategic goals of the enterprise. The data quality governance should be aligned with the existing data governance structure, policies, and processes. The DQ program must have a governance structure with associated management disciplines, including established roles as well as organizational commitment, sponsorship, and leadership at senior management levels.

2.1.2   Skilled Data Quality Resources

These resources correspond to relevant data quality roles, including skilled staff capable of executing the program, projects, and capabilities and managing associated processes. This staff must be knowledgeable about the data and associated processes and empowered to improve processes and systems as needed. Skilled resources, which include data quality analysts, technology and operations leads, and project and pro-gram management professionals, are required to support projects as well as the ongoing operational routines. These include defining, gath-ering, and managing the metadata; performing data quality analytics including root-cause analysis (RCA); conducting profiling and assessment activities; managing ongoing data quality monitoring; and performing issues processing.

2.1.3   Technology Infrastructure and Metadata

This capability includes the methods and tools required to measure, analyze, report, define, collect, and manage information associated with critical data (i.e., data required for critical processes and reporting). This means evaluating and recommending data quality tools (e.g., rules engines, data profiling tools) and developing scorecard and dashboard templates and a data quality metadata repository.

The foundation of any data quality program lies in full understanding of the key processes, systems, and data required to support ongoing business operations. This information provides the context for all subsequent data quality activities and supports repeatable DQ processes. Metadata is gathered in the context of the execution of data quality projects and includes institutionalizing DQ rule descriptions, results, data profiles, error descriptions, and data steward and process ownership information. Successful data quality programs must establish the means to gather, manage, and update this information.

2.1.4   Data Profiling and Analytics

This includes the processes, tools, and skilled resources required to identify the characteristics and understand the meaning and structure of critical data, conduct root-cause and impact analyses, and develop conclusions and recommendations about the state of the critical data. Data quality analysts use data profiling techniques to investigate the characteristics of subject data sets. Data profiling results are essential for completing the activities associated with defining data quality rules for assessment and conducting ongoing analyses of target data sets.

2.1.5   Data Integration

This capability involves determining the lineage of the business, operations, and technology processes by which data enrichment, acquisition, composition, and capture occur. Data integration also addresses the control processes that are used to monitor data integrity as data flows from upstream sources to downstream consumers.

2.1.6   Data Assessment

This capability is the combination of methodologies, analysis, and data quality rules used in measuring the quality of critical data. Assessments establish data quality levels for critical data at specified points within the data flow. This includes pre- and postdata acquisition, postprocessing, and pre–downstream subscription.

Assessment results, including the records whose critical data elements "fail" in one or more data quality rules, are presented for monitoring and analysis on a data quality scorecard. This scorecard, which provides a basis for detailed analyses of data quality across defined measures of data quality, or *dimensions* (discussed later in this chapter), is then used during ongoing monitoring and control activities. Additionally, assessment results form the basis of a formal data quality improvement plan that is developed in order to meet business-driven quality expectations.

2.1.7   Issues Resolution (IR)

The IR process encompasses the identification, triage, tracking, and updating of data quality issues. The IR triage and review processes include root-cause determination and remediation efforts and are executed through a governance process that includes business, operations, and technology. Data quality issues may result from initial (baseline) data quality assessments, from rule breaches detected during assessments performed as part of the periodic monitoring of critical data, or from observations received from business and/or operations personnel during normal business activities and operations. Through this process, the data quality team determines the root cause, proposes solutions, establishes return on investment for those solutions, and gets the data quality improvement projects in the queue with the correct priority based on the business value.

2.1.8   Data Quality Monitoring and Control

Monitoring and control are the ongoing processes and activities of measuring data quality throughout its life cycle. This is the steady state, in which critical data is managed in a controlled environment, where accountabilities, escalations, and actions in response to poor data quality are defined and agreed upon. Data quality teams will establish ongoing routines and processes to monitor the quality levels of defined critical data. These include operational-level review and management of indicators of poor quality, as well as resolution and logging within the IR processes. Also, this steady state includes established change management routines; design, development, and execution of data quality rules; fine-tuning based on subject-matter expert (SME) feedback; identification of the cost of any detected data quality issues; and prioritization of data quality improvement based on return on investment.

2.2   THE DATA QUALITY METHODOLOGY

It is important for an organization to implement the aforementioned strong data quality capabilities to improve the quality of data used in its key processes, with a structured and standardized approach for program implementation and project execution. This includes taking into account of the current state of affairs, building robust program governance and strategy, defining a set of data quality issues and projects, and establishing ongoing steady-state processes. To achieve these, the program should undertake the following four major work streams.

2.2.1   Establish a Data Quality Program

Once the current state of the data quality infrastructure is understood, the executive sponsor needs to build a robust governance structure that includes business, operations, and technology participants. This will be used to facilitate execution of data quality projects and support the eventual steady-state operating environment to be built at later stages. This process includes defining a program charter that states the business value resulting from improved data quality (this is the key measure of success for the program and subsequent efforts), as well as the scope of the program in terms of business processes and systems. In addition, the program should determine the operational support and technology applications through which the data quality capabilities are to be delivered. A detailed discussion on establishing a DQ program is explained in section 2.2.5.

2.2.2   Conduct a Current-State Analysis

This work stream should focus on assessing existing practices, management routines, and reporting and control processes. The results should clearly document data quality practices, key stakeholders, systems, and reporting.

It is important, during this exercise, that the team captures an initial set of issues that may be driving data quality. Any gaps and issues identified in this effort will be accounted for during the execution of data quality projects.

2.2.3   Strengthen Data Quality Capability through Data Quality Projects

The program, led by the executive sponsor, will build an associated data quality capability within the context of executing data quality projects. Here, the focus is on improving the quality of critical data, getting to the root cause, fixing data quality issues, and engaging in proactive measurement as the catalyst for implementing better data quality management practices. The first of these projects is likely to take more time as processes and capabilities are put in place and the organization has its first experience of executing against the methodology. However, as more projects are executed, these capabilities and processes will mature, the execution time will decrease, and the results will have greater impact.

2.2.4   Monitor the Ongoing Production Environment and Measure Data Quality Improvement Effectiveness

In this final stage, the program ensures that ongoing monitoring of production data is leveraged and assessment, profiling results, and scorecards are established during project execution. This stage should also ensure, through a systematic issue resolution (IR) process, that DQ issues are detected and addressed properly. In a steady state, data quality improvement should be prioritized based on the key business value defined during the project initiation.

In the subsequent sections, we discuss the first two work streams: establishing the DQ program and assessing the current state of DQ in greater depth. In Chapter 3, we discuss the remaining two work streams as they are related to the four-phase DAIC (Define, Assess, Improve, and Control) approach.

2.2.5   Detailed Discussion on Establishing the Data Quality Program

In this work stream, the executive sponsor establishes the data quality program with the governance structure (roles, management routines, etc.), the technology environment (assessment tools, analytical tools, metadata environment, etc.), the project portfolio, defined operational resources and procedures including issues management tools and routines, and a resource plan (including a training plan as applicable). At the end of this stage of the program, the team should be able to deliver a robust formal business value–based program charter. This work stream is also responsible for delivering the following four important activities.

Program Communications

Because it is important in any successful program, effective communication of the core objectives and purpose of the program establish the foundation for the work and resource requests to follow. A workshop approach is one effective way to achieve this. The executive sponsor leads the workshop with key stakeholders to introduce the data quality program and helps them start to work on the current-state capabilities analysis. During the kickoff, the stakeholders document business processes, products, and deliverables that are critical for high-quality data. They also document critical data, systems that support business processes and outcomes, and the known data quality issues. The group reviews the data quality project approach and identifies key phase deliverables and roles. The kickoff concludes with a discussion of roles and responsibilities and management routines.

Define Governance Structure with a Charter

The charter is the data quality program's most important document, and it focuses on the business case (i.e., the business value to be realized by improving low-quality data). In addition, the governance structure must be documented by formalizing roles and responsibilities. This enables the executive sponsor to obtain resource commitments. The charter also includes the scope, program strategy, governance and management routines, and operational and technology support.

Configure Technology Environments

This activity focuses on configuring the specific toolsets that will be used for data quality assessments and issues management. The technology team then makes a formal recommendation to the executive sponsor, including the support required for the DQ program. An execution plan is also presented as part of the recommendations. The technology environment should include the functionalities shown in Table 2.1.

Table 2.1 Desired Functionalities in Technology Environment

Functionality	Description
Profiling	Tool selection needs to include a robust profiling tool that allows the analyst to dig into the nature of target data sets to understand the current state of data. There are many tools in the market, but we have seen simple off-the-shelf tools used effectively in the right hands.
Data Quality Rules	Data quality rules help validate various data relationships and identification and correct classification of the majority of data problems. The key here is to discover all data quality rules and make sure they are well understood.
Metadata	A key to the success of the program and subsequent projects is effective metadata governance and management. It is critical to select a tool that allows for the institutionalization of the information you gather as the program matures and projects are executed, as well as one that allows for ease of access and use of that information. *Metadata* is a broad term, so the program team needs to clearly define what metadata needs to be collected. This includes information such as governance and roles (e.g., data stewards); systems; data dictionaries; extract, transfer, load (ETL) and data lineage detail; and data quality profiling and assessment results.
Issues Management	This functionality may also be part of the metadata or reporting environments, but should include a workflow and escalation capability. Here, you should be able to track data quality issues coming from your ongoing assessments as well as other sources, and manage those issues through triage, root-cause analysis, and remediation.
Analytics	As the program matures and larger sets of data quality results are available, it is important to begin to conduct deeper analytics. This includes simple trending to more sophisticated statistical analytics described elsewhere in this book.
Reporting and Project Management	It is important to have strong, automated reporting and project management tools. Programs can get bogged down in too much administrative work and consume precious resources in building reports and communications. Robust tools to automate this work and, wherever possible, formalize and simplify the project and program management activities are important.

Define Monitor and Control Operating Guidelines

Data quality monitoring and issue management are capabilities that require special attention when establishing any data quality program. The operations and technology teams will establish resources and processes to support ongoing data quality assessment and monitoring activities.

2.2.6 Assess the Current State of Data Quality

This work stream provides a baseline understanding of a business area's ability to define, manage, track, and improve data quality. The objective here is to gain a clear documented view of the organization's current data quality capabilities. This will be instrumental in defining the portfolio of projects by prioritizing areas for improvement by leveraging existing processes, tools, and specified gaps. This work stream is responsible for delivering the following three important activities.

Define Scope and Document Current State

The executive sponsor and team will lead the effort to identify and contact individuals and/or groups affected by the data quality efforts. This includes not only data management and technology teams and administrators, but also business line consumers, analysts, and operational users. Documentation and artifacts are solicited from the key stakeholders to support data quality capabilities for the given process or business area. These artifacts should illustrate data quality capabilities, governance and program documentation, existing data quality architecture, data dictionaries and models, assessment results, operational dashboards, and reporting. The assessment of capabilities should be based on the documentation collected and interviews with stakeholders and subject-matter experts. This assessment should rate each business area against the capabilities, as described earlier.

Collect Data Quality Details and Key Issues

While conducting the capability assessment, the team should collect a list of data quality issues (and associated measures where available). This is similar to conducting a survey of data quality. What are the key pain points? Which critical data sets are having particular issues? Are managers confident in the information they are using? Are there customer issues driven by data quality problems? Answers to these questions should be documented and then prioritized.

Prepare a Data Quality Capabilities
Gap Analysis Report

Through this activity, a DQ capabilities gap analysis report has to be prepared to address any weaknesses within current data quality capabilities. This gap analysis is a major input in program building and planning. Identified weaknesses in capability are mitigated through the execution of data quality projects.

2.3   CONCLUSIONS

The following are the conclusions of this chapter:

- This chapter highlights the importance of having a data quality operating model with a program structure with clearly defined objectives and management routines. With the DQ plan in place, it is important to focus on projects that drive business value. Establishment of a data quality program is very important for maximizing business value from good-quality data.
- Sound data quality capabilities are required to increase the effectiveness and efficiency of the operations across the enterprise, thereby increasing the level of confidence in the data that supports products, services, analytics, and reporting.

Chapter 3 describes the four-phase DAIC approach and includes discussions of the last two work streams of the DQ program that are related to the portfolio of DQ projects and monitoring and control aspects.

Chapter 3

The DAIC Approach[1]

3.0   INTRODUCTION

As discussed, DQ programs contribute to building capability with the help of four important work streams to successfully manage and implement data quality. In Chapter 2, we discussed the first two work streams that are related to DQ governance structure. In this chapter, we discuss the remaining two work streams that are focused on the portfolio of DQ projects and the monitoring and control aspects with the Define, Improve, Analyze, and Control (DAIC) approach. This comprehensive approach helps us understand the current state of data quality, organize around information critical to the enterprise and the business, and implementation practices and processes for data quality measurement and improvement.

There are many standard project methodologies, such as Six Sigma approaches (like DMAIC and DMADV), that can be leveraged to create a DQ project approach to ensure good project execution. Before going into the details of the proposed DQ approach, let us briefly discuss Six Sigma methodologies.

3.1   SIX SIGMA METHODOLOGIES

The Six Sigma is a business process methodology that allows companies to drastically improve their operational performance by designing and monitoring their business activities in ways that minimize waste and resource use while maximizing customer satisfaction through a collection of managerial, engineering, design, and statistical concepts. As described in Jugulum and Samuel (2008), Motorola first employed Six Sigma for

[1] **Brian Bramson** is thanked for generously contributing to this chapter.

quality improvement and to gain competitive advantage for its electronic products. AlliedSignal then focused Six Sigma projects on cost reduction to realize over \$2 billion in savings in a four-year period. General Electric's success with Six Sigma in the 1990s convinced other organizations to embrace the methodology. Similarly, finance companies like the Bank of America have also realized the importance of Six Sigma methodology and introduced it in their firms. Many billions of dollars have been saved through the implementation of Six Sigma projects. Six Sigma methodologies revolve around the concept of variation. Variation exists everywhere in nature. No two objects in nature are exactly identical. Variation affects product performance, data quality, service quality, and process outputs, leading to rework, scrap, and premium freight, all of which can cause customer dissatisfaction. Variation causes uncertainty, risk, and potential defects. There are two types of variation: controllable (or assignable) variation and uncontrollable (or chance) variation.

Uncontrollable variation, often referred to as *common cause,* is a stable or consistent pattern of variation over time (predictable). *Controllable variation,* referred to as *special cause variation,* is a pattern that changes over time (unpredictable). To control and reduce variation, we should first understand, quantify, and interpret variation in a process or system. The purpose of Six Sigma methodologies is to identify the areas of variation, isolate root causes, optimize processes, and thereby reduce or minimize the impact of variation in products, processes, and services.

The fundamental approach with Six Sigma is embodied in the equation $Y = f(x)$. Y represents the dependent or the output variable we are interested in for improvement. It can be a quality parameter such as reliability, yield, or market share. x is an independent or input variable that affects the output variable Y. Our objective is to characterize the relationship between Y and x. Once we understand this relationship, we can leverage the key variable to optimize the process and achieve the desired level of performance for Y. Six Sigma has a set of techniques that enables us to characterize and optimize the relationship between Y and x.

The Six Sigma approach helps organizations achieve a rapid rate of improvement in cost, quality, process speed, safety, customer satisfaction, invested capital, and environment. Every Six Sigma project typically follows the "importance of measurement" philosophy. The Six Sigma approach has been successfully applied in almost every type of industry, from retail to financial services to pharmaceuticals to healthcare to high technology and electronics, and to nuclear power generation.

3.1.1   Development of Six Sigma Methodologies

Six Sigma was first developed as a statistics-based methodology to "Define, Measure, Analyze, Improve, and Control" (DMAIC) manufacturing processes. To this end, its ultimate performance target is virtually defect-free processes and products (Six Sigma being the measure of 3.4 defects per million). Over a period of time, Six Sigma has evolved to become a vision, philosophy, goal, metric, improvement methodology, management system, and customer-centric strategy.

In the fields of probability and statistics, *sigma* (σ) represents the standard deviation, a measure of variability. Generally, the term *Six Sigma process* or *sigma level of a process* or *sigma value of a process* means that if we have six standard deviations between the mean of a process and the specification limits, virtually no item will exceed the specification limits or business-defined thresholds.

As shown in Figure 3.1, the commonly accepted definition of a Six Sigma process is one that produces 3.4 defects per million opportunities. The defect calculations are based on normal distribution, as all the quality characteristics are assumed to follow this distribution. In an ideal world, the normally distributed characteristics will be perfectly situated at a mean or nominal value, but in reality that is not the case, as the

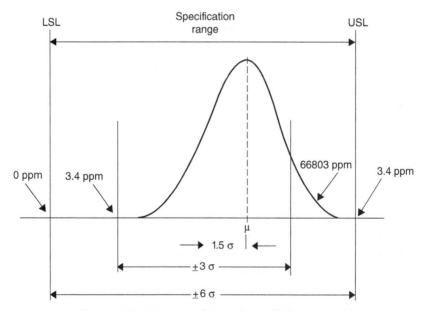

Figure 3.1   Concept of Variation and Sigma Level
Source: Six-Sigma Quality Programs by Fred R. McFadden published in Quality Progress (26)6, June 1993). Reprinted with permission from QP © 1993 ASQ, http://asq.org.

Table 3.1   Magnitude of Sigma Levels

PPM	Sigma Level	PPM	Sigma Level	PPM	Sigma Level
3.4	**6**	233	5.00	30000	3.38
4	5.97	400	4.85	40000	3.25
5	5.91	500	4.79	50000	3.14
6	5.88	600	4.74	66807	3.00
7	5.84	700	4.69	>66807	<3
8	5.82	800	4.66		
9	5.78	900	4.62		
10	5.77	1000	4.59		
20	5.61	2000	4.38		
30	5.51	3000	4.25		
40	5.44	4000	4.15		
50	5.39	5000	4.08		
60	5.35	6210	4.00		
70	5.31	7000	3.96		
80	5.27	8000	3.91		
90	5.25	9000	3.87		

Assumes a process shift of ±1.5 sigma. Calculations are based on Normal distribution and the approach given in (McFadden, 1993) and discussion provided in Quality Digest Column "Six Sigma and Beyond—The 1.5 Sigma Shift" by Thomas Pyzdek. URL for this discussion: www.qualitydigest.com/may01/html/sixsigma.html.

characteristics tend to deviate from the mean or nominal value. There is empirical evidence (McFadden, 1993) that in an average process the mean shifts by 1.5 times sigma over a long period of time. For this reason, all defect calculations are based on a 1.5 sigma (σ) process shift from the mean or nominal value. Table 3.1 shows the magnitude of various sigma levels for any given process, highlighting the importance of Six Sigma.

As mentioned, the Six Sigma approach is a business process–related project-driven methodology. These projects are executed through the DMAIC (Define, Measure, Analyze, Improve, and Control) process. This methodology can be carried out in the steps shown in Figure 3.2.

The DMAIC Six Sigma approach is useful when we are improving a particular process and aim to reduce the defect rate. If a particular process requires major redesign or if we need to design a product or process from the beginning, it is recommended that we use the *Design for Six Sigma* (DFSS) methodology. This DFSS methodology is also called the DMADV (Define, Measure, Analyze, Design, and Verify) approach. The five phases of DMADV are clearly described in Figure 3.3.

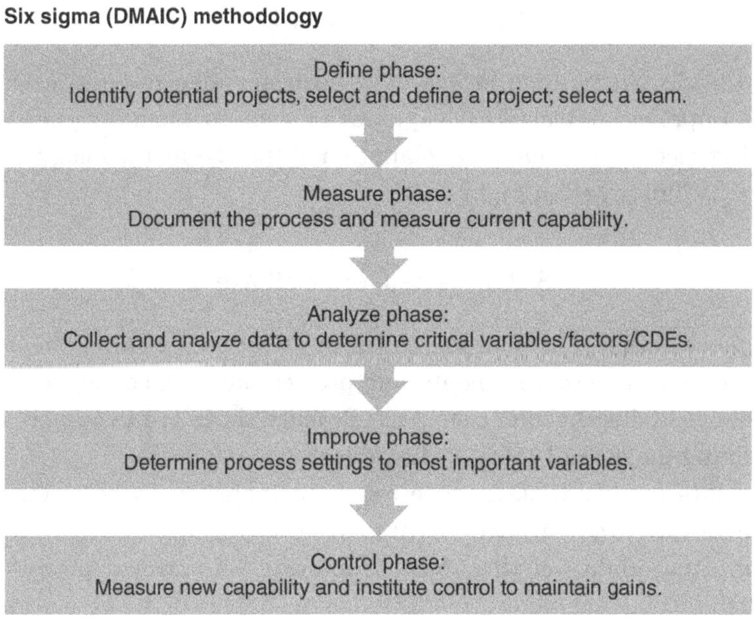

Six sigma (DMAIC) methodology

Define phase:
Identify potential projects, select and define a project; select a team.

Measure phase:
Document the process and measure current capabliity.

Analyze phase:
Collect and analyze data to determine critical variables/factors/CDEs.

Improve phase:
Determine process settings to most important variables.

Control phase:
Measure new capability and institute control to maintain gains.

Figure 3.2 DMAIC Methodology

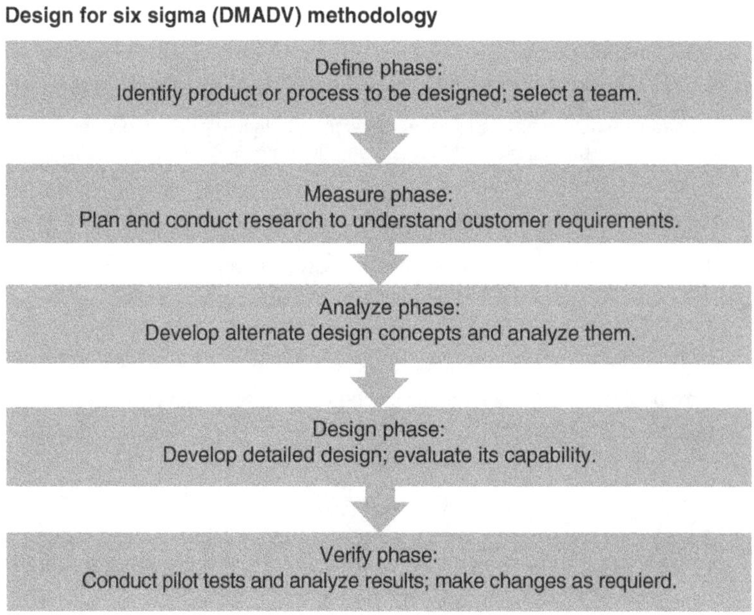

Design for six sigma (DMADV) methodology

Define phase:
Identify product or process to be designed; select a team.

Measure phase:
Plan and conduct research to understand customer requirements.

Analyze phase:
Develop alternate design concepts and analyze them.

Design phase:
Develop detailed design; evaluate its capability.

Verify phase:
Conduct pilot tests and analyze results; make changes as requierd.

Figure 3.3 DFSS Methodology

3.2   DAIC APPROACH FOR DATA QUALITY

Here, the Six Sigma approaches have been modified to build a Define-Assess-Improve-Control (DAIC) approach for improving data quality. The following sections provide an explanation of the DQ methodology and its phases, as illustrated in Figure 3.4.

3.2.1   The Define Phase

This phase focuses on defining the project by establishing the scope, objectives, resource commitments, and project plans, and ensuring strong governance and stakeholder support. Broadly, there are two approaches for defining the overall scope of the project.

The data quality project scope can be established by selecting data critical to the targeted business process. The project focuses on understanding the quality of that data supporting this critical process and establishing ongoing monitoring likewise in support of the given process. Any resulting data quality issues are then investigated via root-cause analysis, and remediation is managed through an established issue management capability.

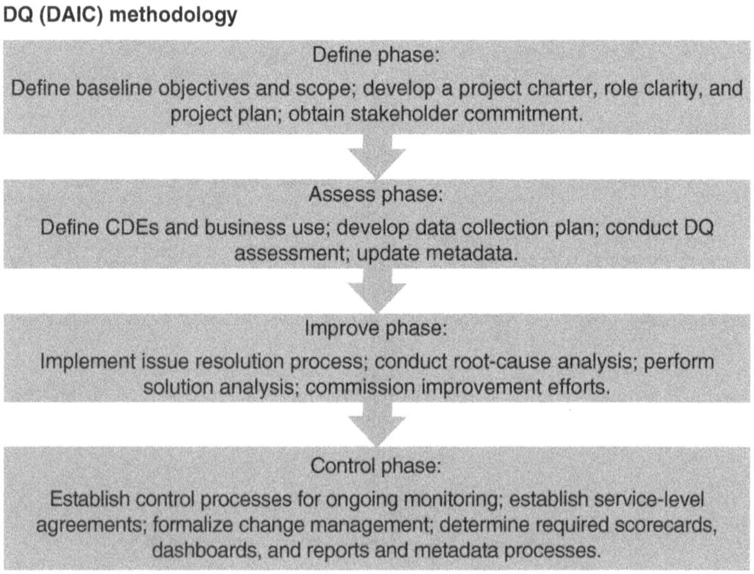

DQ (DAIC) methodology

Define phase:
Define baseline objectives and scope; develop a project charter, role clarity, and project plan; obtain stakeholder commitment.

Assess phase:
Define CDEs and business use; develop data collection plan; conduct DQ assessment; update metadata.

Improve phase:
Implement issue resolution process; conduct root-cause analysis; perform solution analysis; commission improvement efforts.

Control phase:
Establish control processes for ongoing monitoring; establish service-level agreements; formalize change management; determine required scorecards, dashboards, and reports and metadata processes.

Figure 3.4   DQ Methodology (DAIC)

The data quality project scope can also be established by selecting from the set of known DQ issues collected during the current-state analysis. Here, the project focuses on resolving key pain points with the quality of the data used in a given business process. For example, the objective in this case might read:

"In order to ensure the data quality of customer statements, we will define, assess, and measure critical data supporting statements related to products x1 through x4, and establish strong ongoing DQ processes and monitoring in compliance with enterprise DQ standards. The process for gathering and cleansing the required data for these reports is currently estimated at x\$ FTE and takes y days. It is expected that improvement in the data quality will alleviate the resource requirement for cleansing so that these resources may be used for greater value-added customer and product analysis."

Regardless of how the data quality project is scoped, the project will enhance the data quality capability as follows:

- The metadata capability grows stronger through the knowledge obtained.
- The skills of the data quality personnel performing the projects grow stronger as profiling and assessment tools and associated data quality practices are utilized.
- The control capability grows stronger through the addition of new data quality scorecards.
- The issue resolution capability grows stronger through data quality issue logging, root-cause determination, and solution selection.

The following are the activities in the Define phase:

Project charter: The most important activity in the Define phase is the creation of the project charter. The project team establishes the scope and expected business value and creates the project charter. The charter needs to frame the data quality project and determine the objectives, scope, key participants, and resources. It should also outline broad time frames and core deliverables. A typical project charter should have the components shown in Table 3.2.

Role clarity: In the Define phase, the team must clarify the roles related to the DQ project and identify all responsible parties. Typical roles and descriptions of these roles are shown in Table 3.3.

Table 3.2   Project Charter Contents

Charter Content	Description	Example		
Project Objective	Clear objective that can be evidenced by a success measure	"Reduce the number of customer transaction statements that require manual interventions in order to improve straight-through processing by the end of first quarter of 2014. Current manual interventions account for 3 FTEs per month and result in restatements and cost $xxx."		
Scope	Detailed scope statements that define process, systems, and data that will be included in the effort, as well as outlining goals and intended outcomes	The project will review data from customer transaction systems to support statement processing within the reporting operations. The effort will result in implementation of the data quality monitoring and issues management activities.		
Roles	Estimate resource requirements, roles	• DQ Analyst—1FTE • Project Manager—.5FTE • Operations—1FTE • Technology Analyst—1FTE		
Timeline	Project phase timetables, tollgate/milestone dates, and key deliverables	**Define**	**Charter Project Plan**	**dd/mm**
		Assess	• Data dictionary • DQ rules, dimensions, and thresholds • Data collection plan • Assessment results/error records • Data quality scorecard	dd/mm
		Improve	• Issues list • Root-cause results • Solutions/remediation • Recommendations (with ROI)	dd/mm
		Control	• Service-level agreement with transaction systems • Monitoring plan • Management dashboards • Change management routines	dd/mm

Table 3.3 DQ Project Roles and Descriptions

Role	Description
Project Sponsor	Typically, the project executive sponsor plays this role, but it is vital that other key executives and managers also participate, particularly from the given business line.
Project Manager	Strong project management is important to ensure projects are kept on track, issues are identified and raised, and resources are coordinated appropriately.
Data Quality Analyst (DQA)	The DQA is responsible for a majority of the work conducted in the project. The DQA conducts the profiling and assessment activities, leads working sessions, and builds key deliverables. It is essential that the DQA be skilled in data quality and understand how to conduct the associated profiling analytics and build data quality rules.
Technology and Operations Analyst	Data quality efforts are cross-functional. Participation from technology and operations counterparts is essential to success. The technology analyst should help participants understand the flows, identify and gain access to data, and collect metadata. Similarly, the operations analyst should provide operational context and processing details.

Create project plan: Project managers need to prepare a detailed project plan for the four phases of the DAIC approach with the tasks and milestones plan and associated deliverables.

3.2.2   The Assess Phase

During the Assess phase, the project team should focus on establishing and assessing a data quality baseline for the critical data, as outlined in the Define phase. The project team deploys profiling and assessment techniques as well as gathering the business data quality requirements for the given data. This requires the participation of business subject-matter experts (SMEs), data quality analysts, operations managers, and data owners and stewards, as they focus on translating business and operational requirements into data quality rules as well as pulling and analyzing data. The Assess phase ends with the production of data quality scorecards, which provide a clear baseline of the current state of data quality for the given critical data set. The following activities are critical to the Assess phase.

Define Business Use and Critical Data Elements (CDEs)

It can be impractical and a poor use of resources to measure every data element in a given data set or system. It is important to narrow the focus of assessment and monitoring to critical data, that is, to the data required to support the key outcomes and deliverables of the business. Critical data identification is based on assessment of the business process or use that the data supports and the associated key outcomes of that process. Analysis of those key deliverables, such as management reports, client statements, and product analysis, should provide a candidate list of critical data. Subsequently, that list can be prioritized based on existing issues or business goals and statistical analysis, resulting in a finite set of data elements or attributes (Chapters 6 and 7 address the identification and prioritization of CDEs). As with many of the activities in the methodology, this analysis should be done with business, operations, and technology participation. The DQ analyst needs to work through any existing data models and data dictionaries to understand how these attributes are reflected in the given target systems. A simple data dictionary is the primary result, and it is a vital contribution to the metadata collected in the context of the project, as shown in Table 3.4.

This simple data dictionary containing a basic description of the data elements will be the focus of a given data quality assessment. Data dictionaries can (and should) contain additional information, including data types, data model reference, known business and data quality rules, existing integration/normalization, and lineage information.

Table 3.4   Simple Data Dictionary

Attribute/ CDE	Definition	Table	Field/Column Name
Account name	Identified and given to a customer account during account opening. Account names are derived from branch code, type, and customer last name. Used to uniquely identify customer accounts	Transaction_Jan	Account_name
Product	Describes the products provided as described in the enterprise standards.	Product_Ref	Product_type
Address	Primary street address of the customer.	Customer_md	Address_street

Develop a Data Collection Plan

Once business use requirements have been established, the technology and operations teams need to define the data sets and key points in the data and process flows that should be used for profiling and assessment. In addition, the plan for accessing and staging that data for both initial assessment and ongoing monitoring and control going forward needs to be developed. Here, the data quality team must understand where and how data flows from system to system, integration activities (the normalization, mapping, and transformations that occur), and access to existing data models and dictionaries for target systems.

Data Profiling

Data quality analysts use standard data profiling techniques to discover the composition and nature of the data contained in the target data set and for critical data attributes defined in early activities. This includes basic analysis of missing or null values, assessment of validity against known reference sources, and checking of data patterns and formats, as well as any of a number of more sophisticated analytics. (A detailed description of the profiling techniques is given in Chapter 6.)

Specify Data Quality Rules

Leveraging the results of the profiling exercise with input from subject-matter experts in the business, operations, and technology areas, the data quality analyst begins to define and implement a series of data quality rules for the critical data that will drive the baseline measure. Again, these rules define the measurement of data quality based on the requirements established by the business use of the data, and they form the basis for assessing the critical data and understanding its quality. The measures of data quality, and the rules themselves, are expressed in terms of the dimensions of data quality.

Data Quality Dimensions

The DQ dimensions are used to express the quality of data. There are four core data quality dimensions that can be tested by the rules against the given data sets:

- Completeness
- Conformity
- Validity
- Accuracy

Further, these dimensions are hierarchical; that is, higher-level measures such as completeness impact the lower-level measures such as accuracy. Accuracy depends upon validity: It is impossible to be accurate if you are not first valid. Validity depends upon conformity: You cannot be valid unless you first conform to the behavior you are expected to exhibit. If the system expects a three-character code value from a known industry standard and the data presented is a two-character value from an internal standard, then your value cannot possibly be valid. Likewise, conformity depends upon completeness. Table 3.5 shows descriptions of the data dimensions. (Data quality assessment and dimensions are discussed in more detail in Chapter 6.)

There are many tools and methods for writing and executing rules in the data flow to test against these dimensions. These can range from simple SQL queries to SAS tools. There are also dedicated data quality tools that can be used for this purpose.

Regardless of the tool used to execute the rule, the data quality analyst should write the rule in simple English. This allows vetting and review with the subject-matter experts in business and operations, and easier communication with all key players in this exercise. Additionally, it is

Table 3.5   Core Data Quality Dimensions

Dimension	Definition
Completeness	*Completeness* is defined as a measure of the presence of core source data elements that, exclusive of derived fields, must be present in order to complete a given business process.
Conformity	*Conformity* is defined as a measure of a data element's adherence to required formats (data types, field lengths, value masks, field composition, etc.) as specified in either metadata documentation or external or internal data standards.
Validity	*Validity* is defined as the extent to which data corresponds to reference tables, lists of values from golden sources documented in metadata, value ranges, etc.
Accuracy	*Accuracy* is defined as a measure of whether the value of a given data element is correct and reflects the real world as viewed by a valid real-world source (SME, customer, hard-copy record, etc.)

Table 3.6   Examples of Data Quality Rules by Dimensions for Account Names

Data Quality Dimension	Rule Passes When . . .	Rule Fails When . . .
Completeness of account name	There are no null or "0" values in the account_name field.	Any record contains a null or "0" value in the field account_Named.
Conformance of account name	All values in the field account_name are alpha and contain no more than 10 digits.	Any values in the field account_name are not alpha or the field is more than 10 digits in length.
Validity of account name	The value of the field account_name matches any single value from the reference table "Accounts."	The value of the field account_name is not found in the reference table "Accounts."
Accuracy of account name	The values of the fields zip_code, open_date, and account_name match in the same record in the reference table "Accounts."	Any of the values zip_code, open_date, and account name do not match in the same record in the reference table "Accounts."

considered best practice to write the rule in both positive and negative terms, such as "the rule passes when . . ." and "the rule fails when . . . ." As with profiling, executing data quality assessment takes a skilled expert. It is recommended that the program seek out such skilled personnel or take the time to train them appropriately. Table 3.6 shows examples of data quality rules by dimensions for account names.

Conduct Data Quality Assessment

This is the iterative effort involving running the results, validating those results with the subject-matter experts, and refining the data quality rules that drive those results. The DQA plays the lead role, but this work takes input from those who understand the data sets and their uses. At this point, the DQA works with the business to determine the thresholds for any given attribute and dimension. Questions such as "is a completeness score of 95 percent acceptable?" must be answered. (Chapter 8 provides a statistical way to determine thresholds). These statistically determined thresholds should be modified based on SME inputs in order to have more practical numbers to work with. In cases where we cannot statistically determine the thresholds, we must resort to SME inputs to determine this number and refine this process as we collect more and more data.

The result of the assessment is a set of error records, organized by attribute and data quality dimension (or rule). The assessment activity should identify all those records that are incomplete, nonconforming, invalid, and/or inaccurate. These records are the basis for the root-cause analysis conducted in the Improve phase. Also, a data quality scorecard is created in this phase. These scorecards show a summary of the data quality of the given assessment results. Scorecards should be built in such a way that they allow identification of good or problem areas by business area, systems, various points in the data or process flow, and CDEs (including dimensional levels). Typically, the scorecards are populated with percentage errors by attribute and dimension. However, they should also include the details that are reflected in the key business measure, for example, the number of client balances or the number of transactions reflected in the error records. This gives the measure of business context and impact. These scorecards can also reflect the number of records tested versus failed. Scorecards are discussed further in Chapters 6, 7, and 8.

Update metadata

In this activity, metadata collected should be well organized and captured. A strong metadata governance process should be established to include use of standard tools, as well as allowing for general access and use of the information gathered. This effort includes validation and certification from business, operations, and technology.

3.2.3   The Improve Phase

The Improve phase of the DAIC approach focuses on conducting root-cause analysis on DQ issues identified during the Assess phase. These issues should be logged into the issues management system. The data quality and business teams should conduct root-cause analysis and develop process, technology, and/or data cleansing solutions for addressing these issues. For a detailed discussion on resolving DQ issues with a structured methodology, refer to Chapter 9. The Improve phase of a data quality project should include the following.

Implement an Issues Management Process

Thresholds identified by ongoing and periodic data quality assessments need to be recorded in the issues management process along with the necessary information required for use in root-cause analysis, issue status reporting, and ultimate resolution.

Conduct Root-Cause Analysis

The DQA, using standard methods, should conduct analysis of the error records and, where necessary, work with technology and operations teams to find the source of the issue in question. In the end, whenever possible, data quality errors should be remedied at the source.

Conduct Analysis of a Solution through Return on Investment (ROI)

Once a root cause has been identified and discussed with the executive sponsor and the business area, business and technology analysts can begin designing solution alternatives. During this process, they need to pay careful attention to the ROI of each alternative in terms of risk, revenue, cost avoidance, and so on. This then allows the team to prioritize the recommended solution, particularly where there may be competing potential alternatives. The ROI analysis is critical for decision making by leadership, and it is important to note that the analysis may identify areas where the data quality improvement achieved by the resolution may not be financially viable or may not materially affect the associated business.

Commission the Improvement Effort

Prioritized and agreed-upon remediation and improvement efforts must be commissioned, and resulting initiatives are tied to the issues management process. This ensures that management teams and executives have visibility to the data quality improvement.

3.2.4   The Control Phase (Monitor and Measure)

This phase of the DAIC approach marks the business-as-usual implementation of monitoring scorecards, outstanding data quality issues inventory, and the root-cause remediation plan for the outstanding issues and data quality improvement for any projects currently under way. During this phase, production scorecards and dashboards are built, ongoing control and monitoring processes are put into place, and operational owners and escalation routines are formalized. The activities in the Control phase serve as the basis for continuous improvement as ongoing monitoring, analysis, and planning activities drive additional assessment and improvement efforts. This further represents the implementation of the steady-state operating environment (Figure 3.5) in which the data quality capabilities are in place.

In the steady-state monitor and control operating environment, the target data and systems need to be defined. Data quality analysts should conduct profiling and analysis on this data and on collected metadata. Also, the DQAs should execute the initial assessment against critical data attributes and implement the associated scorecards. In the Control phase of the project, the assessment results and scorecard are institutionalized

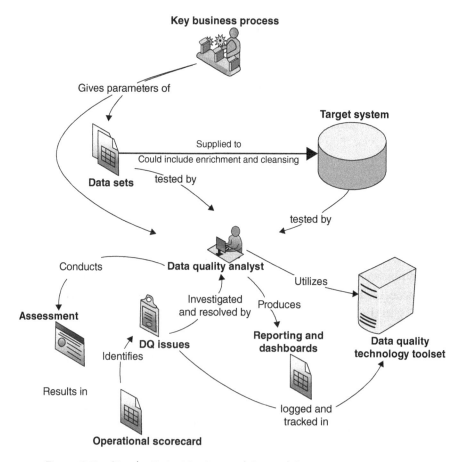

Figure 3.5   Steady-State Monitor and Control Operating Environment

and incorporated into the issues management process. Additionally, ongoing management reporting and change management activities are formalized.

The activities in the Control phase should include the following.

Establish Service-Level Agreements

In many organizations, data flows from system to system in a nonlinear fashion. As data quality capabilities are put in place and assessments are conducted, it is important to establish formal service-level agreements. The control processes need to include the measures and requirements that have been defined during the assessment. The critical data and associated data quality levels should be explicitly discussed along with the management of the issue resolution process.

Formalize Change Management and Metadata Processes

This activity establishes the process for managing changes made to requirements and metadata (data quality rules, critical data, scorecards, stewardship, etc.) on an ongoing basis. This process also manages changes to the data collection plan and technology toolset or the environments in which they are run. The key in this phase is to establish strong governance routines around the management of this metadata. Over time, rules will be enhanced, additional scorecards will be developed, and data models will be collected. All this information is critical for continuous improvement efforts.

Determine Required Scorecards, Dashboards, and Reports

The data quality team needs to work with the various consumers of the results and program participants to define a targeted set of reports and dashboards. They include scorecards with drill-down functionality, dashboards and trending views, system-level metrics, executive dashboards, and issues management reports. It is important that any reporting be actionable so consumers can act upon it. Automation of these reports is highly desirable, as skilled data and process analysts can work on other things rather than working on routine manual reporting activities.

Establish Control Processes for Ongoing Monitoring

This activity focuses on the formalization of the ongoing operational environment in which assessment and scorecards are run. DQAs and business analysts review breaks in data quality and issues management activities and then assign responsibilities. Operationally, the data quality team needs to review the scorecard results and related error records at a set frequency—daily, monthly, or quarterly, depending on relevant processing or business cycles. It is important to establish what is being measured, what constitutes a required action, by whom, and what action needs to be taken. Finally, the data quality monitoring process should be integrated into existing management routines and standard operating procedures.

Thus, we have modified the successful Six Sigma approaches—DMAIC and DMADV—for developing a comprehensive DAIC approach to solve DQ problems. The DAIC is a continuous improvement methodology that has been successfully applied to solve many DQ problems. The ultimate objective is to gain control of the quality of information used in key processes supporting business priorities by establishing an effective and consistent data capability.

3.3   CONCLUSIONS

The conclusions of this chapter can be summarized as follows:

- A four-phase Define, Assess, Improve, and Control approach has been introduced to carry out DQ projects in a systematic way. Having a standardized and structured methodology is important so anyone in the organization can follow the same steps in implementing data quality. This also contributes toward implementing good program controls and project management discipline.
- The DAIC approach is very useful in realizing the value associated with DQ improvements and in helping to sustain the gains of these improvements. The Control phase essentially aims at having controls around the new processes and methods so that gains can be realized to the full extent.

Section II

Executing a Data Quality Program

Chapter 4

Quantification of the Impact of Data Quality[1]

4.0 INTRODUCTION

The key drivers for ensuring data quality in business processes are well known. There are many regulatory, legal, and contractual implications in working with data that is not fit for its intended purpose, and the literature (Redman [1998] and Haug et al. [2011]) suggests that in a large corporation the impact of poor data quality can range between 8 percent and 12 percent of revenue, with an average being 10 percent. Therefore, it is important to design and develop a methodology to quantify the impact of poor-quality data to enable us to understand the factors impacting the data quality and take suitable actions. In this chapter, we describe a framework that can be used to quantify the impact of poor-quality data. This framework is useful in the Define and Assess phases of the DAIC approach.

4.1 BUILDING A DATA QUALITY COST QUANTIFICATION FRAMEWORK

In designing a methodology to quantify the impact of data quality, it is important to understand the paths that data uses to travel throughout an organization by answering the following questions:

- Where (and from whom) is the data element received or created?
- What is the process that it goes through? What are the transfers and transformations?

[1] **Bob Granese** is thanked for generously contributing this chapter.

- How many people touch the process, and what are the systems it goes through?

Answers to these questions are critical to understanding whether a given critical data element (CDE) has a negative impact in more than one area—for example, a joint bank loan application in which the social security number of one of two applicants was either incorrect or omitted. If this is not detected at the very beginning, then a number of things might happen as the application process goes forward. First, the loan could simply be rejected based on incomplete information, or the loan officer might process the application with only one applicant, or it could be delayed on someone's desk along with hundreds of other documents that have information missing. In all these cases, there is at least one cost area affected, which is rework. This rework costs time, money, and resources. In a perfect world, none of these efforts would be necessary. In fact, in quality programs developed for manufacturing, such as Lean Engineering or Six Sigma, any work made necessary due to errors of design or manufacture is deemed waste. This waste, with its direct and indirect costs, creates lost opportunities requiring investigation.

4.1.1   The Cost Waterfall

One of most compelling ways to visualize the negative impacts of poor data quality is a cost "waterfall" (Figure 4.1). In this illustrative example, the total revenue or cost if a cost center is used as the baseline (the tallest column, on the left), and then the dollar costs of the various expense types are captured.

The first column on the left in Figure 4.1 represents revenue and begins at 100 percent. The next is rework, which in this case is the biggest source of unnecessary costs at 3 percent, followed by the impacts of losing customers at 1.5 percent, and so on. The categories of cost are based on each unique situation; there may be some that are not shown here. There will not always be rework costs or marketing costs for every process or business. The key is to try to capture all significant areas so that in the end a true representation of data quality problems as a percentage of revenue is determined. The important takeaway here is that none of these costs are adding value for the customer; therefore, they are just wasted effort. In other words, many things that are considered to be the cost of doing business can be taken out of the business with successful efforts to improve data quality. The various cost elements in Figure 4.1 can be categorized in two ways: cost implications and lost opportunities (as shown in Figure 4.2).

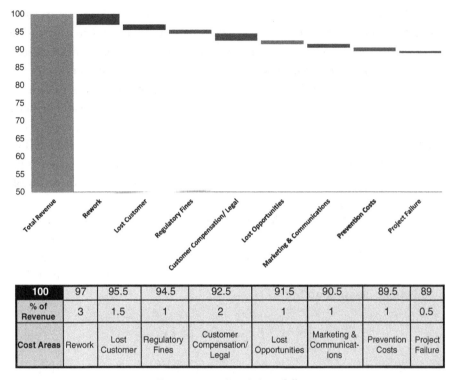

100	97	95.5	94.5	92.5	91.5	90.5	89.5	89
% of Revenue	3	1.5	1	2	1	1	1	0.5
Cost Areas	Rework	Lost Customer	Regulatory Fines	Customer Compensation/ Legal	Lost Opportunities	Marketing & Communicat-ions	Prevention Costs	Project Failure

Figure 4.1   Cost Waterfall

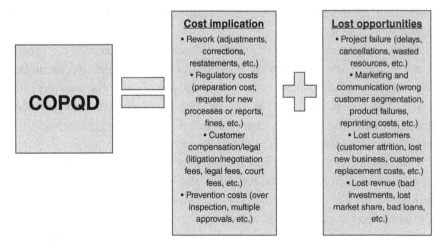

Figure 4.2   Cost Implications and Lost Opportunities
for Cost of Poor-Quality Data (COPQD)

In Figure 4.1, the net impact of these various costs is 11 percent. Once an area of the business has been selected, then we can start to capture the costs. This task is not always an easy one. It requires some work to ascertain which of these seemingly normal cost areas are truly necessary and which are due to bad data. This means working with a cross-functional team including subject-matter experts (SMEs), meaning those who actually perform the process of interest, to identify the correct cost areas. Help from the finance department may be needed to identify the actual dollars spent. Once this information is compiled, it should be relatively simple to calculate the rework costs as shown earlier. Table 4.1 is an example worksheet for capturing the costs for each category.

As an example, this worksheet shows that 500 new statements were reprinted and mailed at a cost of $11.75 each, so the total cost is $5,875.00. By better understanding the costs associated with various processes, an order of execution can be established for prioritizing which type of data needs to be cleaned up first.

4.1.2   Prioritization Matrix

If a large number of processes (or issues within a process) are under consideration, then a prioritization matrix can be used to prioritize the issues. This tool lists all of the processes/issues of concern and then compares them against a cost area. It also focuses on factors such as speed to complete, leadership support, and number of systems affected. Two different scoring mechanisms are then used to complete the worksheet, as shown in Figure 4.3.

First, the criteria are scored on their business importance (or process or taxonomy, if at a lower level). It is helpful to use a scoring scheme that allows for clear separation between the items of interest, and typically 1, 4, 7, and 10 are used as the options. The purpose here is to produce a score by rating the particular process, issue or remediation against those categories using the same 1, 4, 7, and 10 scheme.

This method can produce an estimation of the impact that an issue has on a particular category. For instance, the first scoring column reveals that the Customer Statement Process receives a score of 7 for the amount of rework that it requires. The matrix then multiplies the 7 in that box by the 10 above it for rework, giving that individual cell a value of 70. Repeating this process across each criterion produces a score for each cell, and these are calculated and then added together, producing a total

Table 4.1   Worksheet to Capture Costs in Each Category

Categories of Cost and Lost Opportunities	Number of Units	Cost per Unit	Total Cost
Rework			
How many adjustments are made each month? As a % of all transactions? (EXAMPLE)	500	$11.75	$5,875.00
How many corrections are made each month? As a % of all transactions?			
Reprints or reissue of documents?			
Revised statements with all associated costs?			
Expected output for customers can't be delivered due to data issues?			
Regulatory Impacts			
Preparation costs for meetings and deliverables to regulators?			
Meeting time and materials with regulators?			
Cost of required new reports or process changes?			
Fines levied?			
Loss of right to operate/sell certain areas/products?			
Customer Compensation/Legal			
Making customers whole?			
Customer litigation or negotiation costs?			
Customer legal fees?			
Court costs?			
Class actions?			
Prevention/Overinspection Costs			
Cost of time lost?			
Cost of overhead?			

(*continued*)

Table 4.1   Worksheet to Capture Costs in Each Category (*continued*)

Categories of Cost and Lost Opportunities	Number of Units	Cost per Unit	Total Cost
Project Failure			
Cost of time lost?			
Cost of project cancellation/false start?			
Underutilized resources?			
Productivity losses?			
Marketing and Communication			
Targeting wrong customers?			
Customer segmentation errors?			
Product failures?			
Reputation costs?			
Reprinting and redistribution costs?			
Sending unwanted solicitations?			
Misinformation to analysts?			
Lost Customers			
Customer attrition?			
Loss of new business potential/customer life cycle?			
Loss of recommendations?			
Customer replacement costs?			
Lost Opportunities			
Loss to competition due to lack of capability (DQ related)			
Lost market share?			

score, which is shown in the Score column. The scoring is performed for each process/issue/remediation, with worksheet output providing a score for each issue, as well as a percentage of the total score.

In the example, the statements issue outscores and outranks the marketing issue. While these items are relatively close in score, the exercise is more meaningful when performed with many potential areas of focus.

Process Issue Prioritization Matrix

Legend:
- 10 = Critical to Process Success
- 7 = Important to Process Success
- 4 = Somewhat Important to Process Success
- 1 = Not Important to Process Success

Rank Each Issue vs Each Criterion (How much the issue affects or is affected by the criterion) Use the same 1-4-7-10 scale with 10 the highest impact

Processes/Taxonomy	Issue	Remediation	Impacts (higher is more important)								Implementation Factors (higher is better)						Statistics		Ranking	
			Rework	Lost Customers	Regulatory Risks	Customer	Prevention Costs	Project Failure	Marketing & Communication	Lost Opportunities	Time to Complete	Resources Required	Leadership Support	Technology Support	Costs to Resolve	Supports Strategic Initiative	# of Systems Affected	# of Errors (of all records)	Score	% Score
			10	10	10	7	4	4	4	7	7	4	4	7	7	4	10	10	Score	% Score
Customer Statement Process	Statements are not going to correct address	Synch statement system with CRM	7	1	10	4	1	1	4	1	7	10	7	1	4	7	4	4	499	52.03
Direct Marketing Mailing	Using old customer list	Update customer list	4	1	1	1	1	7	10	10	7	7	7	7	1	10	1	4	460	47.97

Figure 4.3   Example of a Process Issue Prioritization Matrix

49

Even with just these two, it is a worthwhile exercise if a business is constrained by the dollars available to spend. It should be noted that the scoring is a guideline. If a senior manager reviews the output and concludes that regulatory issues are important then we need to make appropriate selection.

4.1.3   Remediation and Return on Investment

Once the areas of focus have been identified, further validation may be performed by calculating the return on investment (ROI). In the prioritization matrix, many criteria were evaluated to rank the various processes and issues. This tool can reduce the list so that a better understanding of the potential payoff from each remediation effort can be achieved. ROI is a well-known concept that simply provides one more way to ensure that maximum benefit is received for improving the quality of the data.

Table 4.2 shows the process for comparing the ROI on several improvement projects. While there are projects with a greater dollar return, it appears that improving data quality in training alone (issues 6 and 7) delivers the greatest return. Figure 4.4 outlines the steps involved in building the DQ quantification framework.

It is important to recognize that in large, complex organizations there will always be poor data quality problems. It is also important to remember that these problems are not simply a source of frustration for customers

Table 4.2   Process for Comparing ROI

Issue	Improvement Opportunity	Spend	Return	Net	ROI	Rank
1	Consolidation	$100	$250	$150	1.50	5
2	Mistake Proofing	$125	$250	$125	1.00	6
3	Integration Project	$275	$375	$100	0.36	8
4	Hiring Freeze	$110	$500	$390	3.55	3
5	Software Upgrade	$195	$500	$305	1.56	4
6	Data Awareness Training	$25	$335	$310	12.40	1
7	DQ Training	$30	$190	$160	5.33	2
8	New System	$475	$800	$325	0.68	7

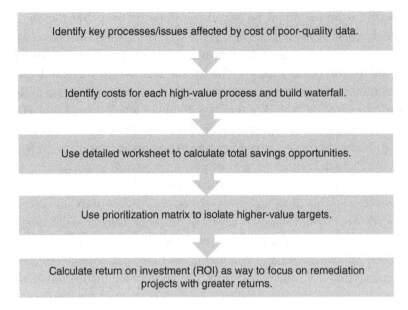

Figure 4.4   Building DQ Quantification Framework

and employees—they, in fact, cost companies a lot of money. This is money that could be spent on growth, research and development, retaining and finding the best people, and reducing prices to become more competitive.

Once the process is completed and remediation efforts are begun, it is important to identify the root cause. This means uncovering the underlying reasons for bad data making its way through the systems. Data problems often originate far upstream and cause pain. The process of tracing each problem to its point of origin is critical to finding a permanent solution. There are many ways to do this, including the Six Sigma process improvement approach.

4.2   A TRADING OFFICE ILLUSTRATIVE EXAMPLE

In a transactional environment, one of the simplest ways to calculate the dollar impacts of poor-quality data is to divide the total operating costs by the total number of transactions (successful and unsuccessful). This produces a cost per transaction. The unit cost is then multiplied by the number of unsuccessful transactions and, theoretically, produces the cost incurred for the failed transactions. This cost should encompass everything required by the transaction process, including the people, infrastructure, tools, office supplies, and electricity needed.

Another example might be a trades processing unit that handles thousands of transactions a day. On a given day, the trades unit could receive 8,000 trades for settlement. Of that number, 10 percent might fail for reasons tied to data quality issues. The bottom line is that those failed trades take as much (and, in many cases, more) time to process. Given a daily unit operating cost of $4,000, this number divided by 8,000 trades produces a processing cost of U.S. $0.50 per trade. The cost of 800 failed trades is $400 per day. If this is the average over time, then operating costs increase by 10 percent, which translates to more people, more infrastructure, and additional costs required to run the business on a daily basis.

Some trades, as well as some loans, will eventually be settled or approved, even if data issues cause them to be temporarily delayed or rerouted. There are, of course, more cost implications, some of which were discussed previously. Angry customers may take their business elsewhere. A company may calculate long-term projections for future business and profitability based on poor-quality information. Table 4.3 describes a complete approach to costing out such an example.

The cost of trades made, failed trades, and eventually settled trades can be established. In addition, a cost determination can be made for lost opportunities, penalties for late settling trades, the loss of customer lifetime value, and the value of their recommendations, as well as the marketing and sales costs needed to replace the lost customers. In addition, there may be regulatory impacts, legal issues with customers, and reputation impacts if the problems continue.

Table 4.3   Costing Out for Trading Office Example

TRADING OFFICE REVENUE		$3,000,000
COST OF REWORK IN TRADING PROCESS		
A	Cost of operations of trading office (includes people, systems, physical plant, etc.)	$1,500,000
B	Total number of trades *attempted (1st attempt)*	100,000
C	Divide total cost by total number of trades *attempted = cost per attempted trade (includes trades attempted more than once)*	$13.64
D	Total number of failed trades	15,000
E	Number of failed trades not data quality related	1,000
F	Number of data quality–related failed trades	14,000

Table 4.3   (*continued*)

G	Trades eventually completed after one or more failed attempts	12,000
H	Cost of rework per trade eventually completed (2/3 of cost of 1st pass at trade)	$9.10
I	Total rework costs of trades eventually completed	$109,143
J	Number of failed trades that never get completed	2,000
K	Multiply cost per attempted trade by total number of DQ-related failed trades	$27,272
L	Regulatory impacts (preparation, fines) for DQ-related errors (factor of 1% of revenue)	$30,000
M	Reputation costs (factor of 1% of revenue)	$30,000
N	Failed trades with additional costs to repair (making customer whole, legal fees)	500
O	Per-trade additional costs to repair	$10.00
P	Total additional costs to repair	$5,000
	Total Failed Trade and Rework Costs	$201,415
COST OF LOST OPPORTUNITY IN TRADING PROCESS		
J	Number of failed trades that never get completed	2,000
Q	Average fees/income for trades completed	$35.00
R	Lost direct revenue from DQ-related failed trades	$70,000
S	Number of lost customers due to DQ-related trade failures	100
T	Lifetime value of customer (LVCT)*	$300.00
U	Marketing and sales costs needed to replace lost customers (per lost customer acquisition costs)	$25.00
V	Loss of customer recommendations to friends and family (per lost customer)	$10
W	Total impact of lost customers (1/5 LVCT + marketing costs + loss of recommendations)	$9,500
	Total Lost Opportunity Costs	$79,500
	Total Cost of Poor-Quality Data	$280,915
	COPQD as % of Revenue	9.36%

*Estimated customer life is five years.

4.3   CONCLUSIONS

The following conclusions can be drawn from this chapter:

- The framework described in this chapter helps identify improvement opportunities. This is not just a case of understanding where most of the data problems lie; it is about making distinctions between high-cost/risk and low-cost/risk data problems so the improvements can positively impact the bottom line.
- The goal is not only to improve data quality but also to improve those areas that have the most immediate and significant payoffs.
- Companies that train their people on these tools and make it widespread practice will outpace their competitors when it comes to keeping customers, employees, and shareholders happy and in place over the long term.
- This should be an ongoing effort. The cycle of "find the issues—prioritize them—fix them" should be followed continuously. New data problems will arise with each new system added and each new business acquired.

Chapter 5

Statistical Process Control and Its Relevance in Data Quality Monitoring and Reporting

5.0 INTRODUCTION

As we have repeatedly mentioned, one of the most important aspects of the data quality operating model (DQOM) is providing a monitoring and control mechanism for critical data elements (CDEs) or process outputs. The monitoring component is useful in the Assess and Control phases, and the control component is useful in the Control phase of the DAIC approach. In this chapter, we discuss statistical process control (SPC) in detail and demonstrate how it can be used in implementing the DAIC approach. Additional uses of SPC include providing a statistical basis to determine business thresholds or specifications. Readers are encouraged to read Chapter 8 to understand how this can be done.

5.1 WHAT IS STATISTICAL PROCESS CONTROL?

Statistical process control is a method for measuring and controlling processes by using numerical facts. Controlling a process means reducing the process variability by clearly distinguishing the controllable variation (or assignable variation) and the uncontrollable variation (natural or chance) of the process. So we can say that the aim of SPC is to understand the variation associated with processes and data elements. Usually, the variation is measured against customer expectations or specifications. Any deviation from the customer expectation is undesirable, and this makes variation the enemy of quality. As discussed in Chapter 1, reducing this deviation is important to reduce the quality loss. The quality loss is directly proportional to the square of this deviation or variation. Deming

(1993) says that variation is life; or life is variation. Because of the inevitable nature of this variation, no two persons are alike, the arrival times of aircraft vary day by day, day-to-day arrival times at the office also vary, and if two people are inspecting the same product, the results will not be the same. Therefore, it is very important to understand the sources of variation so that we can act on them and make the observations as much alike as possible. Variation can come from several factors such as systems, feeds, records, or places, as shown in Figure 5.1. SPC control charts help in detecting these sources and taking appropriate corrective actions.

Traditionally, run charts that graphically represent a variable over time with historical data have been used to monitor the outputs of processes. With the control charts, we can monitor the process outputs as well as identify sources of variation, which in turn helps control process inputs. The control charts enable us to understand whether the process variation is stable or unstable. As long as process observations are within statistically determined control limits, we can say that the process variation is stable. Otherwise, the process variation is unstable, and we need to identify the sources of instability and take suitable corrective measures. If the process is unstable, its performance is not predictable, and therefore the process is not capable of producing desired performance levels. Usually, capability is calculated by comparing the performance levels with specification limits or thresholds after ensuring stability and predictability of the process. The control limits are computed from historical data, and the interpretation of charts is carried out with process knowledge. Therefore, the control chart theory is built on the statistical and process

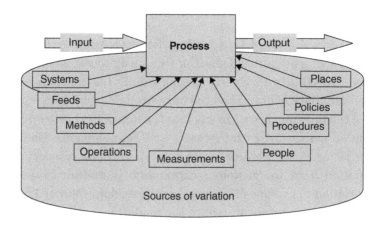

Figure 5.1   Source of Variation

knowledge, and this is the why statistical and process knowledge is so important in successful implementation of SPC.

5.1.1   Common Causes and Special Causes

Dr. Walter Shewhart proposed a new way of thinking about uniformity and nonuniformity. He recognized two kinds of variation: variation from common causes and variation from special causes. The control chart helps us to identify these two types of variation. Special causes are also known as *assignable causes*, and common causes are also known as *chance causes*. Special cause variation is something special, not part of the system of common causes, and it is detected by out-of-control points on the control chart. Common cause variation produces points on the control charts that are within control limits, and they stay the same from day to day, shift to shift, or lot to lot if no change is made to the system.

Common cause variation is also known as the expected variation of the process. The definition of *expected variation* is given as follows.

For any process, if variation due to special causes is not present, then we can say that the process is under the influence of common causes and is expected to have the following behaviors:

- **Behavior 1:** 99.73 percent data points should be within 3 standard deviations from the mean. The statistical control limits are established based on 3 standard deviations on either side of the mean. These limits are known as the *upper* and *lower control limits.* Figure 5.2 shows the distribution of a normal population with 1, 2,

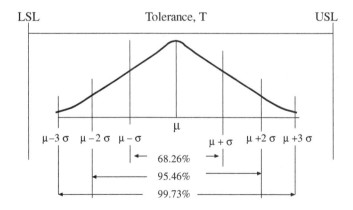

Figure 5.2   Distribution of Normal Population

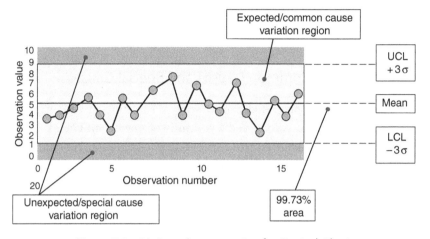

Figure 5.3   Various Components of a Control Chart

and 3 standard deviation distances from the mean. In this figure, we can see how the process performance compares with upper and lower specification limit (USL and LSL, respectively).

- **Behavior 2:** There should not be any trends or patterns. In other words, the data points should exhibit random patterns. There are established rules for evaluating/identifying the trends and patterns associated with control charts.

A process that has only expected variation is said to be statistically "in control." Figure 5.3 describes various components of the control chart and shows a means to find out whether a process is in control or not.

The established conditions based on which we can determine whether the process is in control or not include *Western Electric Run rules* and are listed here:

- Any point outside control limits
- 7 consecutive points on the same side of the center line
- 7 consecutive points increasing or decreasing
- 2 of 3 points beyond 2 standard deviations on either side of the average
- 4 of 5 points beyond 1 standard deviation on either side of the average
- 14 consecutive points alternating up and down
- 14 consecutive points on either side of the average

If data points follow these rules, we can say that the process is out of control.

5.2   CONTROL CHARTS

In this section, we discuss the control charts in detail. In order to use an appropriate control chart, first we need to know the type of data involved. Typically, data can be classified into two types: attribute/discrete data and variable data.

5.2.1   Different Types of Data

Attribute/Discrete Data

Attribute data characteristics have only two states: good/bad, acceptable/ unacceptable, match/no match. They cannot be measured on a continuous scale. Examples of attribute data include go/no go considerations, rejects, and reworks. Note that defective units and defects fall into the category of the attribute type of data.

Defect: A defect is nonconformity. However, not every defect necessarily renders a product unusable or nonfunctional; for example, a scratch on the windshield of a car does not affect its functionality, or a small bug in a software program does not make the program completely unacceptable.

Defective Unit: A defective unit is a unit that is unusable. One defective unit may have more than one defect. For example, if a software program fails to perform its intended function, it is a defective program. It is always better to start controlling the processes that produce defective units. When these processes attain a state of control, we can then concentrate on reducing the defects.

Attribute Control Charts

For monitoring and controlling the defective units we typically use a proportion defective chart (p-chart) or a number of defectives chart (np-chart), and for monitoring and controlling the defects we use a number of defects chart (c-chart) or a number of defects/unit chart (u-chart).

Variable Data

Variable data characteristics can be measured on a continuous scale. Examples of variable data are cycle time, account balance, height, and weight.

Variable Control Charts

There are several types of variable control charts. Individual observation – moving range charts (X-MR charts), average-range charts ($\overline{X}$-R charts), and average-standard deviation charts ($\overline{X}$-s charts) are quite commonly used variable control charts in industrial applications.

The control charts are typically plotted based on sample data that represents the overall population, so it is important to determine the sample size and sampling frequency. These are called *sampling parameters*. Section 5.2.2 discusses sampling.

5.2.2   Sample and Sample Parameters

A sample is a representative of a whole population. Based on a sample, we make several decisions about a population. A sample is also called a *subgroup*. The number of observations or units in a sample is called the *sample size*. The number of times a sample is collected is usually referred to as the *sampling frequency*. In designing a control chart, we must specify both of these parameters.

Selection of Suitable Samples—Rational Subgrouping

The rational subgroup concept means that subgroups should be selected so that if special causes are present, the chance of there being differences between subgroups will be maximized, while the chance of there being differences due to these special causes within a subgroup will be minimized. As a rule of thumb, we should always have at least 20 samples to construct control charts.

Before selecting a subgroup we need to ask the following questions:

1. How is the process currently operated? What are the operating procedures? What is in agreement with best knowledge and best practice? What is questionable? How good is the measurement system? Are there differences between measurement systems?

2. What is known about sources of variation and their effect on the quality of output? How can we verify these effects?

3. What are the actual results of this applied knowledge and current practice? What are the descriptive statistics (means, variation, etc.)? How reliable is the process information? How close is the performance to the target performance? Is the process capable of making the desired parts? Can we replicate process performance? How good are the control systems?

When control charts are applied to the production process, the time order of production usually forms for rational subgrouping. Time order is frequently a good basis for forming subgroups because it allows us to detect special causes that occur over time.

Two approaches to constructing rational subgroups are used. In the first approach, each sample consists of units that were produced at the same time or as closely as possible. This approach minimizes the special cause variability within a sample and maximizes the special cause variability between samples if they are present; it is used when the main goal is to detect the shifts in the process. In the second approach, known as the random sample approach, each sample consists of units of product that are representative of all the units that have been produced since the last sample was taken. The random sample should cover process output over the sampling interval.

How Do We Determine the Frequency of Sampling?

It is always very important to determine the sampling frequency appropriately. Undersampling adversely affects the process with the continued presence of special causes. Oversampling results in waste of time and effort and excess data collection. Although the sampling frequency is determined by the concerned members who own the processes, a preliminary data collection and conduct of variation analysis (an example is shown in Figure 5.4) would be of great help in deciding the sampling frequency.

In the preceding example, the samples are collected on an hourly basis. It is necessary to find the least significant interval, which will determine

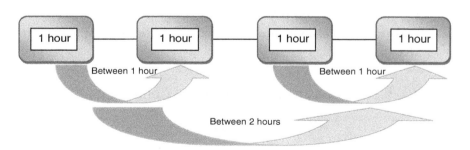

Figure 5.4   Preliminary Data Collection to Find Sampling Frequency

the sampling frequency. The sampling frequency can be determined by looking at the preliminary data. Use of a *nested analysis of variance* (nested ANOVA) technique provides a statistical basis for determining the sampling frequency. The control limits depend on the sample size. Hence, incorrect samples give wrong signals about process variation. After collecting sample observations, we can construct a control chart by using the following guidelines:

1. Construct the control limits based on the sample observations. For attribute charts, if the lower control limit is negative, set it to zero.
2. Check if all the points are within control.
3. If there are a few points beyond the control limits, then there is evidence that abnormalities or special causes are present in the process.
4. The reasons for these abnormalities have to be identified and appropriate actions should be taken to avoid recurrence of these abnormalities.
5. Recalculate the control limits, excluding the points corresponding to abnormalities, as these have by now been eliminated.
6. Repeat steps 2 to 6.
7. When all the points are in control, use the control limits for future control.

   Note that in all iterations, if more than 25 percent of the sample points correspond to abnormalities, then there is something severely wrong with the process. In that case, the process should be modified and fresh data should be collected. Usually, the control limits are shown with dotted lines, and the average or central line is shown with a solid line. Whenever there is a change in the process, the control limits should be revised and the control charts should be operated with the revised control limits. It is always good to have a schedule based on which one can review the control limits and make changes as appropriate. Section 5.2.3 discusses various control charts in detail.

5.2.3   Construction of Attribute Control Charts

p-Chart

A p-chart, known as the proportion or percent defective chart, is used to monitor the proportion of defectives. The control limits for the p-chart can be determined as follows:

$$\text{Upper control limit, } UCL = \bar{p} + A_0$$
$$\text{Central line = average = } \bar{p} \qquad (5.1)$$
$$\text{Lower control limit, } LCL = \bar{p} - A_0$$

where, $A_0 = 3\sqrt{\dfrac{\bar{p}(1-\bar{p})}{n}}$, which is 3 times standard deviation.

After calculating the control limits, they are plotted as in Figure 5.5 to determine whether the process related to know your customer (KYC) is in control.

np-Chart

An np-chart is used to monitor and control the number of defectives (np). The procedure for the construction of the np-chart is similar to that of the p-chart. The equations necessary to construct the control limits are given as follows. The requirement in this case is that the sample size must be equal for all observations.

$$\text{Upper control limit, } UCL = n\bar{p} + A_0$$
$$\text{Central line = average = } n\bar{p} \qquad (5.2)$$
$$\text{Lower control limit, } LCL = n\bar{p} - A_0$$

where $A_0 = 3\sqrt{n\bar{p}(1-\bar{p})}$, which is 3 times standard deviation.

c-Chart

If we want to control the defects rather than the defective units, the c-chart is the simplest tool to capture defect patterns. The requirement in this case

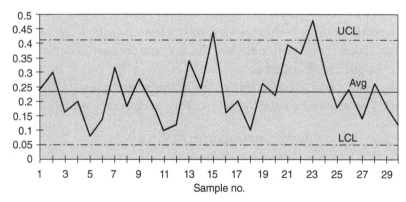

Figure 5.5   p-Chart for Defective KYC Records

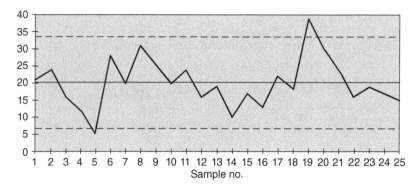

Figure 5.6   c-Chart for Number of Defects in a Sample with 100
Mortgage Accounts

is that the inspection unit must be the same for each sample. An inspection unit is defined as an entity for which it is convenient to keep records. It could be a group of 5 units of product, 10 units of product, and so on. Thus, the number of inspection units (n) determines the sample size, and n need not be an integer. The control limits for the c-chart can be determined as follows:

$$\text{Upper control limit, } UCL = \bar{c} + A_0$$
$$\text{Central line = average} = \bar{c} \qquad (5.3)$$
$$\text{Lower control limit, } LCL = \bar{c} - A_0$$

where $A_0 = 3\sqrt{\bar{c}}$, which is 3 times standard deviation.

After calculating the control limits, they are plotted as in Figure 5.6 to determine whether the process is in control.

u-Chart

When we want to monitor and control the average number of defects per inspection unit, a u-chart is used rather than a c-chart. If c is the total number of defects in a sample, then the average number of defects ($\bar{u}$) per inspection unit is obtained as $u = c/n$.

The procedure for constructing the u-chart is similar to that of the c-chart. The equations used to construct the u-chart are given as follows.

$$\text{Upper control limit, } UCL = \bar{u} + A_0$$
$$\text{Central line = average} = \bar{u} \qquad (5.4)$$
$$\text{Lower control limit, } LCL = \bar{u} - A_0$$

where $A_0 = 3\sqrt{\dfrac{\bar{u}}{n}}$, which is 3 times standard deviation.

5.2.4 Construction of Variable Control Charts

Variable control charts are also known as *twin charts,* since both the process characteristic and its variation are monitored and controlled through them. In this section, we discuss the individual–moving range (X-MR) chart and the average-range ($\overline{X}$-R) chart.

Control Charts for Individual Measurements (X-MR Charts)

There are many situations where we need to monitor the measurement of individual units. An example of this situation is when automated inspection and measurement technology is used, and the performance of every unit/cycle that comes from the technology needs to be analyzed; the production rate is very slow, and it is inconvenient to accumulate more than one measurement before analysis, such as cycle times associated with quarterly reporting; or repeat measurements on the process differ only because of laboratory or analysis error, as in many chemical processes. As the X-MR chart is a combination of two charts, the control limits for both charts should be calculated. First, we calculate the control limits for the moving range (MR) chart. As we know, MRs are obtained by calculating the differences between successive observations. To calculate the control limits for the MR chart, the following set of equations is used.

$$\text{Upper control limit, } UCL = D_4 \overline{MR}$$
$$\text{Central line} = \text{average} = \overline{MR} \qquad (5.5)$$
$$\text{Lower control limit, } LCL = D_3 \overline{MR}$$

When the ranges are in control, we calculate the control limits for the X-chart as shown here:

$$\text{Upper control limit, } UCL = \overline{X} + 3\left(\frac{\overline{MR}}{d_2}\right)$$
$$\text{Central line} = \text{average} = \overline{X} \qquad (5.6)$$
$$\text{Lower control limit, } LCL = \overline{X} - 3\left(\frac{\overline{MR}}{d_2}\right)$$

Note: The values of D_3 and D_4 depend on the sample size and are given in Table 5.1. An example of an X-MR chart for loan processing times is shown in Figure 5.7.

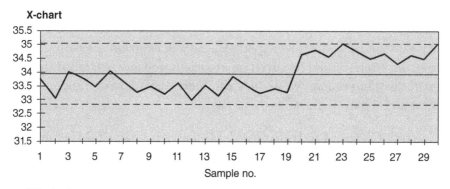

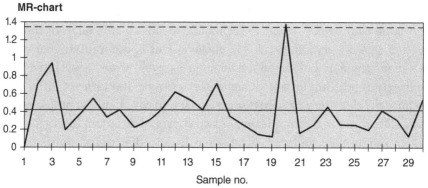

Figure 5.7   Control Chart for Individuals and the Moving Ranges for Loan
Processing Times

Average-Range Chart ($\overline{X}$-R Chart)

This chart is the most commonly used variable twin control chart in manufacturing industry applications. It is applicable in situations where we need to observe drifts in process/CDE performance between time periods. The procedure for construction of this chart is similar to that of the X-MR chart. Here also, we first construct a range chart, and the following set of equations is used to calculate the control limits.

Range Chart

$$\text{Upper control limit, } UCL = D_4 \bar{R}$$

$$\text{Central line = average} = \bar{R} \qquad (5.7)$$

$$\text{Lower control limit, } LCL = D_3 \bar{R}$$

Table 5.1   Variable Control Chart Constants

Sample Size (n)	A_2	A_3	B_3	B_4	D_3	D_4	d_2
2	1.880	2.659	0.000	3.267	0.000	3.267	1.128
3	1.023	1.954	0.000	2.568	0.000	2.575	1.693
4	0.729	1.628	0.000	2.266	0.000	2.282	2.059
5	0.577	1.427	0.000	2.089	0.000	2.115	2.326
6	0.483	1.287	0.030	1.970	0.000	2.004	2.534
7	0.419	1.182	0.118	1.882	0.076	1.924	2.704
8	0.373	1.099	0.185	1.815	0.136	1.864	2.847
9	0.337	1.032	0.239	1.761	0.184	1.816	2.970
10	0.308	0.975	0.284	1.716	0.223	1.777	3.078

When all the ranges are in control, we can calculate the control limits for the averages, as follows.

Average Chart

$$\text{Upper control limit, } UCL = \bar{\bar{X}} + A_2 \bar{R}$$
$$\text{Central line = average = } \bar{\bar{X}} \qquad\qquad (5.8)$$
$$\text{Lower control limit, } LCL = \bar{\bar{X}} - A_2 \bar{R}$$

Note: The values of A_2, D_3, and D_4 depend on the sample size, and they are given in Table 5. 1.

5.2.5   Other Control Charts

Average–Standard Deviation Chart ($\bar{X}$-S Chart)

Range is a good estimator for sample sizes up to 9. The efficiency of the range starts to decline for sample sizes above 9. In those situations, sample standard deviations (s) can be used instead of ranges. The basic procedure for construction of the $\bar{X}$-S chart is almost the same as that of the $\bar{X}$-R chart, but with different equations for evaluating the control limits. These equations are given as follows.

S-Chart

$$\text{Upper control limit, } UCL = B_4\bar{S}$$
$$\text{Central line} = \text{average} = \bar{S} \qquad (5.9)$$
$$\text{Lower control limit, } LCL = B_3\bar{S}$$

Average Chart

$$\text{Upper control limit, } UCL = \bar{X} + A_3\bar{S}$$
$$\text{Central line} = \text{average} = \bar{X} \qquad (5.10)$$
$$\text{Lower control limit, } LCL = \bar{X} - A_3\bar{S}$$

All the constants in these equations are given in Table 5.1. From these discussions, it should be clear that the control limits for various charts depend on parameters such as type of data and sample size. Depending on these parameters, we need to select an appropriate control chart, and Figure 5.8 is intended to serve this purpose.

Control Charts to Detect Small Shifts

Although the control charts discussed here (these are also Shewhart control charts) are useful in several instances, they are relatively insensitive

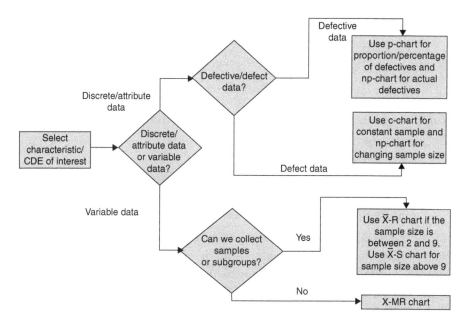

Figure 5.8   Selection of Suitable Control Charts

to small process shifts, say, on the order of about 1.5 sigma or less. This is because these charts use only the information about the process contained in the last plotted point and ignore prior data points. To detect such small shifts, typically a cumulative sum (CUSUM) control chart or exponentially weighted moving average (EWMA) control chart is used.

5.2.6 Multivariate Process Control Charts

The performance of a product often depends on several characteristics or CDEs. The interaction between these characteristics is so important in multivariate situations because patterns are sensitive to the interaction effects. To ensure process stability in cases like these, the following multivariate process control charts are useful:

- Multivariate Shewhart control charts
- Multivariate CUSUM charts
- Multivariate EWMA charts

When using these charts, the analysis is conducted in the same two-phase way as with univariate control charts. Phase 1 concerns the analysis of past data: We want to know whether the process was statistically in control during the time the samples were drawn. Phase 2 then consists of controlling the current process. Some aspects of multivariate analysis are discussed in Chapters 12 and 13.

5.3 RELEVANCE OF STATISTICAL PROCESS CONTROL IN DATA QUALITY MONITORING AND REPORTING

As we know, the purpose of SPC charts is to show the behavior of processes over a period of time with respect to statistical control limits and business-defined specifications or thresholds.

In the data quality methodology described in Chapter 3, there are four phases: Define, Assess, Improve, and Control. Use of SPC is important in the Assess and Control phases. In the Assess phase, after defining the CDEs and updating the CDE metadata, we need to define the fit-for-purpose requirements between the *data consumer* business processes that provide a business capability and the *data producer* business processes that provide data organized into *information objects* (data sets, reports, spreadsheets, etc.) for the purpose of DQ monitoring and control. In order to satisfy the fit-for-purpose requirements, we need to study the CDE performance, and SPC charts are very useful for this purpose. Statistical process charts in the Assess phase aid in examining the CDE outputs and taking corrective action if the output is out of control. These two activities are sometimes referred to as *statistical process monitoring* (SPM).

Further SPC is also useful in isolating focus areas as part of the root-cause analysis. For discussion of this, see Chapter 8 on data quality monitoring and reporting scorecards, where it is shown how SPC can be used to isolate problem areas so that we can perform remediation efforts. The use of SPC is extremely important even in the Control phase in activities such as establishing a monitoring and control environment; formalizing the change management process; determining scorecards, dashboards, and reports; and putting control processes into place.

As you can see, SPC charts, along with the DQ scorecard framework, can create a lot of value in establishing the monitoring and control environment. Once again, readers are encouraged to refer to Chapter 8 for a detailed discussion of the DQ scorecards and relevant examples.

5.4   CONCLUSIONS

The following conclusions can be drawn from this chapter:

- Statistical process control is extremely important for monitoring CDE performance and building control mechanisms around it.
- SPC is also quite important in measuring the successful implementation of DQOM, as it provides a means to measure the impact of improvement activities on CDEs.
- As mentioned in Chapter 8, an analytical framework with tools such as SPC, Pareto analysis, heat maps, and ANOVA is extremely important to identify focus areas for improvement and conduct drill-down analysis.
- Standardization and automation of SPC charts in technology platforms are essential to handle large numbers of DQ operations with multiple CDEs.

Chapter 6

Critical Data Elements: Identification, Validation, and Assessment[1]

6.0 INTRODUCTION

The data quality assessment and improvement initiative begins with identifying the data elements that need to be monitored, assessed, and improved from tens of thousands of data elements. The data elements that are selected are called critical data elements (CDEs). In this chapter, we discuss how to identify CDEs, how to validate them, and how to conduct CDE assessment with the help of data quality rules and data quality scores. The techniques proposed in this chapter are useful in the Assess phase of the DAIC approach.

6.1 IDENTIFICATION OF CRITICAL DATA ELEMENTS

6.1.1 Data Elements and Critical Data Elements

Data elements are data attributes used in running a business. For example, the name of a customer is a data element that can be used in account management, marketing, and customer service. From a technical standpoint, a data element is defined as an aspect of an individual or object that can take on varying values among individuals (Herzog et al. 2007).

Critical data elements (CDEs) are defined as "the data that is critical to success" in a specific business area (line of business, shared service, or group function), or "the data required to get the job done." Note that data

---

[1] **Chuan Shi** is thanked for generously contributing this chapter and **Ian Joyce** is thanked for making edits to this chapter and their help is greatly appreciated.

that is critical in one business area may not be critical in another. Also note that when identifying CDEs, we often look at reports that may present values derived from underlying data; derived values are calculated from the underlying CDEs.

In addition, CDEs that are necessary in multiple business areas are considered to be enterprise CDEs that must have an associated data standard. Examples of enterprise CDEs include data elements used to uniquely identify customers, data elements used to derive values that appear in key management reports, unique identifiers of information important to the business (customer ID, contract ID, etc.), input data elements for use in financial calculators (loan loss reserve, risk capital, etc.), and so forth.

A standard CDE definition typically contains:

- The element name
- A business description
- A business driver
- Data quality dimensions
- The source of the data
- An information subject with which the CDE is associated
- Stakeholders
- Privacy criteria
- Other key relationships

The identification of CDEs typically follows an engagement model that involves a coupling of the functional areas, or the business areas, with the data quality or data standards experts. They work together to identify CDEs that are associated with information subjects (such as the customer or employee) or support one or more functional or business areas. The input from business subject-matter experts is crucial in order to understand the business process, classify the process outputs, select important values derived from the process output, and eventually decompose derived values into potential CDEs.

6.1.2   CDE Rationalization Matrix

Although business SMEs decide on the initial list of CDEs, the CDE rationalization matrix is an invaluable tool for prioritizing the proposed CDEs according to different business criteria. In particular, the CDE

Table 6.1   Business/Function-Level CDE Rationalization Matrix

Critical Data Element Rationalization						
Ranking Criteria (Weights)	10	7	7	7	10	
Proposed CDE/Criteria	Criterion 1	Criterion 2	Criterion 3	Criterion 4	Criterion 5	Total
1 CDE1	7	7	7	10	10	338
2 CDE2	10	10	10	10	10	410
3 CDE3	10	4	10	4	10	326
4 CDE4	10	4	4	7	4	245
5 CDE5	7	7	4	4	4	215

rationalization matrix is used at the business or function level as well as at the enterprise level.

First, we'll discuss the business/function-level CDE rationalization matrix with the example shown in Table 6.1. At the business/function level, a set of criteria (that fit the business purpose) is chosen. Then, each criterion is weighted on a scale of 1, 4, 7, and 10, which represents their importance relative to the other criteria. After this step, each proposed CDE is scored in relation to each of the criteria (again) on a scale of 1, 4, 7, and 10. Once we determine both the weights of the criteria and the scores of a CDE in relation to those criteria, we can derive a total score, which is a sum product of all criteria weights and their corresponding scores. The total score is used to rank the importance of that CDE against others for that business/function.

Similar to the business/function-level CDE rationalization matrix, the enterprise CDE rationalization matrix compares and prioritizes CDEs that are important across multiple functions. In this case, we consider criteria that are grouped in the categories of Organizational Relevance and Business Values. These are strategic criteria essential to the successful running of businesses.

Figure 6.1 illustrates the enterprise CDE rationalization matrix. In addition to the total scores that rank all the proposed enterprise CDEs, percentages for Organizational Relevance and percentages for Business Values are also computed. For a given enterprise CDE candidate, the

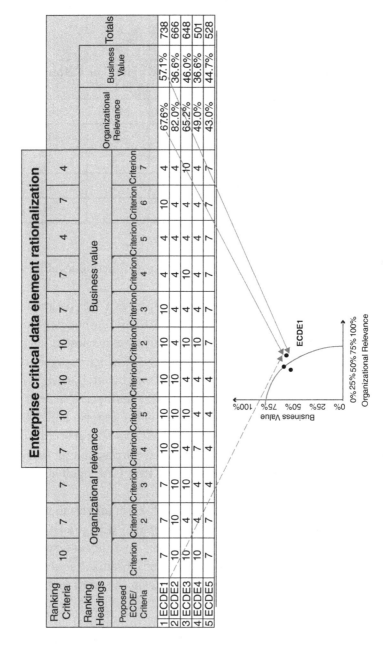

Enterprise critical data element rationalization

Ranking Criteria	10	7	7	7	4	10	10	10	7	7	4	7	4			
Ranking Headings	Organizational relevance						Business value							Organizational Relevance	Business Value	Totals
Proposed ECDE/ Criteria	Criterion 1	Criterion 2	Criterion 3	Criterion 4	Criterion 5	Criterion 1	Criterion 2	Criterion 3	Criterion 4	Criterion 5	Criterion 6	Criterion 7				
1 ECDE1	7	7	7	10	10	10	10	10	4	4	10	4		67.6%	57.1%	738
2 ECDE2	10	10	10	10	10	10	4	4	4	4	4	4		82.0%	36.6%	666
3 ECDE3	10	4	4	4	4	4	10	4	10	4	4	10		65.2%	46.0%	648
4 ECDE4	10	4	4	7	4	4	10	4	7	4	4	4		49.0%	36.6%	501
5 ECDE5	7	7	4	4	4	4	7	7	7	7	7	7		43.0%	44.7%	528

Figure 6.1 Enterprise CDE Rationalization Matrix

percentage of any category (i.e., either Organizational Relevance or Business Values) is calculated by

Percentage of a category

$$= \frac{\sum_{i=1}^{c} \text{Weight of criterion } i \times \text{Score of criterion } i}{\text{Maximum weight} \times \text{Maximum score} \times c} \times 100\% \quad (6.1)$$

where c is the number of criteria for that category, and both the maximum weight and maximum score are 10. For example, the percentage of Organizational Relevance of CDE 1 is

$$(7 \times 10 + 7 \times 7 + 7 \times 7 + 7 \times 10 + 10 \times 10)/500 \times 100\% = 67.6\%$$

Note that Equation (6.1) can lead to the fact that even if the scores of all criteria are 10, the percentage is still not 100 percent. This is because it is possible that the weights of all criteria are not 10, while in the denominator of Equation (6.1), the maximum score is multiplied by the maximum weight. In other words, the denominator is the maximum aggregated score that a CDE may be graded in a category, assuming that all criteria are of equal importance with the highest weight. However, in reality, these criteria do not all have the highest weight. Such a denominator is chosen because neither the criteria value scores nor the criteria themselves are set in stone, and they are therefore subject to change. Once these criteria and their relative weights have been agreed upon, the denominator should be changed to reflect the maximum possible score of that category for each CDE.

The two percentages are used to plot each CDE in a two-dimensional coordinate system, with Organizational Relevance representing the horizontal axis and Business Values representing the vertical axis. In Figure 6.1, enterprise CDE 1 is labeled to illustrate this. It provides a quadrant view of all the CDEs. To determine which CDEs to select, we can either choose a qualifying numeric threshold for the total scores of CDEs or, from an engineering perspective, a quarter of an arc can be drawn in a two-dimensional coordinate system selecting any CDEs plotted above the arc (see Figure 6.1).

6.2   ASSESSMENT OF CRITICAL DATA ELEMENTS

The goal of any data quality effort is to be able to objectively measure data quality. Data quality assessment is a process that is used to measure

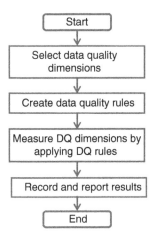

Figure 6.2   Flowchart of Data Quality Assessment

the data quality of CDEs. The broad steps involved in a data quality assessment are provided in Figure 6.2.

6.2.1   Data Quality Dimensions

Data quality assessment starts with selecting data quality dimensions of relevance to the specific business process that the data quality effort addresses. A data quality dimension, as defined by Wang and Strong (1996), is a set of data quality attributes that represent a single aspect or construct of data quality. Table 6.2 lists four core data quality dimensions that are typically used. Although these dimensions were explained in Chapter 3, the explanations are repeated here for the convenience of readers.

Some other data quality dimensions that may be widely used by the financial services industry are provided in Table 6.3. Definitions of data quality dimensions are qualitative in nature. Shanks and Darke (1998) provide a semiotic-based data quality framework. Batini and Scannapieco (2006) emphasize the need to recognize whether the dimensions refer to either the value or the intention. The challenge for data quality analysts lies in transforming these qualitative definitions into data quality measurements.

Translating dimension definitions into a set of data quality rules is a technique that is used to measure data quality. In what follows, we provide, with the help of examples, an overview of data quality rules and the role they play in producing data quality scores.

Table 6.2   Four Core Data Quality Dimensions

Dimension	Definition
Completeness	*Completeness* is defined as a measure of the presence of core source data elements that, exclusive of derived fields, must be present in order to complete a given business process.
Conformity	*Conformity* is defined as a measure of a data element's adherence to required formats (data types, field lengths, value masks, field composition, etc.) as specified in either metadata documentation or external or internal data standards.
Validity	*Validity* is defined as the extent to which data corresponds to reference tables, lists of values from gold sources documented in metadata, value ranges, etc.
Accuracy	*Accuracy* is defined as a measure of whether the value of a given data element is correct and reflects the real world as viewed by a valid real-world source (SME, customer, hard-copy record, etc.)

Table 6.3   Other Data Quality Dimensions Used by Industry

Dimension	Definition
Timeliness	A measure of current data available for business use as defined by established service level agreements (SLAs) for delivery/receipt.
Duplicate avoidance	A measure of erroneous duplicated records and data elements across or within systems
Integrity	An entity-level measure of the existence of a unique primary key field, as well as a measure of whether foreign keys in one table reference a valid primary key in the respective parent table
Consistency and synchronization	A measure of data elements or records being equivalent across systems and sources, to include continuity of the data elements and records through its life cycle
Data decay	A measure of how current the data is, to include the frequency at which the data is refreshed/updated

6.2.2   Data Quality Business Rules

Data quality business rules (DQ rules) take us one step further in measuring data quality. Data quality defects arise when data does not conform to domain constraints and business rules (Chiang and Renee 2008). Data quality rules are structured representations of these constraints and business rules, and they help us quantify how good or how bad the data is. By applying the data quality rules to CDEs, we classify them as good or bad in the context of a chosen dimension.

For demonstration purposes, suppose we are tasked with quantifying the data quality of CDEs that have an impact on Basel II[2] reports for calculating risk-weighted assets (RWAs). Assume that the following business rules have been provided by the business subject-matter experts:

- **Business Rule 1:** The CDE "seniority of claim" always takes a two-digit value; the valid values of this CDE are restricted and they can be mapped to Seniority of Claim Code, Senior Secured, Senior Unsecured, Subordinated Secured, and Subordinated Unsecured.
- **Business Rule 2:** The CDE "country of risk" is always the same as the "obligor country of risk," the facility country where the obligor is most directly exposed to economic, financial, sociopolitical, or legal risk.

We map these business rules to data quality rules for different data quality dimensions:

- **Data Quality Rule 1:** The CDE "seniority of claim" takes values from the set {10, 20, 30, 40}. As a result, this CDE is valid and its validity is 100 percent, as it takes predefined values. This rule maps to the validity dimension of data quality.
- **Data Quality Rule 2:** The CDE "country of risk" is required, and therefore any null values are considered data defects. This thereby addresses the completeness dimension of data quality.

---

[2] Basel II, initially published in June 2004, was intended to create an international standard for banking regulators to control how much capital banks need to put aside to guard against the types of financial and operational risks banks (and the whole economy) face (http://en.wikipedia.org/wiki/Basel_II).

After defining business rules, we first need to conduct profiling to understand the behavior patterns of CDEs, and after this step we can calculate data quality scores for CDEs. Section 6.2.3 briefly discusses data profiling.

6.2.3 Data Profiling

Data profiling is an important activity for improving data quality by way of identifying, interpreting, and validating data patterns and data formats from various data sources. Data profiling also helps us to understand the gap between actual data and expected data. Profiling also assists in the creation of new business rules and the validation of the data with existing business rules.

Data profiling involves the calculation of descriptive statistics such as minimum, maximum, mean, mode, percentile, standard deviation, variance, and frequency. During data profiling, we can also obtain more information on metadata, such as data type, blanks, null values, seasonality patterns, and cyclical patterns associated with data. Data profiling is extremely important in the preparatory type of analytics discussed in Chapter 13 of this book.

Maydanchik (2007) considers the following four types of profiling to be most useful in DQ assessment.

Attribute profiling: Attribute profiling helps us understand distributions and patterns associated with CDEs (attributes) by using descriptive statistics. This also helps us understand outliers and the completeness of data sets. Through this exercise, we can also identify aggregate statistics such as sums and counts.

Relationship profiling: Relationship profiling aims at identifying entity keys and various relationships in the data model.

State-transition model profiling: This type of profiling helps us understand the cycle of level- or state-dependent objects as it appears in data. For an employee, the level could be "active," "termination," or "retired."

Dependency profiling: This type of profiling helps us understand the hidden relationships among the attribute values or CDEs.

The benefits of data profiling also include understanding whether the data is fit for its purpose, reducing cycle times for important projects, and comparing the data with user expectations.

6.2.4   Measurement of Data Quality Scores

At this point, we have selected the data quality dimensions and measured them using associated DQ rules. The measurement results are called *data quality scores* (DQ scores). DQ scores are the direct indicators of the performance of the data. A DQ score may reflect the quality of the data at a certain level. In particular, it can be a score for a given data quality dimension of a CDE, an aggregated score of multiple data quality dimensions of a CDE, or even an aggregated score of multiple CDEs (across all related data quality dimensions) at either the function/business unit level or the enterprise level. A DQ score is a percentage between 0 and 100. It can generally be interpreted as the percentage of nondefect data entries out of all data entries.

Data quality scores at multiple levels need to be populated in a logical manner. In other words, we cannot get a DQ score at the CDE level without first getting DQ scores at the DQ dimension level. Similarly, we cannot derive a DQ score at the function/business level without first getting DQ scores at the CDE level. This is why we need to determine DQ dimensions and the related DQ rules first. They are used to profile the data and to calculate the DQ scores for different DQ dimensions. Once the dimension-level scores are available, DQ scores at the CDE, taxonomy, function, and enterprise levels can be derived accordingly. Figure 6.3 describes the roll-up process that can be used to obtain DQ scores at various levels.

6.2.5   Results Recording and Reporting (Scorecard)

A scorecard is a management tool that summarizes and displays data quality scores. It can be used at the CDE level for a specific business/ function project, as well as at the enterprise level to provide an overview of the data quality performance within the organization. In the latter case, it is called an *enterprise (data quality) scorecard.*

In this section, we provide a brief example of scorecards at the CDE level. Consider four CDEs called CDE 1, CDE 2, CDE 3, and CDE 4. In addition, the four core dimensions mentioned in Section 6.2.1 are included. Table 6.4 illustrates the scorecard.

This chapter does not explain in detail how to compute the scores. However, a specific sequence for measuring data quality dimensions is used, and it plays an important role in computing the DQ scores of different data quality dimensions. For instance, the example in Figure 6.3 displays the following scores for CDE 1: Completeness 100 percent, Conformity

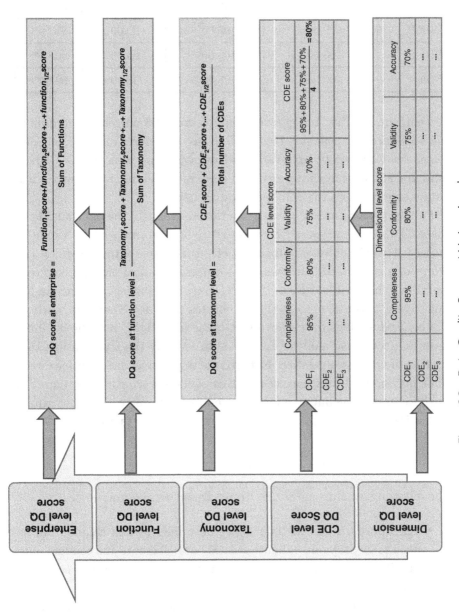

Figure 6.3 Data Quality Scores at Various Levels

Table 6.4 A CDE-Level Scorecard Example

	Completeness	Conformity	Validity	Accuracy
CDE 1	100.00%	100.00%	100.00%	95.00%
CDE 2	99.00%	99.00%	90.00%	85.00%
CDE 3	100.00%	100.00%	95.00%	90.00%
CDE 4	100.00%	95.00%	95.00%	92.00%

100 percent, Validity 100 percent, and Accuracy 95 percent. According to the scorecard, we conclude that CDE 1 has no defects in terms of Completeness, Conformity, and Validity. However, 5 percent of this CDE is inaccurate. The scorecard provides a summary of data quality by critical data element across the data quality dimensions.

Finally, a scorecard is used to monitor and control the data quality of these CDEs. For the set of CDEs in Figure 6.3, we can produce a regular scorecard (weekly, biweekly, monthly, etc.) that displays these results. The scores of a given CDE can be used to construct a statistical process control (SPC) chart. An outlier in the SPC chart may suggest a change in the underlying business process that generates the data. Therefore, outliers can be used as flags to trigger a root-cause investigation of the business process. Root-cause analysis is applied to identify the true reasons that created the process deviation. Note that both positive and negative deviations may occur. In the case of negative deviation or poorer data quality, the necessary remediation efforts are conducted to correct the root causes and to improve the business process as well as the data quality.

6.3   CONCLUSIONS

The following conclusions can be drawn from this chapter:

- The approach and methodologies described in this chapter can be used to identify and validate critical data elements and conduct data quality assessment and improvement by calculating DQ scores at various levels.
- High-quality data helps in the formulation of risk management decisions based on increasingly accurate data that reflects the reality of both the company itself and the market.

Chapter 7

Prioritization of Critical Data Elements (Funnel Approach)[1]

7.0 INTRODUCTION

In Chapter 6, we discussed how to identify, validate, and assess critical data elements through subject-matter expertise, the rationalization matrix, profiling, DQ rules, and DQ scores. In this chapter, we discuss how to prioritize these CDEs and reduce the number of CDEs to be measured and monitored, using the funnel approach. We demonstrate the applicability of this approach with the help of a case study. The funnel approach presented in this chapter is useful in the Assess and Improve phases of DAIC.

7.1 THE FUNNEL METHODOLOGY (STATISTICAL ANALYSIS FOR CDE REDUCTION)

With the input from business SMEs and the CDE rationalization matrix, we can derive a set of CDEs for a given business case. This aspect was discussed in Chapter 6. However, the size and complexity of a big company's data population make it economically infeasible to carry out 100 percent data quality checks for all CDEs for any ongoing operational process. Therefore, it is not only desirable but also necessary to reduce the number of CDEs being measured. To this end, sampling methodologies are employed. This allows for efforts to be concentrated on monitoring and improving the data quality of the CDEs that are of the greatest business or organizational importance.

[1] **Chuan Shi** is thanked for his generous contribution to this chapter and **Ian Joyce** is thanked for making edits to this chapter. Their help is greatly appreciated.

In this section, we discuss how to reduce the number of CDEs using sampling-based statistical analysis as part of the funnel methodology. By applying statistical analysis, we can reduce the number of CDEs by using correlation and regression analyses for continuous CDEs (Section 7.1.1), and by using association analysis for discrete CDEs (Section 7.1.2). This application allows us to identify CDEs that have close relationships. Next, a signal-to-noise (S/N) ratios analysis is conducted for each pair of highly correlated CDEs. The CDEs with lower S/N ratios are chosen for future assessment, as a lower S/N ratio indicates a greater variation of the data. Greater variation of the data implies that the process that generates the data is unstable. This instability may represent a risk to the running of the business. The structure of this section and the approach used to reduce the number of CDEs are illustrated in Figure 7.1.

In Figure 7.1, the process starts with a set of CDEs that we have after obtaining SME inputs and applying the CDE rationalization matrix. An example of funneling CDEs is shown on the right side of this figure. Suppose that we have 100 CDEs before applying the funnel methodology. After prioritization through Pareto analysis (see Chapter 11 for a discussion of Pareto analysis), we might reduce the number of CDEs to 50. After applying statistical analysis such as correlation and association analysis, this number might come down to 25. Through application of S/N ratio analysis, this can be further reduced to a manageable list of 5 to 10, on which we can perform DQ assessment and which we can proactively monitor and control.

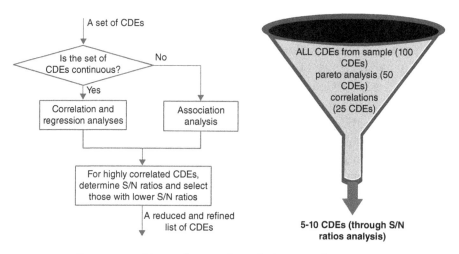

Figure 7.1   CDE Reduction through the Funnel Approach

7.1.1   Correlation and Regression Analysis for Continuous CDEs

Correlation Analysis

The purpose of conducting (linear) correlation and regression analysis for CDEs is to identify dependencies and relationships between any pair of CDEs, and eventually to reduce the number of CDEs to be analyzed. Linear correlation coefficients are a good approximation of second-order interaction between the variables. Since higher-order effects are usually insignificant with financial data, we decide to build relationships based on linear correlation coefficients. Suppose there are two CDEs called X and Y. If they are highly correlated, the value of X can help us to predict the value of Y with a high degree of confidence. For example, if X is within its normal range, then Y is most likely within its normal range as well.[2] On the other hand, if X sits outside its normal range due to a data quality defect, then it is also very likely for Y to be an outlier from its normal range. Therefore, for a pair of highly correlated CDEs, as long as we guarantee the data quality of one CDE, then by their highly dependent nature, the data quality of the other CDE is most likely guaranteed as well.

We discuss this idea formally by considering multiple CDEs. In addition, it is important to note that correlation analysis and regression analysis are used to analyze CDEs comprising continuous data whose correlations and regression coefficients can be computed. To study the dependency of pairs of discrete CDEs, we apply a similar approach called *association analysis* (see Section 7.1.2).

Suppose we have a set of (continuous) CDEs from a given business case. To reduce the number of CDEs, we must first conduct a correlation analysis for each pair of CDEs and summarize them in a correlation analysis matrix. To compute the correlation of a pair of CDEs (e.g., X and Y), we select two samples of X and Y, from which their correlation is calculated. Let r_{XY} be their correlation, and it is computed by (Albright et al. 2009):

$$r_{XY} = \frac{\dfrac{\sum (X_i - \bar{X})(Y_i - \bar{Y})}{(n-1)}}{s_X s_Y} \tag{7.1}$$

---

[2] However, to quantify the relationship between X and Y, correlation analysis alone is not enough. A large correlation indicates a definitive (linear) relationship between the two variables. A (linear) regression analysis is needed to tell us how Y would change given a unit change of X (and vice versa).

where $\overline{X}$ is the sample mean of X,

$\overline{Y}$ is the sample mean of Y,

s_X is the sample standard deviation of X,

s_Y is the sample standard deviation of Y, and n is the size of both samples.

Given this definition, the range of a correlation is between -1 and 1, inclusively. In particular, for two underlying variables, a correlation close to 1 indicates a large positive linear relationship, while a correlation close to -1 indicates a large negative linear relationship. A correlation close to 0 indicates a weak or no linear relationship. To generalize this idea to multiple CDEs, consider a business process that has six CDEs called CDE 1, CDE 2, . . ., and CDE 6. Equation (7.1) is then used to compute the correlations between all pairs of CDE i and CDE j ($i = 1, 2, . . ., 6$, and $j = 1, 2, . . ., 6$), and this leads to a correlation analysis matrix as shown in Table 7.1.

Note that the correlation of one CDE with itself is always 1. This explains why all the diagonal elements in Table 7.1 are 1. In addition, the correlation analysis matrix is symmetric since the correlation between CDE i and CDE j is exactly the same as that between CDE j and CDE i. Therefore, if we have n CDEs, the number of correlations we need to compute is $n(n - 1)/2$ (instead of n^2).

Once we build the correlation analysis matrix, it is a straightforward task to identify the pairs of CDEs that are highly correlated. As mentioned previously in this section, a correlation close to 1 or -1 indicates a strong (linear) relationship. Therefore, we can choose thresholds and

Table 7.1   Correlation Analysis Matrix of Six Continuous CDEs

	CDE 1	**CDE 2**	**CDE 3**	**CDE 4**	**CDE 5**	**CDE 6**
CDE 1	1.000	−0.169	0.952**	−0.048	0.997**	0.882**
CDE 2	−0.169	1.000	−0.149	0.093	−0.169	−0.169
CDE 3	0.952**	−0.149	1.000	−0.051	0.952**	0.837*
CDE 4	−0.048	0.093	−0.051	1.000	−0.048	−0.045
CDE 5	0.997**	−0.169	0.952**	−0.048	1.000	0.882**
CDE 6	0.882**	−0.169	0.837*	−0.045	0.882**	1.000

*Moderately correlated

**Highly correlated

segment pairs of CDEs according to which threshold segment their correlations fall into. For instance, in the preceding example, we choose 0.85 (and –0.85) as a threshold; therefore, any pair of CDEs whose correlation falls into the 0.85 and 1 segment (and the –0.85 and –1 segment) is considered highly correlated. The pairs of highly correlated CDEs are subject to further investigation to determine, for each pair, which CDE to select for data quality assessment and improvement efforts. The signal-to-noise ratios analysis is used to select one CDE from a pair of highly related CDEs. We will discuss this further in Section 7.1.3.

Regression Analysis

While correlation analysis tells us how definitively two CDEs (e.g., X and Y) are related, (linear) regression analysis quantifies the relationship between them. To see this, consider the two CDEs that are perfectly (linearly) correlated. In other words, their correlation is 1.

We consider three different scenarios, demonstrated by the scatter plots in Figure 7.2. In all these scenarios, the correlations are 1. However, the impact on Y brought by a unit change of X would not be the same in all scenarios. Since scenario (a) has the steepest slope while scenario (c) has the gentlest slope, the impact of a unit change of X to Y would be greater in scenario (a) and less in scenario (c). Regression analysis helps us to quantify the relationship between two variables. In particular, the slope (denoted by b) in linear regression is used and it is computed by (Albright et al. 2009):

$$b = \frac{\sum (X_i - \bar{X})(Y_i - \bar{Y})}{\sum (X_i - \bar{X})^2} = r_{XY} \frac{s_Y}{s_X} \tag{7.2}$$

Correlation is 1 in all scenarios

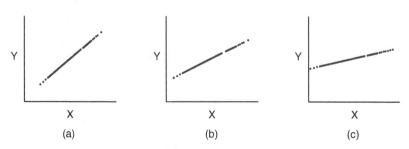

Figure 7.2   Examples of Variable Pairs with Correlations of 1

To explain why running regression analysis is a logical next step after correlation analysis, we need to recall our ultimate purpose in running this set of analyses on CDEs. We have recognized a practical need to reduce the number of CDEs in instances where they are numerous. As a result, once we identify a pair of highly correlated CDEs, we may choose to monitor only one and improve its data quality.[3] However, it is possible that both of them are necessary inputs of some *business impacting decision variable* (BIDV), such as the risk-weighted asset (RWA).[4] Alternatively, we may say that a BIDV can be a function of multiple CDEs, in the form of:

$$BIDV = f(CDE\ 1, CDE\ 2, \ldots) \tag{7.3}$$

In this case, if we were to analyze only the data quality of CDE 1 and its impact on that specific BIDV, a regression analysis between CDE 1 and CDE 2 would allow us to quantify the impact of CDE 2 on that BIDV without having to monitor its data quality. This is because, according to the linear regression equation, CDE 1 can be expressed as a function of CDE 2:

$$CDE\ 1 = a + b \times CDE\ 2 \tag{7.4}$$

Equation (7.4) enables us to reflect the unit change of CDE 2 in terms of CDE 1. Since we monitor CDE 1 and its impact on that BIDV, the regression analysis between CDE 1 and CDE 2 allows us to quantify the impact of CDE 2 on that BIDV indirectly. The argument presented previously explains why we would take a step further to conduct the regression analysis for a pair of CDEs that are proven to be highly correlated by the correlation analysis. In summary, regression analysis provides us with the ability to quantify the business impacts of associated CDEs. This is done through the correlation with those CDEs whose data quality is well controlled.

7.1.2 Association Analysis for Discrete CDEs

Association analysis with discrete CDEs plays a similar role to the role correlation analysis plays with continuous CDEs. Due to the discrete nature of some critical data elements, we are not able to compute their

---

[3] We explain how to choose one CDE from a pair in Section 7.1.3, where we discuss the signal-to-noise ratios.
[4] A risk-weighted asset (RWA) is a bank's assets or off-balance-sheet exposures, weighted according to risk (http://en.wikipedia.org/wiki/Risk-weighted_asset).

correlation matrix numerically. However, their dependence can be analyzed by counting the number of data quality defects of one CDE, given the occurrence of data quality defects of another CDE.

Association analysis is widely used in transaction pattern recognition: When given a set of transactions, we can find the rules that will predict the occurrence of an item based on the occurrences of other items in the transaction (Tan et al. 2005). We extend the term *association analysis* in our context, but will focus more on identifying highly correlated discrete CDE pairs, rather than building association rules.

Again, suppose that there are six discrete CDEs: CDE 1, CDE 2, . . ., CDE 6. We construct the association analysis matrix as follows. For each CDE, we count the number of its data quality defects given the coexistence of the data quality defects of another CDE. See Table 7.2 for illustration. Suppose that we have 1,000 records that contain these six CDEs.

Note that we only count the number of data quality defects of a CDE given the coexistence of the data quality defects of a different CDE. This is why we put N/A in all diagonal elements of this matrix. In addition, the association analysis matrix is symmetric. As a result, if we have n CDEs, the number of counts we need to compute is $n(n - 1)/2$ (instead of n^2).

In the example in Table 7.2, the data quality defects of CDE 1 and CDE 2 happen together 100 times out of 1,000 records. However, the numbers of occurrences of data quality defects of CDE 1 and another CDE (other than CDE 2) are relatively small compared to 100. This suggests that CDE 1 and CDE 2 have a strong dependence. In other words, whenever CDE 1 fails for a data quality reason, we may expect that CDE 2 will also fail. Likewise, if we improve the data quality of CDE 1 to reduce its data quality defects, we would also expect to observe fewer data quality

Table 7.2   Association Analysis Matrix of Six Discrete CDEs

	CDE 1	CDE 2	CDE 3	CDE 4	CDE 5	CDE 6
CDE 1	N/A	100	16	3	22	0
CDE 2	100	N/A	178	2	15	4
CDE 3	16	178	N/A	10	1	12
CDE 4	3	2	10	N/A	20	80
CDE 5	22	15	1	20	N/A	5
CDE 6	0	4	12	80	5	N/A

defects associated with CDE 2. Similar pairs in this example are CDE 1 and CDE 3 (178 coexistences) and CDE 4 and CDE 6 (80 coexistences). The pairs of highly correlated CDEs are subject to further investigation to determine, for each pair, which CDE to select for data quality assessment and improvement. As mentioned in the case of a continuous CDE, the signal-to-noise ratios analysis is applied to select one CDE from each pair of highly correlated CDEs. We discuss this next, in Section 7.1.3.

7.1.3   Signal-to-Noise Ratios Analysis

Signal-to-noise (S/N) ratios are used as the last step in the funnel methodology to finally determine which CDE to study for each pair of highly correlated (continuous or discrete) CDEs. The application of S/N ratios was pioneered by Dr. Taguchi in the field of quality engineering and functions as a measure that is used in science and engineering to compare the level of a desired signal with the level of background noise (Taguchi 1986, Taguchi and Jugulum 1999). In our approach, we compute an S/N ratio as follows:

$$\text{S/N ratio} = 10 \log \left(\frac{\text{Mean of the CDE}^2}{\text{Standard Deviation of the CDE}^2} \right) \quad (7.5)$$

which is similar to the reciprocal of the coefficient of variation, that is, the ratio of the mean to standard deviation of a CDE. Signal-to-noise ratios measure the magnitude of the square of the mean over the variance of a given CDE. Specifically, a smaller S/N ratio indicates a higher variability for the CDE under consideration. The larger variability may suggest that the business process that generates values of that CDE is not stable and therefore requires investigation.

As an example, consider CDE 1 and CDE 2 in Figure 7.3. They are highly correlated since they follow the same trend (i.e., for a given record, a large CDE 1 comes with a large CDE 2, and a small CDE 1 comes with a small CDE 2). However, it is obvious that the values of CDE 1 present much larger variability than the values of CDE 2. Therefore, we dedicate our effort to eliminating the data quality defects of CDE 1 by improving its business process and reducing its variability, since the large variability of CDE 1 is a bigger concern than that of CDE 2. When two CDEs are (highly) correlated, we keep the one with the lower S/N ratio for the purpose of data quality assessment and improvement, while leaving the other one unmonitored.

After reducing the CDEs, we should start to assess them by using business rules, DQ dimensions, and DQ scores. See Chapter 6 for the assessment.

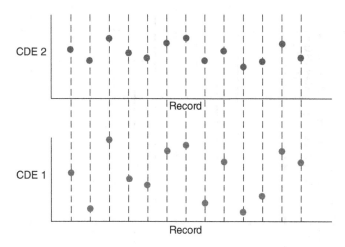

Figure 7.3   A Pair of Highly Correlated CDEs

7.2   CASE STUDY: BASEL II

In 2008 a global banking crisis hastened the adoption of regulatory measures outlined in the 2004 Basel II Accords. Essentially, these accords
promoted the application of risk and capital management requirements
designed to ensure that banks follow a process to set aside sufficient capital
to offset the risks created through their lending and investment practices. A
good company should incorporate data quality measurement in its continuous efforts to identify, assess, and manage all risks, be they of the liquidity,
credit, market, insurance, or operational variety.

7.2.1   Basel II: CDE Rationalization Matrix

In an early Basel II data quality assessment, subject-matter experts
(SMEs) from the functional area were able to identify 35 data elements
that would be likely candidates for consideration as the critical data
elements that, when measured, would provide the best assessment of
the quality of data used in the particular Basel II function. While the
35 data elements were recognized as being important, the consensus
among the SMEs was that not all the elements could be regarded as
equally significant. In the absence of an existing tool, the *critical data
element rationalization matrix*, as shown in Table 7.3 was devised as
a means for rank-ordering CDE candidates by scoring them against
weighted ranking criteria and deriving a total that is a sum product of

Table 7.3   Basel II Rank-Ordered CDE Rationalization Matrix

Weightings		10	7	7	7	10	10	10	7	7	4	
Ranking Criteria	Proposed CDE/ Criteria	Ease of Access (Easiest = 10)	% of Reports (High% = 10)	% Customers (High% = 10)	Total Incidences (High incidence = 10)	Business Support (Strong support = 10)	Technology Support (Strong support = 10)	Regulatory Risk (High risk = 10)	Financial Risk (High risk = 10)	Reputation Risk (High risk = 10)	Operations Risk (High risk = 10)	Totals
1	CDE22	4	4	4	10	10	10	7	10	7	10	595
2	CDE21	7	10	4	7	7	10	4	4	10	4	541
3	CDE11	4	7	7	7	10	10	4	7	4	7	532
4	CDE27	4	7	10	10	4	10	4	7	10	1	532
5	CDE29	7	10	10	1	10	7	1	7	10	4	532
6	CDE31	7	7	10	7	4	1	7	10	10	4	514
7	CDE19	1	7	4	1	10	10	7	7	10	7	511
8	CDE24	7	1	10	4	7	10	7	7	1	10	511
9	CDE10	7	7	7	1	7	10	7	7	4	1	496
10	CDE20	1	7	10	1	7	7	7	10	10	1	490
11	CDE5	4	1	10	7	7	7	10	7	4	1	487
12	CDE1	7	10	7	10	1	7	4	7	4	7	484
13	CDE17	1	4	4	4	7	10	7	7	10	7	481

Table 7.3 (Continued)

14	CDE8	4	7	10	7	4	7	1	10	7	7	475
15	CDE12	7	1	1	7	10	10	1	10	4	7	469
16	CDE26	1	1	4	10	7	10	10	7	1	7	469
17	CDE15	10	1	4	1	10	4	7	10	4	1	454
18	CDE16	4	10	1	4	7	10	1	4	7	10	442
19	CDE2	1	10	7	7	1	4	7	10	4	10	436
20	CDE25	10	1	7	10	7	1	4	1	4	10	421
21	CDE33	7	1	7	10	1	10	1	10	1	7	421
22	CDE4	10	7	7	1	1	4	7	7	10	4	418
23	CDE6	1	7	10	4	10	4	1	10	4	1	409
24	CDE13	10	10	7	7	1	1	4	7	4	1	409
25	CDE14	1	1	10	7	4	10	7	4	1	4	397
26	CDE18	4	7	7	7	10	4	1	7	7	1	397
27	CDE7	10	4	4	4	4	7	4	1	4	10	391
28	CDE3	7	7	1	1	10	4	4	1	1	7	388
29	CDE28	4	4	7	7	7	7	1	4	1	4	385
30	CDE30	7	7	1	1	7	1	10	4	1	1	364
31	CDE35	4	10	7	7	1	7	1	4	1	7	361
32	CDE9	4	4	4	1	7	4	4	4	4	10	349
33	CDE23	4	4	1	4	10	1	4	4	7	1	292
34	CDE34	1	1	4	10	7	1	4	1	1	4	265
35	CDE32	1	1	1	1	10	1	4	1	1	7	216

all criteria weights and their corresponding scores. The creation and use of the function-specific evaluation criteria afforded the SMEs the opportunity of conducting a high-level potential-CDE filtering exercise that was based on more than just experiential quantification. With totals ranging from 595 to 223 for the 35 data elements under consideration, it rapidly became evident that the CDE rationalization matrix was indeed a value-adding tool in the CDE identification and selection process. The tool provided a means for the business SMEs to quickly differentiate between CDE candidates based on a numeric valuation derived from an evaluation process common to all the data elements being considered. Equipped with the output of the rationalization matrix, the SMEs were able to reduce the number of CDE candidates under consideration from 35 to 21.

7.2.2   Basel II: Correlation and Regression Analysis

Linear correlation and regression analysis and association analysis were next applied to the 21 remaining Basel II CDE candidates with the intent of identifying existing relationships and dependencies between pairs of potential CDEs. In cases where strong correlations can be established between two CDEs, then relationships can be built based on linear correlation coefficients. In these instances, the value of one CDE in a pair can help predict the value of the second CDE with a high level of confidence. Consequently, given two highly correlated CDEs, what falls within the normal range for one member of the pair will very likely be reflected in the range of the pair's second member. If high data quality can be demonstrated for one CDE in a pair, then it is highly likely that the data quality of the second CDE can also be guaranteed. In the case of attribute-type data element variables, such dependencies can be established through the measure of association. Since CDE 5 and CDE 8 are attribute variables, an association analysis was performed to determine the relationship between these two potential CDEs. The analysis demonstrated that there was no relationship between CDE 5 and CDE 8. This led to the decision to keep both of these variables for data quality assessment.

For the remaining 19 CDEs, a correlation analysis was performed. In the Basel II correlation coefficient table (Table 7.4), 8 strongly correlated pairs of CDEs (with correlation coefficients greater than 0.85) are in evidence: CDE4-CDE7, CDE4-CDE10, CDE4-CDE12, CDE10-CDE7,

Table 7.4   Basel II CDE Correlation Analysis

	CDE4	CDE6	CDE7	CDE9	CDE10	CDE12	CDE13	CDE15	CDE16	CDE18	CDE19	CDE20	CDE23	CDE24	CDE27	CDE28	CDE29	CDE30	CDE33
CDE4	1	-0.15845	0.94097	-0.07018	1	0.86733	-0.00246	-0.04753	-0.05935	-0.35508	-0.06459	0.10137	0.05222	-0.02656	0.12077	0.05713	0.33052	0.10466	-0.00246
CDE6	-0.15845	1	-0.13644	0.0939	-0.15845	-0.15704	-0.17101	0.03401	0.03274	-0.05505	0.01219	-0.11871	0.03316	-0.01205	0.27657	0.05029	-0.04143	0.276	-0.17101
CDE7	0.94097	-0.13644	1	-0.06981	0.94097	0.82212	-0.02544	-0.04437	-0.05632	-0.33977	-0.06029	0.09216	0.04597	-0.02544	0.12763	0.04429	0.29684	0.18697	-0.02544
CDE9	-0.07018	0.0939	-0.06981	1	-0.07018	-0.06621	-0.0392	0.01547	0.01437	0.00636	-0.02117	-0.10284	-0.00655	-0.01231	0.07685	-0.01646	-0.04959	-0.03429	-0.0392
CDE10	1	-0.15845	0.94097	-0.07018	1	0.86733	-0.00246	-0.04753	-0.05935	-0.35508	-0.06459	0.10137	0.05222	-0.02656	0.12077	0.05713	0.33052	0.10466	-0.00246
CDE12	0.86733	-0.15704	0.82212	-0.06621	0.86733	1	0.03862	-0.04795	-0.05977	-0.21516	0.00756	0	0.04801	-0.01776	0.12155	0.04582	0.30342	0.08684	0.03862
CDE13	-0.00246	-0.17101	-0.02544	-0.0392	-0.00246	0.03862	1	0.0195	0.02068	0.36822	0.21715	-0.05971	-0.00388	0.03347	-0.23989	-0.21814	-0.16975	0.04383	1
CDE15	-0.04753	0.03401	-0.04437	0.01547	-0.04753	-0.04795	0.0195	1	0.86875	0.02558	0.09905	-0.0278	-0.00345	-0.00024	-0.01297	-0.03147	-0.02818	0.02013	0.0195
CDE16	-0.05935	0.03274	-0.05632	0.01437	-0.05935	-0.05977	0.02068	0.86875	1	0.02811	0.09475	-0.01989	-0.00378	-0.00243	-0.01775	-0.03592	-0.032	0.01305	0.02068
CDE18	-0.35508	-0.05505	-0.33977	0.00636	-0.35508	-0.21516	0.36822	0.02558	0.02811	1	0.23408	-0.11422	0.12123	0.04595	-0.18859	-0.14566	-0.27597	-0.05236	0.36822
CDE19	-0.06459	0.01219	-0.06029	-0.02117	-0.06459	0.00756	0.21715	0.09905	0.09475	0.23408	1	-0.15119	-0.05775	0.01507	-0.06781	-0.10286	-0.0929	0.03891	0.21715
CDE20	0.10137	-0.11871	0.09216	-0.10284	0.10137	0	-0.05971	-0.0278	-0.01989	-0.11422	-0.15119	1	0.02849	-0.08168	0.15763	-0.01778	0.0249	-0.13074	-0.05971
CDE23	0.05222	0.03316	0.04597	-0.00655	0.05222	0.04801	-0.00388	-0.00345	-0.00378	0.04595	-0.05775	0.02849	1	-0.00365	0.04247	0.06274	0.08707	-0.01669	-0.00388
CDE24	-0.02656	-0.01205	-0.02544	-0.01231	-0.02656	-0.01776	0.03347	-0.00024	-0.00243	0.04595	0.01507	-0.08168	-0.00365	1	-0.03828	-0.03277	-0.03514	-0.04288	0.03347
CDE27	0.12077	0.27657	0.12763	0.07685	0.12077	0.12155	-0.23989	-0.01297	-0.01775	-0.18859	-0.06781	0.15763	0.04247	-0.03828	1	-0.03218	0.1152	0.1743	-0.23989
CDE28	0.05713	0.05029	0.04429	-0.01646	0.05713	0.04582	-0.21814	-0.03147	-0.03592	-0.14566	-0.10286	-0.01778	0.06274	-0.03277	-0.03218	1	0.86716	0.13217	-0.21814
CDE29	0.33052	-0.04143	0.29684	-0.04959	0.33052	0.30342	-0.16975	-0.02818	-0.032	-0.27597	-0.0929	0.0249	0.08707	-0.03514	0.1152	0.86716	1	0.10582	-0.16975
CDE30	0.10466	0.276	0.18697	-0.03429	0.10466	0.08684	0.04383	0.02013	0.01305	-0.05236	0.03891	-0.13074	-0.01669	-0.04288	0.1743	0.13217	0.10582	1	0.04383
CDE33	-0.00246	-0.17101	-0.02544	-0.0392	-0.00246	0.03862	1	0.0195	0.02068	0.36822	0.21715	-0.05971	-0.00388	0.03347	-0.23989	-0.21814	-0.16975	0.04383	1

CDE10-CDE12, CDE15-CDE16, CDE13-CDE33, and CDE28-CDE29. Regression analysis helped the Basel II data quality practitioners to establish relationships between business-impacting decision variables by building mathematical equations for highly correlated CDEs. Determining which of the candidate CDEs in a correlated pair to disregard and which candidate CDEs to retain for further assessment became the final step in applying the funnel process to the Basel II potential CDEs. This determination was made by applying the signal-to-noise ratio methodology first introduced by Dr. Taguchi (1987).

7.2.3   Basel II: Signal-to-Noise (S/N) Ratios

The final step for reducing the number of the 35 original Basel II CDE candidates was achieved through the application and analysis of signal-to-noise (S/N) ratios. Through S/N ratio analysis, Basel II data quality practitioners were able to choose which CDE in a related pair needed to be retained for data quality assessment. CDEs with low S/N ratios have higher variability and, consequently, need more attention with regard to data quality monitoring and control. Table 7.5 shows S/N ratios for highly correlated CDEs.

Table 7.5   S/N Ratio Analysis for Highly Correlated Variables

CDE	S/N Ratio (decibel units)
CDE 4	6.42
CDE 7	6.27
CDE 10	6.47
CDE 12	6.54
CDE 13	11.96
CDE 15	−18.66
CDE 16	−18.57
CDE 28	−4.65
CDE 29	−6.03
CDE 33	11.96

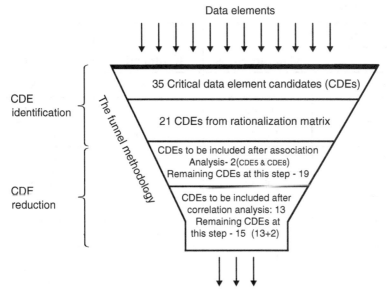

Figure 7.4   Process of Reducing the CDEs from 35 to 15

Examination of the correlation matrix (Table 7.4) reveals that CDE 4, CDE 7, CDE 10, and CDE 12 have mutually high correlations. CDE 7, with an S/N ratio of 6.27 decibels, has the lowest S/N ratio of the four CDEs. For this reason, CDE 7 was selected for data quality assessment. Similarly, CDE 15 was chosen from the pair CDE 15 and CDE 16. For the pair CDE 28 and CDE 29, CDE 29 was selected. In the example of the pair CDE 13 and CDE 33, the S/N ratios were the same. In this case, business reasons dictated that CDE 13 be designated for data quality assessment.

Following the performance of the signal-to-noise ratio analysis, 15 of the original 35 data elements qualified for and were selected as the critical data elements for the particular Basel II function. These 15 CDEs were then chosen for data quality assessment as shown in Figure 7.4.

For the final list of CDEs, data quality assessment was performed by evaluating DQ scores using business rules and conducting profiling. Table 7.6 shows a summary of the DQ assessment.

In summary, by applying the funnel methodology for CDE determination, the Basel II data quality practitioners were able to examine an initial

Table 7.6   DQ Assessment Summary for Final 15 CDEs

Dimension CDE	Completeness	Conformity	Validity
CDE5	100.00%	100.00%	100.00%
CDE6	100.00%	100.00%	100.00%
CDE7	100.00%	100.00%	100.00%
CDE8	100.00%	100.00%	100.00%
CDE9	99.80%	99.20%	99.28%
CDE13	0.20%	0.00%	0.00%
CDE15	84.40%	86.60%	86.87%
CDE18	100.00%	100.00%	100.00%
CDE19	100.00%	100.00%	100.00%
CDE20	98.40%	98.00%	98.20%
CDE23	0.60%	0.14%	0.36%
CDE24	100.00%	100.00%	100.00%
CDE27	39.00%	38.00%	32.01%
CDE29	100.00%	100.00%	100.00%
CDE30	100.00%	100.00%	100.00%

35 potential critical data elements and reduce them to a final 15 CDEs. The methodology proved extremely useful for the following reasons:

1. It eliminated redundancy and reduced the number of data elements to be monitored so that attention could be focused on the right elements. In later data quality assessment initiatives, the Basel II DQ practitioners were to encounter hundreds of data elements associated with a given functional area or line of business. Having a proven systematic and valid process to reduce the candidate pool for CDEs became an operational necessity of paramount importance.
2. It ensured the identification and selection of the data elements that were best qualified to be the CDEs and whose data quality was then to be assessed and monitored for a given line of business or functional area. Critical to this process was the active participation of

the Basel II SMEs. This was achieved from the very outset by including subject-matter experts from the Basel II functional area. Their specialized knowledge and experience contributed greatly to the evaluation and rank-ordering of the initial 35 data elements when using the CDE rationalization matrix. It further ensured that the conduct of the data quality assessment methodology was continuously framed within the context of the functional area's business objectives.

7.3 CONCLUSIONS

The following are the conclusions that can be drawn from this chapter:

- The chapter primarily introduces a funnel methodology to reduce the number of CDEs that require proactive monitoring and control. In this process, SME inputs, use of the CDE rationalization matrix, and statistical analysis help select the critical data elements from a large list of data elements.
- Statistical process control (SPC) charts, as described in Chapter 5, are typically used to monitor the data quality scores of CDE dimensions.
- Finally, given the presence of an undesired data quality of a CDE, root-cause analysis must be performed to identify the underlying causes and make suitable improvements.

Chapter 8

Data Quality Monitoring and Reporting Scorecards

8.0 INTRODUCTION

The most important aspect of the data quality effort is the monitoring and reporting (M&R) function. An effective M&R function is absolutely necessary for successful DQ deployment. This function is usually carried out with the help of scorecards. The DQ scorecard is a strategic tool that can be used by data quality teams and technology teams to understand the behavior of CDEs in relation to the performance of business function, capability, business unit, or operational data source (ODS).

As we all know, it's very difficult to plan on things if we cannot measure them. To this end, the scorecards provide the necessary measurement and tracking methodology so that teams can identify what should be done and measured as part of planning process. Besides assisting with planning activities, the scorecards also help to prioritize areas of focus so that a business can work in those areas as part of its root-cause analysis activities. The most important aspect of the scorecard is its design. We need to collect all user inputs so that we can develop simple, informative, and easy-to-understand scorecards. In this chapter, we describe a mechanism to construct and implement effective scorecards. Through this mechanism, a user can store, sort, and retrieve DQ defect information and perform remediation through failure pattern analysis. The framework presented in this chapter is quite useful in the Improve and Control phases of the DAIC approach.

8.1   DEVELOPMENT OF THE DQ SCORECARDS

The purpose of designing and developing the DQ scorecards is to have a mechanism by which users can store, sort, and retrieve DQ defect information and perform the required analytics to identify and prioritize areas of focus for conducting root-cause analysis. The scorecards serve the following functions:

- Deliver monitoring and reporting capability by using DQ metrics to drive the data management discipline across the enterprise
- Provide a reporting framework for structured identification of critical data elements (CDEs) and associated business rules supporting specific business capabilities
- Produce reporting metrics enabling root-cause analysis of data quality issues by performing analytics on CDEs and/or issue-related data

The development of the DQ scorecards involves designing an analytical framework that can perform variation analysis, statistical process control (SPC) analysis, generation of heat maps, and determination of thresholds, in addition to having the capability of storing the defect information. Section 8.2 outlines the analytics framework used in building the DQ scorecards.

8.2   ANALYTICAL FRAMEWORK (ANOVA, SPCs, THRESHOLDS, HEAT MAPS)

We have worked on a generalized approach to developing a standard analytical framework so that it can be applied to all the CDEs of interest. The description of this methodology is as shown in Figure 8.1.

In the analytics framework, we start off by identifying the CDEs of interest. For a discussion of CDE definition, selection, and prioritization, please refer to Chapters 6 and 7. The next step is to collect the information on the CDEs, build associated business rules, and conduct profiling. DQ business rules are one of the most important aspects of DQ assessment. These rules validate the data relationships and can be executed by using computer queries/programs. Building DQ rules and executing them require a systematic approach. The greater the number of rules that consider all data types, sources, and design strategies

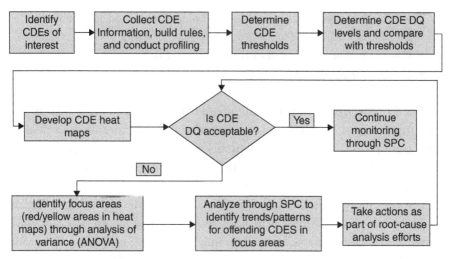

Figure 8.1   Analytics Framework for DQ Scorecards

we have, the better it is for evaluating DQ levels. (A detailed discussion of DQ rules is provided in Chapter 6.) The next step after developing and executing business rules is to conduct data profiling using these rules. Profiling enhances understanding of the distributional patterns associated with CDEs and provides their descriptive statistics. It enables us to understand the data, its actual structure, and dependencies. Furthermore, we can establish a baseline for improvement by measuring existing data quality levels. For a detailed discussion on profiling, readers are again encouraged to read Chapter 6. After profiling, we need to establish thresholds for DQ levels either by means of business inputs or through statistical analysis of historical data, or through both. Section 8.2.1 describes a methodology to determine thresholds.

8.2.1   Thresholds and Heat Maps

Threshold, in the DQ context, is defined as the allowable defect rate for a given CDE. It helps to identify CDEs that are outside the specification limit for one or more dimensions. Thresholds may be created with consideration given to business value and the consumer's and producer's risk. Where multiple threshold values exist, threshold selection is determined by using the highest threshold standard currently in use.

The determination of thresholds can be accomplished in two ways:

- Based on business inputs and benchmarking
- Using historical data analysis with SPC

The first approach is relatively straightforward: Business SMEs provide inputs based on their process knowledge and experience in dealing with the process. Of course, benchmarking techniques—comparing with the best in class in the industry or internally with a division—can also be used in this approach, along with the SME inputs.

The second approach is based on the use of statistical process control on historical data. If historical data is not available, we can use SME insights/experience as a starting point and begin collecting data and refining thresholds once there is sufficient data. (For SPC-related discussions and construction of SPC charts, please refer to Chapter 5.) The steps for using an SPC-based approach to determine thresholds are as follows:

1. Based on CDE business rules, calculate the DQ scores at the dimensional level.
2. Identify a suitable control chart and construct control limits based on historical data. The upper control limit corresponding to this control chart can be referred to as the *current CDE capability* with respect to the dimension of interest.
3. Compare DQ scores corresponding to various samples used against the control limits.
4. Identify the points that are out of control limits. Discard out-of-control points and recalculate the upper limit with the points within control. This upper limit is called the *process CDE potential index* for the dimension of interest.
5. After determining the CDE dimension potential index, obtain SME feedback on this and modify this index as appropriate. This modified CDE potential index can be considered as the threshold for the CDE dimension under examination.

These steps should be repeated for other CDE dimensions of interest. An illustrative example is provided here with the help of Figure 8.2. In this figure, we can see that the current process allows 0.925 (92.5 percent) quality (1 – 0.075, or LCL in the figure) for the validity dimension. After removing the points above the UCL, the process can produce 99.2 percent

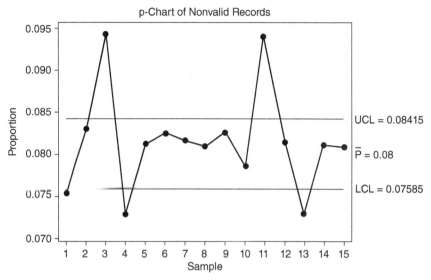

Figure 8.2   SPC Analysis for Determining Thresholds

quality. Therefore, we recommend that the initial threshold for the validity dimension be 99.2 percent, or an allowable defect rate of 0.8 percent (8,000 parts per million, or PPM). Of course, this number should be validated by business SME inputs, and, if necessary, adjustments should be made as appropriate.

After the threshold analysis, we need to construct heat maps for the CDE under examination. The heat maps can be constructed at the system level or region level from which the CDEs come.

A heat map is a graphical or tabular representation of data in which the individual values contained in a matrix are represented in different colors. In this case, the purpose of a heat map is to identify the problematic areas so that we can do a drill-down analysis as part of the root-cause analysis (RCA) process. The typical color code scheme employed is as follows:

Green: Areas with good DQ (with scores between 98 percent and 100 percent)

Yellow: Vulnerable DQ areas where drill-down analysis is required (with scores between 95 percent and 98 percent)

Red: At-risk areas where we should focus and perform drill-down analysis (with scores less than 95 percent)

Table 8.1 shows an example of a heat map as used in this framework.

Table 8.1   Example of Heat Map Used in the Analytical Framework

CDEs	CDE1		CDE2		CDE3		CDE4		CDE5	
Operational data source (ODS)	% Valid Records	% Valid Balance	% Valid Records	% Valid Balance	% Valid Records	% Valid Balance	% Valid Records	% Valid Balance	% Valid Records	% Valid Balance
ODS1	95.54%	7.71%	92.59%	41.91%	90.39%	99.78%	100.00%	100.00%	99.88%	99.91%
ODS2	63.09%	21.62%	92.68%	98.22%	99.88%	99.91%	95.54%	7.71%	99.88%	99.92%
ODS3	87.59%	31.05%	90.39%	99.78%	99.88%	99.92%	63.09%	21.62%	99.96%	99.94%
ODS4	92.59%	41.91%	99.88%	99.91%	99.96%	99.94%	87.59%	31.05%	99.76%	99.98%
ODS5	92.68%	98.22%	99.88%	99.92%	99.76%	99.98%	92.59%	41.91%	99.92%	100.00%
ODS6	90.39%	99.78%	99.96%	99.94%	99.92%	100.00%	92.68%	98.22%	100.00%	100.00%
ODS7	99.88%	99.91%	99.76%	99.98%	100.00%	100.00%	90.39%	99.78%	95.54%	7.71%
ODS8	99.88%	99.92%	99.92%	100.00%	95.54%	7.71%	99.88%	99.91%	63.09%	21.62%
ODS9	99.96%	99.94%	100.00%	100.00%	63.09%	21.62%	99.88%	99.92%	87.59%	31.05%
ODS10	99.76%	99.98%	95.54%	7.71%	87.59%	31.05%	99.96%	99.94%	92.59%	41.91%
ODS11	99.92%	100.00%	63.09%	21.62%	92.59%	41.91%	99.76%	99.98%	92.68%	98.22%
ODS12	100.00%	100.00%	87.59%	31.05%	92.68%	98.22%	99.92%	100.00%	90.39%	99.78%

From Table 8.1, it is clear that some data sources with red zones require immediate attention, as the DQ levels corresponding to CDEs coming out of these operational data sources are at unacceptable levels. So efforts should be focused on these areas by doing drill-down analysis using ANOVA and SPC. After analyzing red areas, we need to look at yellow areas and do drill-down analysis as required. For all green areas, we should continue to monitor and control the performance through SPC charts. Section 8.2.2 describes the roles of ANOVA and SPC charts in this framework.

8.2.2   Analysis of Variance (ANOVA) and SPC Charts

Analysis of variance, or ANOVA, is a technique to find out the effect of the factors that are being studied, based on overall variation. ANOVA provides information on the magnitude as well as the statistical significance of the factor effects. Based on the results of ANOVA, the optimal levels of the significant factors are chosen to improve the performance of a process.

The results of ANOVA are presented in tabular form. The elements in ANOVA table are shown in Table 8.2.

Source: The column in the ANOVA table labeled "Source" contains a list of sources of variation that contribute to the variation in the experimental data.

Sum of Squares (SS): The sum of squares reflects the variation that can be attributed to each source listed in the ANOVA table.

Degrees of Freedom (df): The degrees of freedom reflect the amount of information from the experiment that was used to calculate the sum of squares. Usually, the df of a factor is equal to the number of its levels minus 1. The df corresponding to an interaction between two or more factors is equal to the product of dfs of the corresponding factors. In ANOVA, total df is equal to total number of observations minus 1. The error df is obtained by subtracting the sum of all dfs from total df.

Table 8.2   ANOVA Table

Source	Degree of Freedom (df)	Sum of Square (SS)	Mean Square (MS)	F-Ratio/p-Value

Mean Square (MS): The mean square is the sum of squares divided by the respective degrees of freedom.

F-Ratio: The F-ratio is the mean square of an effect divided by mean square error. In each case, the amount of variation that occurs as the result of adjusting a factor (as captured by its mean square) is compared to the amount of variation observed when the other factors are held constant (mean squared error). A large F-ratio would therefore indicate a significant effect. Usually, F-ratios are compared with critical values (available in standard F-tables) to discover significant factors.

p-Value: In statistical hypothesis testing, we can reasonably state that the p-value is the probability of obtaining a test statistic as extreme as the one that was actually observed. We reject the null hypothesis when the p-value is less than the significance level α (Greek alpha), which is often 0.05 or 0.01. Here, a low value of p indicates the significance of the factor. We can use either F-ratio or p-value to determine the significance of a factor.

Figure 8.3 shows an example of an analysis of variance. From this figure, it is clear that the F-ratio is high and the p-value is low. This indicates that there is significant variability between the countries. Country 5 has higher variability and lower DQ scores, and country 4 has lower DQ scores as compared to other countries, so efforts should be focused in these regions to start with. Also, box plot patterns corresponding to countries with large variation in DQ scores should be examined in order to understand the reasons for the high variability. Usually with ANOVA, box plots are used. They show the distribution of data points in a given region or operational data source. Using box plots, we can graphically compare variability across the regions or operational data sources.

After identifying the areas of focus, we can conduct SPC analysis in those areas to understand the behavior patterns of the CDEs. As we know, the purpose of SPC charts is to show the behavior of processes over a period of time with respect to statistical control limits. If the performance is within the control limits, then we say that process is in statistical control and under the influence of natural variation. On the other hand, if the performance is outside of the control limits, then we can say that process is out of control and is under the influence of special cause of variation. (Please see Chapter 5 for a detailed discussion of SPC.) After understanding the behavioral patterns and isolating focus areas, actions

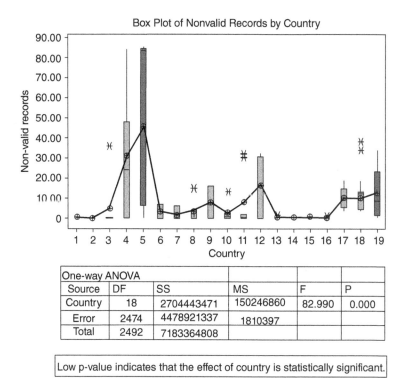

Figure 8.3   Analysis of Variance (ANOVA)

must be taken to improve the DQ levels. This should be done as part of RCA activities. After improving the performance levels, we need to continuously monitor the CDE performance on an ongoing basis, as shown in Figure 8.1.

8.3   APPLICATION OF THE FRAMEWORK

In this section, we will describe how the framework was applied for an important enterprise-level CDE. The data on this CDE (valid records and balance amounts) was collected for three months from 12 operational data sources in 10 countries. After collecting this information and determining the thresholds, Pareto analysis was performed to identify operational data sources with high nonvalid balance amounts. The Pareto analysis was as shown in Figure 8.4.

From Figure 8.4, it is clear that five combinations of countries and operational data sources account for more than 90 percent of nonvalid

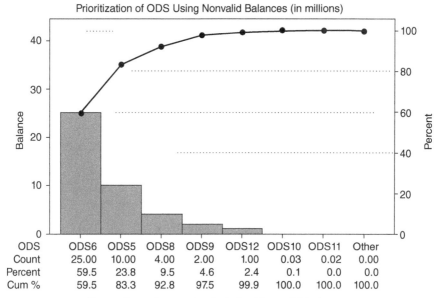

ODS	ODS6	ODS5	ODS8	ODS9	ODS12	ODS10	ODS11	Other
Count	25.00	10.00	4.00	2.00	1.00	0.03	0.02	0.00
Percent	59.5	23.8	9.5	4.6	2.4	0.1	0.0	0.0
Cum %	59.5	83.3	92.8	97.5	99.9	100.0	100.0	100.0

Figure 8.4　Pareto Analysis for Nonvalid Balances

balances, and they are as shown. After this, a heat map was constructed with nonvalid balances and records to indicate areas that require immediate focus. This is shown in Figure 8.5. Even in this heat map, the following color scheme was used:

Green: Areas with good DQ (with scores between 98 percent and 100 percent)

Yellow: Vulnerable DQ areas where drill-down analysis is required (with scores between 95 percent and 98 percent)

Red: At-risk areas where we should focus and perform drill-down analysis (with scores less than 95 percent)

After identifying areas on which to focus (red and yellow zones), analysis of variance (ANOVA) was performed to determine the statistical significance of the variation and to drill down into problem areas. Then SPC analysis was performed to determine patterns and trends associated with the problem areas and take appropriate actions.

The analysis that was performed for this CDE can be replicated and applied to other CDEs. Efforts should be also on to standardize the analytical framework and automate the same so that it can be done with

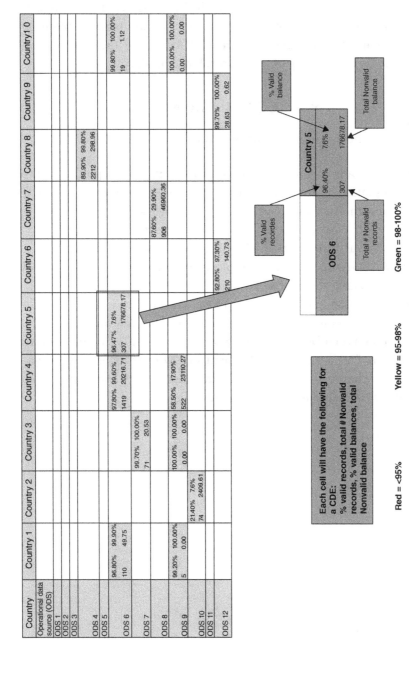

Figure 8.5   Heat Map for an Enterprise-Level CDE—Records and Balances[1]

[1] **Jagmeet Singh** is thanked for generously contributing to the art work for Figure 8.5.

111

the click of few buttons. It is important to note that the information on CDEs has been housed in a database (data-related platform), and automation efforts are being performed through this platform. Thus, the user can store, sort, and retrieve DQ defect information and perform required analytics to identify and prioritize areas of focus and to conduct root-cause analysis with the help of the data-related platform.

8.4   CONCLUSIONS

The following conclusions can be drawn from this chapter.

- It is important to have DQ scorecrads housed in a platform like the DQ platform by which the user can store, sort, and retrieve DQ defect information and perform the required analytics to identify and prioritize areas of focus for conducting root-cause analysis.
- An analytical framework with tools such as Pareto analysis, heat maps, ANOVA, and SPC is extremely important for identification of focus areas and to conduct drill-down analysis.
- Standardization and automation of this framework are essential so that analytics can be easily run with the click of few buttons.
- Development of a DQ scorecards as described in this chapter is quite important for successful deployment of DQ operations in an organization. This also increases data awareness and transparency in dealing with issues across the organization.

Chapter 9

Data Quality Issue Resolution

9.0 INTRODUCTION

The issue resolution (IR) process encompasses issue identification, tracking, and the resolution of issues through root-cause analysis. The issues involved can be data quality–related, process quality–related, or technology-related. If we identify the category to which a particular issue belongs, we can resolve the issue with the help of the data quality methodology (as described in Chapter 3) or process quality (Six Sigma approach). This is how we can demonstrate the linkage between data quality and process quality approaches. This linkage further benefits the data quality initiative from a methodology and toolset that increases data quality by improving process quality. In this chapter, we explain the structured linkage between data quality and process quality by understanding the processes related to CDEs and using process engineering and data quality tools and techniques. The linkage process explained in this chapter is quite valuable in the Improve phase of the DAIC approach.

9.1 DESCRIPTION OF THE METHODOLOGY[1]

As mentioned earlier, a major component of this effort is the issues resolution (IR) process. This process is focused on identifying the sources of data quality issues and working to prevent them by root-cause remediation. By approaching the work from the standpoint of IR, we can see the way some issues cut across the various businesses and units of the business. This suggests that, in many cases, the solution will take more than the effort of any one group. Therefore, the approach that needs to be considered is

[1] **Ian Joyce** is thanked for editing this section. This help is greatly acknowledged.

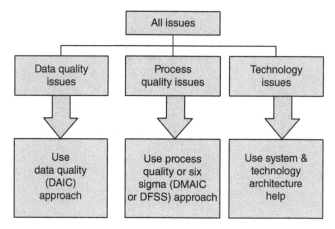

Figure 9.1   Issue Resolution—Linkage of Data Quality and Process Quality

IR approach that cuts across silos and should encourage various parts of the organization to work together to solve these problems. Figure 9.1 describes the way issues need to be looked at and how they can be worked to resolution with different approaches, thereby improving transparency, cooperation among groups, and data quality.

Section 9.2 briefly discusses the DQ approach and process quality (Six Sigma) approach. Please note that we are not providing any description of the third category (technology) shown in Figure 9.1, since the purpose here is to demonstrate the linkage of DQ and process quality (PQ) approaches.

9.2   DATA QUALITY METHODOLOGY

As mentioned in previous section, if the issue is related to data quality, then we recommend that the DQ methodology as described in Chapter 3 should be used. The DQ methodology consists of four phases: Define, Assess, Improve, and Control.

The *Define* phase focuses on establishing scope, objectives, resources, commitments, and project plans, and ensuring strong governance and stakeholder support.

In the *Assess* phase, the project team focuses on establishing and assessing a data quality baseline for the critical data as outlined in the Define phase. The project team deploys profiling and assessment techniques as well as gathering business data quality requirements for the given data. This work requires the participation of business subject-matter experts, data quality analysts, operations managers, and data owners and stewards as they focus on translating business and operational requirements into data quality rules as well as pulling and analyzing data. The phase ends with the production a of data quality scorecard, which provides a clear baseline of the current state of data quality for the given critical data set.

The *Improve* phase focuses on conducting root-cause analysis on issues identified during the Assess phase or known data quality issues obtained from other sources, all of which have been logged into the issues management process and system. This is the practical implementation of the issues management processes established previously. The data quality and business teams conduct root-cause analysis and develop process, technology, and/or data cleansing solutions for addressing these issues.

The *Control* phase marks the business-as-usual implementation of monitoring the scorecards, outstanding data quality issues inventory, plus root-cause remediation and data quality improvement for any projects currently under way. Figure 9.2 shows the approach to use to resolve DQ-related issues. The business requirements and analytical tools and techniques are also shown in this figure.

9.3 PROCESS QUALITY/SIX SIGMA APPROACH

The Six Sigma approach is a business process methodology that allows companies to drastically improve their operational performance by designing and monitoring their business activities in ways that minimize waste and resources while maximizing customer satisfaction through a collection of managerial, engineering, design, and statistical concepts. As discussed in Chapter 3, the Six Sigma approach is a business process–related, project-driven methodology. These projects are executed through the DMAIC (Define, Measure, Analyze, Improve, and Control) process. The DMAIC Six Sigma approach is useful when we are improving a particular process and want to reduce the defect rate. If a particular process requires major redesign or if we need to redesign a product or process from the beginning, it is recommended that we use the Design for Six Sigma (DFSS) methodology. This methodology is also called the DMADV (Define, Measure, Analyze, Design, and Verify) approach. Although detailed discussions of these two approaches are provided in Chapter 3, for the benefit of the readers, let us briefly summarize their important aspects here.

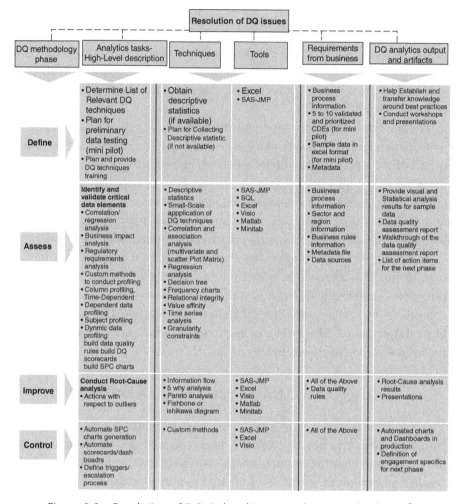

Resolution of DQ issues					
DQ methodology phase	Analytics tasks-High-Level description	Techniques	Tools	Requirements from business	DQ analytics output and artifacts
Define	• Determine List of Relevant DQ techniques • Plan for preliminary data testing (mini pilot) • Plan and provide DQ techniques training	• Obtain descriptive statistics (if available) • Plan for Collecting Descriptive statistic (if not available)	• Excel • SAS-JMP	• Business process information • 5 to 10 validated and prioritized CDEs (for mini pilot) • Sample data in excel format (for mini pilot) • Metadata	• Help Establish and transfer knowledge around best practices • Conduct workshops and presentations
Assess	**Identify and validate critical data elements** • Correlation/regression analysis • Business impact analysis • Regulatory requirements analysis • Custom methods to conduct profiling • Column profiling, Time-Dependent • Dependent data profiling • Subject profiling • Dynmic data profiling build data quality rules build DQ scorecards build SPC charts	• Descriptive statistics • Small-Scale apppplication of DQ techniques • Correlation and association analysis (multivariate and scatter Plot Matrix) • Regression analysis • Decision tree • Frequency charts • Relational integrity • Value affinity • Time series analysis • Granularity constraints	• SAS-JMP • SQL • Excel • Visio • Matlab • Minitab	• Business process information • Sector and region information • Business rules information • Metadata file • Data sources	• Provide visual and Statistical analysis results for sample data • Data quality assessment report • Walkthrough of the data quality assessment report • List of action items for the next phase
Improve	**Conduct Root-Cause analysis** • Actions with respect to outliers	• Information flow • 5 why analysis • Pareto analysis • Fishbone or ishikawa diagram	• SAS-JMP • Excel • Visio • Matlab • Minitab	• All of the Above • Data quality rules	• Root-Cause analysis results • Presentations
Control	• Automate SPC charts generation • Automate scorecards/dash boadrs • Define triggers/escalation process	• Custom methods	• SAS-JMP • Excel • Visio	• All of the Above	• Automated charts and Dashboards in production • Definition of engagement specifics for next phase

Figure 9.2   Resolution of DQ-Related Issues with DQ Methodology[2]

Six Sigma (DMAIC) Approach

Define Phase: Identify potential projects; select and define a project; select a team.

Measure Phase: Document the process and measure current capability.

Analyze Phase: Collect and analyze data to determine critical variables/factors/CDEs.

Improve Phase: Determine process settings to most important variables.

[2] **Raji Ramachandran** is thanked for the generous help in creation of the art work for Figure 9.2.

Control Phase: Measure new capability and institute control to maintain gains.

Design for Six Sigma (DMADV) Methodology:
  Define Phase: Identify product or process to be designed; select a team.
  Measure Phase: Plan and conduct research to understand customer requirements.
  Analyze Phase: Develop alternate design concepts and analyze them.
  Design Phase: Develop detailed design and evaluate its capability.
  Verify Phase: Conduct pilot tests and analyze results; make changes as required.

9.4 CASE STUDY: ISSUE RESOLUTION PROCESS REENGINEERING

A financial company's functional group wanted to be able to prioritize issues stored in the issue resolution (IR) database. The group needed to know which issues to work on first and therefore decided to develop a single view that would allow to see the priority ranking of the issues based on the number of occurrences and the number of days the issues had been around. Based on such prioritization, the IR process will be reengineered, and issues that are considered high priority will be addressed first.

Using this approach, the group wanted to classify the issues into data quality–related, process quality–related, and technology-related categories. Study of 152 IR items by the team revealed that 61 items were believed to have process-related issues, 51 were believed to have data quality issues, and the remaining 40 had technology-related issues (see Figure 9.3). Appropriate personnel were assigned to resolve each issue group.

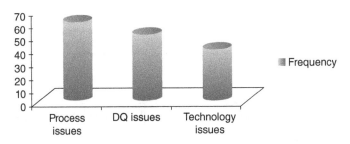

Figure 9.3   Distribution of 157 Issues

In each of these groups, the issues were further classified based on number of issue occurrences and age of the issue, which is the number of days that issue had been around. Figure 9.4 shows the distribution of the 51 data quality–related issues. Each cell in this figure shows issue IDs corresponding to age and occurrence buckets. This figure highlights the focus areas for issue remediation. To begin with, the team focused on the issues that had been around longest (higher age) and that occurred with greater frequency (higher occurrence), as indicated at the lower right gray section in Figure 9.4. These were followed by the other prioritized issues,

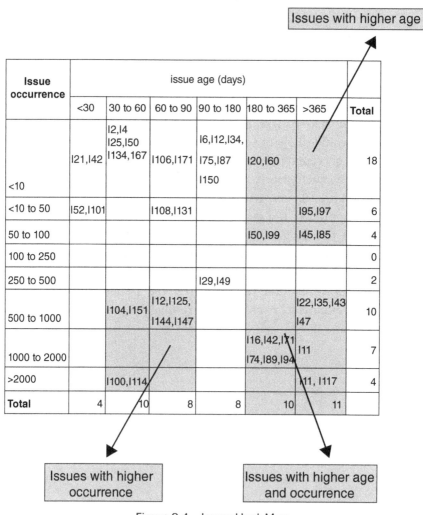

Issue occurrence	issue age (days)						Total
	<30	30 to 60	60 to 90	90 to 180	180 to 365	>365	
<10	I21,I42	I2,I4 I25,I50 I134,I167	I106,I171	I6,I12,I34, I75,I87 I150	I20,I60		18
<10 to 50	I52,I101		I108,I131			I95,I97	6
50 to 100					I50,I99	I45,I85	4
100 to 250							0
250 to 500				I29,I49			2
500 to 1000		I104,I151	I12,I125, I144,I147			I22,I35,I43 I47	10
1000 to 2000					I16,I42,I71 I74,I89,I94	I11	7
>2000		I100,I114				I11, I117	4
Total	4	10	8	8	10	11	

Issues with higher age

Issues with higher occurrence

Issues with higher age and occurrence

Figure 9.4   Issues Heat Map

as shown in the other gray areas in the figure. Regardless of issue classification, root-cause analysis, a systematic problem-solving approach aimed at identifying the upstream causes of problems or events, was performed for high-priority issues in each group.

As we all know, data quality issues can be resolved using many techniques available within the DQ methodology. Resolution of issues related to process inefficiencies can be accomplished through Lean and Six Sigma techniques. Technology issues need to be resolved by technology and architecture teams. Being able to prioritize the issues and assign them to the person with the appropriate knowledge resulted in a more efficient and effective issue resolution process in that function.

9.5   CONCLUSIONS

The conclusions of this chapter can be summarized as follows:

- It is important to understand that there is a linkage between DQ and PQ methodologies, which can be demonstrated through the issue management process.
- Upfront classification of issues into DQ, PQ, or technology groups assists teams to quickly resolve issues using proven methods. This can significantly reduce issue resolution cycle times.
- This approach cuts across silos and encourages various parts of an organization to work together to solve problems quickly.

Chapter 10

Information System Testing

10.0   INTRODUCTION

In previous chapters, we described methods to improve the quality of the data coming from various operational data sources and systems. If there are errors in these systems, then we might be working on the wrong data for evaluating DQ scores and initiating improvement activities. In order to verify that these systems are defect-free, we should perform measurement system analysis to ensure that the systems are highly reliable. Usually, the errors related to the systems can be fixed by studying the main effect of the factors or the combination effect of the factors interacting with these systems. The "system" here can be any software, analytical platform, or operational data source.

This chapter describes a methodology that can be used to test the performance of a given system and identify failing factors or signals that are responsible for poor information/data quality. The methodology described here uses the principles of robust engineering and orthogonal arrays to study two-factor interactions (combination effects) and main effects. Usually, it is sufficient to study two-factor combinations, because higher-order effects are small; hence, they can be neglected. This methodology aptly applies in the Improve phase of the DAIC approach because the main aim of this phase is to identify the failing factors and take suitable actions.

Generally, the technology teams or designers test the performance of a system by studying one factor at a time. Even after such tests, the system can fail and affect the information quality because of the presence of interactions between the factors. Therefore, the designers must study all the interactions and take appropriate corrective actions before the release of the product. The presence of interactions can be calculated by studying two-factor combination effects. To obtain these effects, the software or system should be tested under various combinations of the factors.

The different states of factors are referred to as different *levels*. For a given factor, the number of levels may be very high. If the number of such signals is very high, then the number of possible combinations can be of the order of hundreds. Since it is not feasible to test the system under all the combinations, a procedure is necessary to minimize the number of combinations. By using orthogonal arrays (OAs), we can minimize the number of combinations to be tested. This facilitates the study of all possible two-factor combination effects.

10.1   TYPICAL SYSTEM ARRANGEMENT

A typical testing arrangement is shown in Figure 10.1. This is similar to a p-diagram (parameter diagram) showing various components of the system. In Figure 10.1, the noise factors correspond to the hardware conditions (for example, the same system can be used in different countries under different rules and regulations). Control factors refer to system specifications. Here, we are basically interested in user conditions (or test factors or signals), as they are primarily used to develop test procedures with the help of orthogonal arrays.

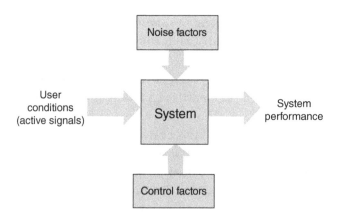

Figure 10.1   P-Diagram for System Testing

10.1.1   The Role of Orthogonal Arrays

The purpose of using orthogonal arrays in the design for robustness is to estimate the effects of several factors and required interactions by minimizing the number of experiments. In the case of software testing, the purpose of using the OAs is to study all the two-factor combinations with a minimum number of experiments. Note that, the number of combinations with OAs is equal to the number of experiments to be conducted using one factor at a time.

Suppose there are 23 active signals, 11 with two levels and the remaining 12 with three levels. If we want to study all the two-factor combinations, the total number of experiments in this case would be 1,606. For this example, if a suitable OA is used, the number of experimental runs needed to obtain all two-factor combinations would be 36. The corresponding array is $L_{36}(2^{11} \times 3^{12})$, where L denotes the Latin square design, 36 is the number of test runs, 11 is the number of two-level signal factors, and 12 is the number of three-level signal factors that can be used.

10.2   METHOD OF SYSTEM TESTING

For the purpose of explanation, let us consider the same example with 23 signals. Let A, B, C, ..., L, M, ..., U, V, W represent these 23 factors. The signal factors are allocated to the different columns of the L_{36} array, as shown in Table 10.1. In the array, the numbers 1, 2, 3 correspond to the different levels of the signals. The 36 test runs in Table 10.1 need to be performed to obtain the effect of two-factor combinations. The response for each combination is 0 or 1. 0 means the software function is satisfactory, and 1 means the software has some problems or there are some bugs.

10.2.1   Study of Two-Factor Combinations

Since the L_{36} array contains two-level and three-level factors, the following three types of two-factor combinations need to be studied.

Two-level factor combinations
Three-level factor combinations
Two-level and three-level factor combinations

Table 10.1   Signal Factor Allocation in $L_{36}(2^{11} \times 3^{12})$ Array

Signal Factor	A	B	.....	L	M	.....	V	W	
Run/Column	1	2	.....	12	13	.....	22	23	Response
1	1	1		1	1	.....	1	1	0 or 1
2	1	1		2	2	.....	2	2	0 or 1
3	1	1		3	3	.....	3	3	0 or 1
4	1	1		1	1	.....	3	3	0 or 1
5	1	1		2	2	.....	1	1	0 or 1
6	1	1		3	3	.....	2	2	0 or 1
7	1	1		1	1	.....	2	3	0 or 1
8	1	1		2	2	.....	3	1	0 or 1
9	1	1		3	3	.....	1	2	0 or 1
10	1	2		1	1	.....	3	2	0 or 1
11	1	2		2	2	.....	1	3	0 or 1
...	...	...	...	...	...	.....	...	...	...
32	2	2		2	1	.....	2	2	0 or 1
33	2	2		3	2	.....	3	3	0 or 1
34	2	2		1	3	.....	3	1	0 or 1
35	2	2		2	1	.....	1	2	0 or 1
36	2	2		3	2	.....	2	3	0 or 1

For factors A and B, the total number of a particular two-factor combination in an OA can be obtained by the following equation:

$$n_{ij} = (n_i * n_j)/N \qquad (10.1)$$

where n_{ij} = number of combinations of ith level of A and jth level of B
n_i = number of ith levels of A in a column assigned to A
n_j = number of jth levels of B in a column assigned to B
N = total number of experimental runs in the array

10.2.2   Construction of Combination Tables

Let us explain the procedure for constructing combination tables by considering the two-level factors A and B. These factors are assigned to columns 1 and 2 of the OA. For these factors, the possible combinations are A1B1, A1B2, A2B1, and A2B2, where A1 and A2 correspond to the first and second levels of factor A and B1 and B2 are the first and second levels of factor B. The number of these combinations can be obtained by Equation (10.1). For

Table 10.2   Interaction Table for Two-Level Factors

Factor A/Factor B	B1	B2
A1	# of 1s	# of 1s
A2	# of 1s	# of 1s

this example, the number of combinations of A1B1 is equal to $(18 \times 18)/36$, which is 9. Similarly, the number of other combinations is also equal to 9. For obtaining combination effects, we need to check how many times the system failed in a given combination. If the system fails at all times, then there is something wrong with that combination and the designer needs to fix this combination. In this example, for a particular combination if the system fails every time (9 times), then the designer must look into this combination and take appropriate corrective measures. Since the responses for the combinations of the OAs are 0s or 1s, the number of 1s will determine the combinations to be fixed. The number of 1s can be obtained by constructing the tables as outlined here. In the L_{36} array, the number of such tables is $^{11}C_2$, which is 55. For the two factors A and B, Table 10.2 is such a table.

In similar fashion, combination tables for three-level factors and combination tables for two-level and three-level factors can be constructed. Examples of three-level factors and two-level and three-level factors are shown in Tables 10.3 and 10.4, respectively.

The total number of two-factor combinations for the L_{36} array is = 55 (for two-level factors) + 66 (for three-level factors) + 132 (for two-level and three-level factors) = 253. Thus, using the L_{36} array, we can study all 1,606 combinations by conducting only 36 experiments and constructing the combination tables.

To summarize, the following steps outline the procedure for system testing:

1. Identification of active signals and their levels
2. Selection of a suitable OA for testing and performing required experimental runs

Table 10.3   Interaction Table for Three-Level Factors

Factor L/Factor M	M1	M2	M3
L1	# of 1s	# of 1s	# of 1s
L2	# of 1s	# of 1s	# of 1s
L3	# of 1s	# of 1s	# of 1s

Table 10.4   Interaction Table for Three-Level Factors

Factor A/Factor W	W1	W2	W3
A1	# of 1s	# of 1s	# of 1s
A2	# of 1s	# of 1s	# of 1s

3. Construction of the combination tables and identification of combinations with higher error rates to focus on

Even if the number of active signals is large, orthogonal arrays of greater size can be constructed to accommodate the signals.

10.3   MTS SOFTWARE TESTING

Since software design is a good example of system design, we will show how this testing methodology is useful in testing software. This particular software is intended to perform a multivariate data analysis called the Mahalanobis-Taguchi Strategy (MTS). MTS is a pattern analysis tool, which is useful for recognizing and evaluating various patterns in multidimensional cases. Examples of multivariate systems are medical diagnosis systems, face/voice recognition systems, and inspection systems. In this technique, Mahalanobis distance and robust design principles (Taguchi methods) are integrated; hence, its name.

Basically, there are four stages in MTS (Taguchi and Jugulum, 2002). They are:

- Stage I: Develop Measurement Scale
  - Select a Mahalanobis space or reference group with suitable variables and observations that are as uniform as possible.
  - Use the Mahalanobis space as a base or reference point of the scale.
- Stage II: Validate Measurement Scale
  - Identify the conditions outside the Mahalanobis space.
  - Compute the Mahalanobis distances for these conditions and check whether they are compatible with the decision maker's judgment.
- Stage III: Optimize Measurement Scale
  - Optimize the scale by identifying the useful set of variables using orthogonal arrays and signal-to-noise ratios.
- Stage IV: Conduct Future Diagnosis
  - Monitor the conditions using the scale, which is developed with the aid of the useful set of variables. Based on the values of Mahalanobis distances, take appropriate corrective actions.

In MTS, the Mahalanobis distance (MD) can be calculated by using the following equation:

$$\text{MD} = D^2 = (1/k)\, Z_i C^{-1} Z_i{}^T \qquad (10.2)$$

where Z_i = standardized vector obtained by standardized values of
$\qquad X_i\,(i = 1...k)$
$Z_i = (X_i - m_i)/s_i$
X_i = value of ith characteristic
m_i = mean of ith characteristic
s_i = standard deviation of ith characteristic
k = number of characteristics/variables
T = transpose of the vector
C = correlation matrix

A detailed description of the MTS method, along with case studies, is provided in Chapter 12 of this book.

Once the software has been designed, it is tested by using orthogonal arrays. As mentioned earlier, the most important aspect of this type of testing is selection of suitable usage conditions. Since this software is intended to perform a particular type of multivariate analysis, the following usage conditions (factors) are selected:

- Operating system (OS)
- Number of variables
- Sample size
- Correlation structure
- Data type

For these conditions, suitable levels were selected as shown in Table 10.5.

Since there are 4 factors at 3 levels and 1 factor at 2 levels, an $L_{18}(2^1 \times 3^7)$ array with 18 experimental combinations was selected for testing. The layout for this experimentation along with the results are shown in Table 10.6.

In Table 10.6, for columns where the factors A, B, C, D, and E are assigned, 1, 2, and 3 are used to denote level 1, level 2, and level 3, respectively. In the column for test results, "0" indicates satisfactory performance and "1" indicates failure. This data was analyzed by evaluating all two-factor effects. The details of the analysis are shown in Table 10.7.

Table 10.5   Factors and Levels for Testing

	Factors	Level 1	Level 2	Level 3
A	Operating system (OS)	OS 1	OS 2	
B	Number of variables	14	60	96
C	Sample size	50	200	500
D	Correlations	Weak	Mild	Strong
E	Data type	Qualitative (2 levels)	Qualitative (10 levels)	Continuous

Table 10.6   Layout and Results of Experimentation

L_{18} Array	Operating System (OS)	Number of Variables	Sample Size	Correlations	Data Type	Test Result
Run Number	A	B	C	D	E	
1	1	1	1	1	1	0
2	1	1	2	2	2	0
3	1	1	3	3	3	1
4	1	2	1	1	2	0
5	1	2	2	2	3	0
6	1	2	3	3	1	1
7	1	3	1	2	1	1
8	1	3	2	3	2	0
9	1	3	3	1	3	0
10	2	1	1	3	3	0
11	2	1	2	1	1	0
12	2	1	3	2	2	0
13	2	2	1	2	3	1
14	2	2	2	3	1	1
15	2	2	3	1	2	0
16	2	3	1	3	2	1
17	2	3	2	1	3	0
18	2	3	3	2	1	0

Table 10.7   Data Analysis (Two-Factor Combinations in Percent Failures)

	B1	B2	B3	C1	C2	C3	D1	D2	D3	E1	E2	E3
A1	33.33	33.33	33.33	33.33	0.00	66.67	0.00	33.33	66.67	66.67	0.00	33.33
A2	0.00	66.67	33.33	66.67	33.33	0.00	0.00	33.33	66.67	33.33	33.33	33.33
B1				0.00	0.00	50.00	0.00	0.00	50.00	0.00	0.00	50.00
B2				50.00	50.00	50.00	0.00	50.00	100.00	100.00	0.00	50.00
B3				100.00	0.00	0.00	0.00	50.00	50.00	50.00	50.00	0.00
C1							0.00	100.00	50.00	50.00	50.00	50.00
C2							0.00	0.00	50.00	50.00	0.00	0.00
C3							0.00	0.00	100.00	50.00	0.00	50.00
D1										0.00	0.00	0.00
D2										50.00	0.00	50.00
D3										100.00	50.00	50.00

From Table 10.7, we can see that B2D3, B2E1, B3C1, C1D2, C3D3, and D3E1 have 100 percent failures. These failures are related to a higher number of variables, lower sample sizes, and strong correlations (multicollinearity problems). For example, B2D3 is a case with a higher number of variables and strong correlations, and D3E1 is a case of strong correlations with qualitative variables at two levels. With these problems, the Mahalanobis distances cannot be computed precisely because the correlation matrix tends to become singular, causing problems with inverting the matrix. After identifying these problems, necessary actions were taken to change the algorithm for computing the Mahalanobis distances. This resulted in a significant reduction in the number of bugs. After taking the necessary actions, the program worked successfully in all 18 combinations of the OA.

10.4   CASE STUDY: A JAPANESE SOFTWARE COMPANY

This study was conducted by a software company in Japan. The software performance was required to be analyzed with 23 signals. These signals were designated as A, B, C..., U, V, W. For these factors, suitable levels were selected. Table 10.8 shows the layout and some signal factors with their selected levels.

The factors A, B, C,..., U, V, W were assigned to the different columns of the L_{36} array, as described before. The results of the 36 combinations are shown in Table 10.9.

Analysis of Results

With the help of the results shown in Table 10.10, the two-way interaction tables were constructed. As mentioned, for the signals in the L_{36} array, the total number of two-way tables is 253. Out of all two-factor combinations, only two combinations were considered important, as these had 100 percent errors. These two combinations are K2W1 and Q1S1 and are shown in Tables 10.11 and 10.12.

Table 10.8   Signal Factors and Number of Levels

Signal	A	B	M	N	O	P	J	...	W	K
Number of levels	2	3	3	3	3	3	2	...	3	2

Table 10.9   Results of the Different Combinations of the L_{36} Array

Experiment number	Response	Experiment number	Response
1	1	19	0
2	0	20	0
3	0	21	0
4	0	22	1
5	1	23	0
6	1	24	1
7	0	25	0
8	1	26	0
9	0	27	0
10	0	28	0
11	1	29	1
12	1	30	0
13	0	31	1
14	0	32	0
15	0	33	0
16	0	34	0
17	0	35	0
18	0	36	0

In Table 10.11, the different combinations of K and W are obtained (from the L_{36} array) as follows: K1W1 from the runs 1, 15, 16, 20, 27, 34; K1W2 from the runs 2, 13, 14, 21, 25, 35; K1W3 from the runs 3, 14, 18, 19, 26, 36; K2W1 from the runs 5, 8, 12, 24, 29, 31; K2W2 from the runs 6, 9, 10, 22, 30, 32; and K2W3 from the runs 4, 7, 11, 23, 28, 33. The combinations in Table 10.12 are likewise obtained in a similar way. The combinations Q1S1 (which has 100 percent errors) is obtained from the runs 1, 6, 11, 23 of the L_{36} array.

After identifying the significant interactions, suitable corrective actions were taken. Once the corrective actions were taken, 36 runs of the L_{36} array were again conducted. It was found that in these runs, all the responses were 0s, indicating that there were no bugs in the software.

Table 10.10   Two-Way Interactions

	B1	B2	...	C1	C2	...	D1	D2	...	S1	S2	S3	...	W1	W2	W3
A1	4	2		5	1		3	3						4	1	1
A2	2	2		1	3		2	2						3	1	0
B1				3	3		3	3						4	2	0
B2				3	1		1	3						3	0	1
C1							3	3						4	1	1
C2							3	1						3	1	0
...																
...																
K1														1	0	0
K2														6	2	1
...																
...																
Q1										4	0	0				
Q2										1	1	0				
Q3										1	1	2				
...																
S1																
S2																
S3																
...																
V1														3	0	1
V2														3	1	0
V3														1	1	0

Table 10.11   Combinations of K and W

	W1	W2	W3	Total
K1	1	0	0	1
K2	6	2	1	9
Total	7	2	1	10

Table 10.12   Combinations of Q and S

	S1	S2	S3	Total
Q1	4	0	0	4
Q2	1	1	0	2
Q3	1	1	2	4
Total	6	2	2	10

10.5   CASE STUDY: A FINANCE COMPANY

This study was conducted in a financial institution. The purpose of this project was to roll out error-free pricing software by eliminating performance-related errors and minimizing the number of cases to be tested. The financial institution selected 14 items as signal factors for testing (8 at 2 levels and 6 at 3 levels). Table 10.13 shows the layout of factors and levels.

The factors shown in Table 10.13 were assigned to the different columns of the L_{36} array as described previously. The results of the 36 combinations are shown in Table 10.14.

With the help of the results in Table 10.15, the two-way interaction tables were constructed. Suitable actions were taken on the combinations with 100 percent failure rates. This resulted in two additional versions of the software with improvements. These details are provided in Table 10.16. In the last version, the error was drastically reduced to 0 percent.

Table 10.13   Factor-Level Layout

Factor	Level 1	Level 2	Level 3
A	A1	A2	
B	B1	B2	
C	C1	C2	
D	D1	D2	
E	E1	E2	
F	F1	F2	
G	G1	G2	
H	H1	H2	
I	I1	I2	I3
J	J1	J2	J3
K	L1	L2	L3
L	K1	K2	K3
M	M1	M2	M3
N	N1	N2	N3

Table 10.14 L_{36} Array Layout and Test Results

L_{36} Array															
	1	2	3	4	5	6	7	8	9	10	11	12	13	14	
Run Number	A	B	C	D	E	F	G	H	I	J	K	L	M	N	Test Result
1	1	1	1	1	1	1	1	1	1	1	1	1	1	1	0
2	1	1	1	1	1	1	1	1	2	2	2	2	2	2	0
3	1	1	1	1	1	1	1	1	3	3	3	3	3	3	0
4	1	1	1	1	1	2	2	2	1	1	1	1	2	2	1
5	1	1	1	1	1	2	2	2	2	2	2	2	3	3	1
6	1	1	1	1	1	2	2	2	3	3	3	3	1	1	1
7	1	1	2	2	2	1	1	1	1	1	2	3	1	2	1
8	1	1	2	2	2	1	1	1	2	2	3	1	2	3	1
9	1	1	2	2	2	1	1	1	3	3	1	2	3	1	1
10	1	2	1	2	2	1	2	2	1	1	3	2	1	3	1
11	1	2	1	2	2	1	2	2	2	2	1	3	2	1	1
12	1	2	1	2	2	1	2	2	3	3	2	1	3	2	1
13	1	2	2	1	2	2	1	2	1	2	3	1	3	2	1
14	1	2	2	1	2	2	1	2	2	3	1	2	1	3	1
15	1	2	2	1	2	2	1	2	3	1	2	3	2	1	1
16	1	2	2	2	1	2	2	1	1	2	3	2	1	1	1
17	1	2	2	2	1	2	2	1	2	3	1	3	2	2	1
18	1	2	2	2	1	2	2	1	3	1	2	1	3	3	0
19	2	1	2	2	1	1	2	2	1	2	1	3	3	3	0
20	2	1	2	2	1	1	2	2	2	3	2	1	1	1	1
21	2	1	2	2	1	1	2	2	3	1	3	2	2	2	1
22	2	1	2	1	2	2	2	1	1	2	2	3	3	1	1
23	2	1	2	1	2	2	2	1	2	3	3	1	1	2	1
24	2	1	2	1	2	2	2	1	3	1	1	2	2	3	1
25	2	1	1	2	2	2	1	2	1	3	2	1	2	3	1
26	2	1	1	2	2	2	1	2	2	1	3	2	3	1	1
27	2	1	1	2	2	2	1	2	3	2	1	3	1	2	0
28	2	2	2	1	1	1	1	2	1	3	2	2	2	1	1
29	2	2	2	1	1	1	1	2	2	1	3	3	3	2	0
30	2	2	2	1	1	1	1	2	3	2	1	1	1	3	1
31	2	2	1	2	1	2	1	1	1	3	3	3	2	3	1
32	2	2	1	2	1	2	1	1	2	1	1	1	3	1	1
33	2	2	1	2	1	2	1	1	3	2	2	2	1	2	1
34	2	2	1	1	2	1	2	1	1	3	1	2	3	2	1
35	2	2	1	1	2	1	2	1	2	1	2	3	1	3	0
36	2	2	1	1	2	1	2	1	3	2	3	1	2	1	1

Table 10.15 Two-Way Interactions

	B1	B2	B3	C1	C2	C3	D1	D2	D3	E1	E2	E3	F1	F2	F3	G1	G2	G3	H1	H2	H3
A1	66.67	88.89	0.00	66.67	88.89	0.00	66.67	88.89	0.00	55.56	100.00	0.00	66.67	88.89	0.00	66.67	88.89	0.00	55.56	100.00	0.00
A2	77.78	77.78	0.00	77.78	77.78	0.00	77.78	77.78	0.00	77.78	77.78	0.00	66.67	88.89	0.00	77.78	77.78	0.00	88.89	66.67	0.00
A3	0.00	0.00	0.00	0.00	0.00	0.00	0.00	0.00	0.00	0.00	0.00	0.00	0.00	0.00	0.00	0.00	0.00	0.00	0.00	0.00	0.00
B1				55.56	88.89	0.00	66.67	77.78	0.00	55.56	88.89	0.00	55.56	88.89	0.00	55.56	88.89	0.00	66.67	77.78	0.00
B2				88.89	77.78	0.00	77.78	88.89	0.00	77.78	88.89	0.00	77.78	88.89	0.00	88.89	77.78	0.00	77.78	88.89	0.00
B3				0.00	0.00	0.00	0.00	0.00	0.00	0.00	0.00	0.00	0.00	0.00	0.00	0.00	0.00	0.00	0.00	0.00	0.00
C1							55.56	88.89	0.00	66.67	77.78	0.00	55.56	88.89	0.00	55.56	88.89	0.00	55.56	88.89	0.00
C2							88.89	77.78	0.00	66.67	100.00	0.00	77.78	88.89	0.00	88.89	77.78	0.00	88.89	77.78	0.00
C3							0.00	0.00	0.00	0.00	0.00	0.00	0.00	0.00	0.00	0.00	0.00	0.00	0.00	0.00	0.00
D1										55.56	88.89	0.00	44.44	100.00	0.00	55.56	88.89	0.00	55.56	88.89	0.00
D2										77.78	88.89	0.00	88.89	77.78	0.00	88.89	77.78	0.00	88.89	77.78	0.00
D3										0.00	0.00	0.00	0.00	0.00	0.00	0.00	0.00	0.00	0.00	0.00	0.00
E1													44.44	88.89	0.00	55.56	77.78	0.00	55.56	77.78	0.00
E2													88.89	88.89	0.00	88.89	88.89	0.00	88.89	88.89	0.00
E3													0.00	0.00	0.00	0.00	0.00	0.00	0.00	0.00	0.00
F1																55.56	77.78	0.00	55.56	77.78	0.00
F2																88.89	88.89	0.00	88.89	88.89	0.00
F3																0.00	0.00	0.00	0.00	0.00	0.00
G1																			66.67	77.78	0.00
G2																			77.78	88.89	0.00
G3																			0.00	0.00	0.00

(Continued)

135

Table 10.15 (Continued)

J1	J2	J3	K1	K2	K3	L1	L2	L3	M1	M2	M3	N1	N2	N3
83.33	83.33	66.67	66.67	83.33	83.33	83.33	66.67	83.33	66.67	83.33	83.33	83.33	83.33	66.67
83.33	66.67	83.33	66.67	66.67	100.00	66.67	83.33	83.33	100.00	100.00	33.33	66.67	100.00	66.67
0.00	0.00	0.00	0.00	0.00	0.00	0.00	0.00	0.00	0.00	0.00	0.00	0.00	0.00	0.00
66.67	83.33	66.67	83.33	50.00	83.33	50.00	83.33	83.33	83.33	83.33	50.00	66.67	83.33	66.67
100.00	66.67	83.33	50.00	100.00	100.00	100.00	66.67	83.33	83.33	100.00	66.67	83.33	100.00	66.67
0.00	0.00	0.00	0.00	0.00	0.00	0.00	0.00	0.00	0.00	0.00	0.00	0.00	0.00	0.00
83.33	66.67	66.67	66.67	66.67	83.33	66.67	66.67	66.67	83.33	83.33	50.00	50.00	83.33	83.33
83.33	83.33	83.33	66.67	83.33	100.00	83.33	83.33	100.00	83.33	100.00	66.67	100.00	100.00	50.00
0.00	0.00	0.00	0.00	0.00	0.00	0.00	0.00	0.00	0.00	0.00	0.00	0.00	0.00	0.00
83.33	50.00	83.33	50.00	83.33	83.33	83.33	66.67	66.67	83.33	83.33	50.00	66.67	83.33	66.67
83.33	100.00	66.67	83.33	66.67	100.00	66.67	83.33	100.00	83.33	100.00	66.67	83.33	100.00	66.67
0.00	0.00	0.00	0.00	0.00	0.00	0.00	0.00	0.00	0.00	0.00	0.00	0.00	0.00	0.00
66.67	66.67	66.67	50.00	66.67	83.33	66.67	66.67	66.67	66.67	83.33	50.00	83.33	83.33	33.33
100.00	83.33	83.33	83.33	83.33	100.00	83.33	83.33	100.00	100.00	100.00	66.67	66.67	100.00	100.00
0.00	0.00	0.00	0.00	0.00	0.00	0.00	0.00	0.00	0.00	0.00	0.00	0.00	0.00	0.00
66.67	66.67	66.67	66.67	66.67	83.33	66.67	66.67	66.67	66.67	83.33	50.00	66.67	83.33	50.00
100.00	100.00	83.33	83.33	83.33	100.00	83.33	83.33	100.00	100.00	100.00	66.67	100.00	100.00	83.33
0.00	0.00	0.00	0.00	0.00	0.00	0.00	0.00	0.00	0.00	0.00	0.00	0.00	0.00	0.00
83.33	66.67	66.67	66.67	66.67	83.33	66.67	83.33	66.67	83.33	83.33	50.00	66.67	83.33	66.67
83.33	83.33	83.33	66.67	83.33	100.00	83.33	66.67	100.00	83.33	100.00	66.67	83.33	100.00	66.67
0.00	0.00	0.00	0.00	0.00	0.00	0.00	0.00	0.00	0.00	0.00	0.00	0.00	0.00	0.00

Table 10.15 (Continued)

	H1	H2	H3	J1	J2	J3	K1	K2	K3	L1	L2	L3	M1	M2	M3
H1	83.33	66.67	66.67	50.00	83.33	83.33	83.33	50.00	83.33	66.67	83.33	66.67	66.67	83.33	66.67
H2	83.33	83.33	83.33	83.33	66.67	100.00	66.67	100.00	83.33	100.00	100.00	50.00	83.33	100.00	66.67
H3	0.00	0.00	0.00	0.00	0.00	0.00	0.00	0.00	0.00	0.00	0.00	0.00	0.00	0.00	0.00
J1				75	75	100	50	100	100	75	100.00	75	75	100	75
J2				50	75	100	100	50	75	100.00	75	50.00	75	75	75
J3				75	75	75	75	75	75	75	100.00	50.00	75	100	50
K1							75	50	75	50	100	50	50.00	100.00	50.00
K2							50	75	100	100	75	50	75	75	75
K3							100	100	75	100	100	75	100.00	100.00	75
L1										75	100	50	75	100	75
L2										75	75	75	75	75	75
L3										100	100	50	100	100	50
M1													75	100	75
M2													100	75	100
M3													50	100	25

Table 10.16   Calculator Performance Improvement

Version	Error Rate	100% Failure Combinations
V1	75%	81
V2	33%	24
V3	0%	0

10.6   CONCLUSIONS

The conclusions from this chapter are as follows:

- If the issue is technology-related, we can look at the factors or combinations of factors affecting the issue by using the methodology described in this chapter and take necessary actions to fix the factors so as to obtain accurate information from the system or operational data source.
- While testing the system or operational data source performance, it is important to study the effect of two-factor combinations in addition to the main factor effects.
- This simple and cost-effective methodology helps reduce most, but not all, system bugs.
- Methods like these are important in improving the quality of the data coming from the systems or operational data sources.

Chapter 11

Statistical Approach for Data Tracing

11.0 INTRODUCTION

Centralized data quality assessment can perform reasonability, boundary, and validity checks, but centralized accuracy checks are difficult to perform. Tracing operations back to the source and validating the data with source data is the best way to perform accuracy checks. However, given the vast quantity and complexity of data passing through the organization, it becomes economically unfeasible to carry out full, 100 percent data accuracy checks for ongoing operational processes. Therefore, there is a need to apply a statistical approach in tracing operations that includes sampling schemes and statistical process control (SPC) to prioritize top critical data elements, trace them back to the source system, and take proactive measures to monitor and control them. Further, a good data tracing approach also helps in data lineage activities. Data lineage is about understanding where data is and how it flows and transforms across the corporate network. In this chapter, we describe the tracing methodology, its important aspects, and how it can be linked to data lineage. As we can see, the tracing methodology is quite useful in the Assess and Improve phases of the DAIC approach.

11.1 DATA TRACING METHODOLOGY

A data tracing operation can be defined as an end-to-end activity to perform data quality accuracy checks for CDEs, prioritize CDEs, trace prioritized CDEs to source systems, and proactively monitor and control them through statistical methods. The most important aspects of data tracing are statistical sampling and use of SPC for monitoring and controlling. A generalized approach was developed to conduct statistical analysis and

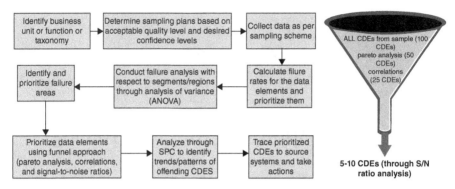

Figure 11.1 Generalized Data Tracing Approach (the CDE numbers in funnel are only for illustration)

recommend a suitable sampling plan. The description of this methodology is shown in Figure 11.1.

The first step in the methodology is to define the characteristics of a test case and identify the business units or functions that require tracing operations. After this step, we need to define sampling schemes based on acceptable quality levels and desired level of confidence. Section 11.1.1 provides a detailed discussion of statistical sampling. Then we need to collect data related to CDEs and DQ-based statistics (failure rates with respect to accuracy) of these CDEs to prioritize them with Pareto analysis.

The Pareto principle states that it is possible for many performance measures, such as defect rate and data quality, to separate the "vital few" CDEs/causes from the "trivial many." Historically, this concept was also known as the *80/20 rule,* which states that 80 percent of problems can be solved by focusing on 20 percent of CDEs/causes. The concept of the "vital few" and "trivial many" was first stated by J. M. Juran, a well-known expert in the field of quality. Juran (Juran and Godfrey, 1999) noted that the performance can be significantly improved by focusing the attention on the "vital few" causes.

A Pareto diagram consists of Pareto bars arranged in descending order and may use the failures due to CDEs/causes on the left-hand side and cumulative percentages on the right-hand side, as shown in Figure 11.2. This figure shows that about 10 CDEs are causing 80 percent of the problem. In other words, if we focus on these CDEs, we can solve 80 percent of the problem related to data quality performance.

The next step after prioritizing CDEs is to perform failure analysis for business units or functions through analysis of variance (ANOVA). This information helps in determining focus areas for tracing operations. ANOVA is a technique for identifying the significance or importance of

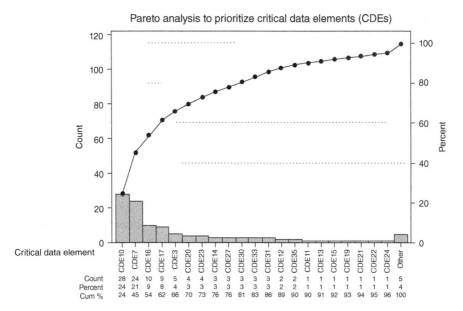

Figure 11.2   Pareto Analysis to Prioritize the CDEs

factors. ANOVA provides information on the magnitude as well as the statistical significance of the factor effects. Based on the results of ANOVA, we can prioritize focus areas. A detailed discussion of ANOVA is provided in Chapter 8.

In addition to identifying the main effects of important factors (functions, business units, or products), we need to look at the combination effect of these factors, since there may be CDE failures resulting from a particular combination that might not show up when we look at only the main effects. The combination effects are also tested using ANOVA (usually referred to as two-way ANOVA, since two factors are tested). A detailed discussion of two-factor combination effects is provided in Chapter 8. Once we know the areas to focus on, we can use the funnel approach (as shown in Figure 11.1) for further prioritization of CDEs through statistical techniques such as correlation analysis and signal-to-noise (S/N) ratios. (These techniques are described in Chapter 7.) After we finalize the list of prioritized CDEs, we can perform SPC analysis to identify associated trends or patterns that will help us understand abnormalities, trace them to the appropriate source system, and take actions to improve data quality.

As mentioned, one of the most important aspects of tracing is the selection of suitable sampling schemes. For determining appropriate sampling schemes, we need to know the acceptable defect rate, the factors with high failure rates, and the desired level of confidence (usually 95 percent or 99 percent). Section 11.1.1 provides a detailed discussion of sampling plans.

11.1.1   Statistical Sampling

Let us suppose that we are conducting analysis on the proportion p of the population (of all Basel II data elements) that potentially has errors. To do that, we sample the elements randomly and let $\bar{P}$ represent the sample proportion of the data elements with errors. We want to use $\bar{P}$ to infer p.

According to the *central limit theorem,* for a sufficiently large population, the sampling distribution of $\bar{P}$ is approximately normal, with mean p and standard deviation $\sqrt{p(1-p)/n}$, where n is the sample size. Because p is the unknown parameter, we substitute $\bar{P}$ for p in the standard deviation to obtain the standard error:

$$\text{SE}(\bar{p}) = \sqrt{\frac{p(1-p)}{n}} \qquad (11.1)$$

The multiple used to obtain the confidence interval for the population error rate p is a Z-value. For a 95 percent confidence interval, it is 1.96. Then, in order to find the confidence interval for the population error rate, we use the following formula, which is based on the assumption of a large sample size:

$$\bar{p} \pm 1.96 \times \sqrt{\frac{p(1-p)}{n}} \qquad (11.2)$$

We want to point out one assumption considered when we analyze the population by statistical sampling: The error rates of all data elements are assumed to follow the same distribution. This is the underlying assumption that sample data is identically, independently distributed (i.i.d.). In other words, we treat different data element errors in the same way. We care more about the total number of errors in the sample, but less about the specific data elements that have errors, since their error rates are assumed to be the same.

Sample Size

Given the methodology we've explained, the sample size depends on the three factors: the sample error rate $\bar{P}$, the confidence interval (95 percent), and the desired margin of error (which is equal to half the confidence interval). Let m be the margin of error, then the sample size can be computed by

$$n = \frac{z^2 \times p \times (1-p)}{m^2} \tag{11.3}$$

For instance, suppose the sample error rate $\bar{p}$ is 3.96 percent, and let us choose the margin of error to be 3 percent. Then a desired sample size is 162. However, in order to get a more accurate estimated result, a larger sample size is highly desirable. This point is further demonstrated when we discuss the assumption of a large sample size.

The 95 percent confidence interval of the population error rate can be computed by

$$\left[\bar{p} - Z \times \sqrt{\frac{p(1-p)}{n}}, \bar{p} + Z \times \sqrt{\frac{p(1-p)}{n}} \right] \tag{11.4}$$

where $Z = 1.96$ is the test statistic. Plugging in those numbers, we derive that the 95 percent confidence interval of the population error rate is [0.0016, 0.0776] or [0.16 percent, 7.76 percent].

Therefore, we are at least 95 percent sure that the population error rate is between 0.16 percent and 7.76 percent.

Now let's discuss the assumption of a large sample size, which is a prerequisite of the sampling methodology. A rule of thumb for checking the validity of this assumption is the following. Let PL and PU be the lower and upper limits of the confidence interval. Then the sample size is sufficiently large, and the confidence interval is valid if

$$n \times \text{PL} > 5, \quad n \times (1 - \text{PL}) > 5, \, n \times \text{PU} > 5, \text{ and } n \times (1 - \text{PU}) > 5 \tag{11.5}$$

It can be seen that the first condition is violated with the sample testing results, though the other three are satisfied. This indicates a desire to increase the sample size. Once the sample size is increased, n will be larger and the confidence interval will be narrower, which means that PL will be larger as well. A larger n and a larger PL will help meet the first condition.

After determining the suitable sampling scheme and sample size, the next step is to compare the samples that are collected for tracing and the defect rate. If these requirements are satisfied, then tracing operations can be shifted to the other areas. While doing this shift, we need to continually focus on prioritized CDEs and maintain proactive

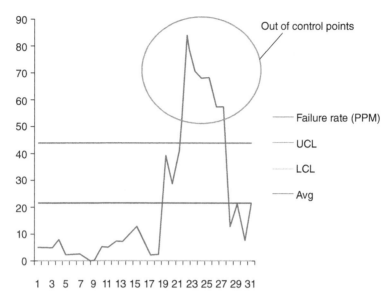

Figure 11.3   Example of an SPC Chart

controls using SPC. An effective process control system can be developed through control charts.

The purpose of control charts is to show the behavior of processes over a period of time with respect to statistical control limits. If the performance is within the control limits, then we say that process is in statistical control and under the influence of natural variation. On the other hand, if the performance is outside of the control limits, then we can say that process is out of control and is under the influence of a special cause of variation.

Figure 11.3 shows an example of an SPC chart. With the SPC schemes, we ensure the stability, predictability, and capability of a process. (A detailed discussion of SPC is provided in Chapter 5.)

11.2   CASE STUDY: TRACING

This section describes a tracing case study in which the methodology described in Figure 11.1 was used.

11.2.1   Analysis of Test Cases and CDE Prioritization

Over the past two years, 274 traces (test cases) were performed against 42 data elements (in total, 11,508 data elements). Table 11.1 shows examples of the test case layout used in the data analysis.

Table 11.1 Example of Test Case Layout

Based on Test Cases	
Test Cases	Pass/Fail
Test Case 1	0
Test Case 2	1
Test Case 3	0
Test Case 4	1
Test Case 5	1
...	...
Test Case 270	0
Test Case 271	0
Test Case 272	1
Test Case 273	0
Test Case 274	1

Only 1.004 percent of the data elements (out of 11,508) failed. However, the test case failure rate is 12.57 percent. These failures are driven by 22 data elements. Figure 11.4 shows the prioritization of the CDEs through Pareto analysis.

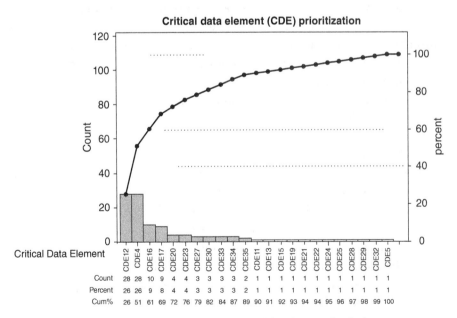

Figure 11.4 CDE Prioritization Using Pareto Analysis

The next step is to identify focus areas through ANOVA (main effects and two-factor combinations). Figures 11.5a and 11.5b show the summary of the analyses.

From Figure 11.5, we can conclude that the effects of the factors are statistically significant, as p-values are very small. In other words, at least one segment and at least one exposure type have significantly higher error rates as compared to the others. We can conclude the same through combination analysis as well (see Table 11.2).

After this step, we moved on to a different phase of the analysis, which is selection of a suitable sampling scheme. Using the procedure described earlier in this chapter, we determined sample size for the 90 percent and 95 percent levels of confidence. The details are shown in the Table 11.3.

Table 11.3 provides sample size corresponding to 90 percent and 95 percent bounds. In this case, it was decided that the 95 percent level of confidence would be used, for which the sufficient sample size is 169, with 95 percent confidence limits of 134 and 201. Please note that we have collected 274 samples, although 169 samples are sufficient for the desired defect rate of less than 2 percent. Figure 11.6 shows the defect rate is in statistical control and is at the level of less than 2 percent.

So this analysis helps us conclude that for this tracing exercise 169 samples are sufficient, and the remaining effort can be allocated to the other areas where tracing has not been started. While doing so, we need to perform proactive monitoring of the 22 CDEs that have failure rates through SPC on an ongoing basis. It is important to note that reducing samples from 274 to 169 translates into a 38 percent reduction of tracing effort in the given area.

After conducting the analysis, the following were proposed for deploying this statistical approach:

- Track the performance of 22 CDEs using control charts.
- As the error rate decreases, you can reduce the effort of tracing accordingly (as shown in Figure 11.7 with an illustrative control chart).
- Leverage this effort to target or predict likely failures associated with the data elements having defects.
- Leverage learnings to develop and continuously update business rules for automated testing of important CDEs.
- Develop an automated testing scheme identified by sampling methodology with business rules and a data quality operating model (DQOM).

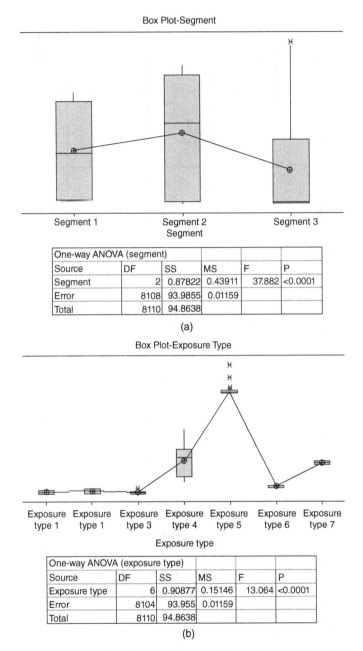

Box Plot-Segment

One-way ANOVA (segment)

Source	DF	SS	MS	F	P
Segment	2	0.87822	0.43911	37.882	<0.0001
Error	8108	93.9855	0.01159		
Total	8110	94.8638			

(a)

Box Plot-Exposure Type

One-way ANOVA (exposure type)

Source	DF	SS	MS	F	P
Exposure type	6	0.90877	0.15146	13.064	<0.0001
Error	8104	93.955	0.01159		
Total	8110	94.8638			

(b)

Figure 11.5   ANOVA to test the significance of main factor effects. Low P-value in both cases indicates that the effects are statistically insignificant.

Table 11.2 Effect of Combinations of the Factors (shaded areas indicate important combinations)

Based on Test Cases			
Business Segment/ Exposure type	Segment 1	Segment 2	Segment 3
Exposure Type 1		19.23%	
Exposure Type 2	100.00%	11.82%	0.00%
Exposure Type 3	22.20%	15.55%	7.14%
Exposure Type 4		0.00%	
Exposure Type 5		7.69%	
Exposure Type 6		0.00%	
Exposure Type 7	0.00%	10.00%	

Based on DQ Errors			
Business Segment/ Exposure type	Segment 1	Segment 2	Segment 3
Exposure Type 1		1.37%	
Exposure Type 2	55.17%	0.62%	0.00%
Exposure Type 3	1.53%	1.18%	0.49%
Exposure Type 4		0.00%	
Exposure Type 5		0.78%	
Exposure Type 6		0.00%	
Exposure Type 7	0.00%	0.05%	

Table 11.3 Statistical Sampling Scheme

Confidence Level	Lower Bound	Sample Size	Upper Bound
90%	34	42	50
95%	134	169	201

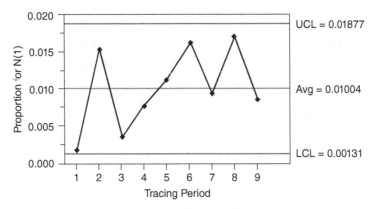

Figure 11.6 Control Chart for the Defect Rate

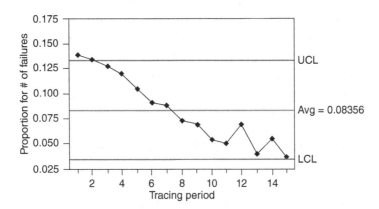

Figure 11.7 Illustrative Example to Show the Reduction in Failure Rate

11.3 DATA LINEAGE THROUGH DATA TRACING

As stated, data tracing is an end-to-end activity to perform DQ accuracy checks for CDEs across functions or business units. Since tracing helps measure the accuracy of CDEs starting from the source system and various transformational points, it is extremely useful in data lineage activities.

The lineage of data is quite important for businesses such as financial institutions that must abide by government regulations. Data lineage refers to the data life cycle that includes the data origination points and various points at which data undergoes transformations over time. Data lineage also helps us understand various diverse processes that the data goes through. Data lineage can help organizations in several different ways:

More efficient and cost-effective compliance and audits: Many financial institutions spend a lot of time in preparing information for data lineage audits, which takes a lot of time and effort. Through proper lineage activities, we can reduce the time and effort required for those audits.

More reliability of exposure risks reported by banks: Lineage also plays an important role in determining the reliability of the exposure risk reported by financial institutions.

Data loss prevention: Data lineage helps in combining data from various sources and effectively using such data in various decision-making activities. This is useful in preventing data losses in data aggregation situations and allows good data control. Prevention of data loss reduces the impact of poor data quality.

Sound data analytics: As described in Chapter 13, good data is very important for running data analytics and obtaining meaningful insights. If we fail to understand the data, its sources, and its transformational points, we will not able to use such data in obtaining meaningful business outcomes.

Therefore, employing a good and confident tracing approach enables us to understand the data lineage, identify CDEs of interest, and perform root-cause analysis to improve data quality levels as well as perform several other business-related activities as follows:

- Perform data operations
- Create and modify data
- Understand data uncertainties and risks
- Understand business processes/systems that touch the data
- Compare data with business-defined specifications

11.4 CONCLUSIONS

The following conclusions can be drawn from this chapter:

- Statistical analysis (Pareto analysis, sampling plans, ANOVA, and SPC analysis) helps us to follow a systematic process for end-to-end DQ assessment.
- The statistical framework developed in this chapter can be used to reduce the tracing effort required for performing DQ operations by identifying areas on which to focus.
- The framework also helps in proactive monitoring of important CDEs.
- Automation of the toolset used in this chapter assists in the rapid application of this methodology in many areas.
- The data tracing approach can be generalized for defining a statistical sampling methodology and for end-to-end data quality accuracy testing.
- Using a sound tracing approach enables us to understand data lineage, which helps businesses in many ways to increase speed and efficiency in data-related decision activities.

Chapter 12

Design and Development of Multivariate Diagnostic Systems

12.0 INTRODUCTION

In previous chapters, we have described the importance of data quality and how it can be measured and improved with the critical data element (CDE) view. After ensuring high-quality and reliable data, the data should be used in a meaningful way to derive important insights. The methodology described in this chapter is useful in ensuring high information quality that will help up us to formulate important insights. We usually have to deal with the information based on more than one variable or CDE in order to draw insights, which will need to be used in relation to one another to make important decisions. Systems with more than one CDE or variable can be called *multivariate systems*. Examples of multivariate systems include medical diagnosis systems, client relationship mechanisms, fraud detection systems, and fire alarm sensor systems. This chapter describes the Mahalanobis-Taguchi Strategy (MTS) and its applicability to developing a multivariate diagnostic system with a measurement scale. The Mahalanobis distance (MD) is used to measure the distances in a multivariate system, and Taguchi's principles are used to measure accuracy of the system and identify important variables that are sufficient for the measurement system. This methodology is becoming increasingly popular, evidenced by the many case applications around the globe.

12.1 THE MAHALANOBIS-TAGUCHI STRATEGY

The Mahalanobis-Taguchi Strategy (MTS) is a pattern analysis technique, which is used to conduct system diagnosis through a multivariate

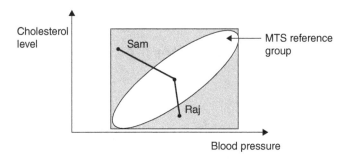

Figure 12.1   Importance of Correlations in Multivariate Systems

measurement scale. In multivariate systems, patterns are difficult to represent in quantitative terms and they are extremely sensitive to correlations between the variables. The importance of correlations in multivariate systems is illustrated by Figure 12.1.

In Figure 12.1, if we look at the variable blood pressure and cholesterol levels independently of each other, then we can conclude that both Sam and Raj are normal (within the rectangular area). However, if we consider the correlations between the variables, then we can say that they are somewhat abnormal, as they do not fall within the elliptical area that forms the reference group. Furthermore, we can precisely state that Sam is sicker than Raj, since his distance from the center of the ellipse is larger than that of Raj. Through MTS analysis, we can obtain such insights by expressing patterns in quantitative terms.

The Mahalanobis distance (MD), which was introduced by well-known Indian statistician P. C. Mahalanobis, measures distances of points in multidimensional spaces. Taguchi methods have been successfully applied in many engineering applications to improve the performance of the products/processes/systems. They are proved to be extremely useful and cost effective. In the context of MTS, following two aspects of Taguchi methods are used:

- Signal to noise ratios or S/N ratios: they are used to measure the accuracy of MTS diagnostic system
- Orthogonal arrays: they are used to optimize the diagnostic systems by minimizing the number of variable combinations to study.

In the subsequent sections of this chapter, a detailed discussions on S/N ratios and orthogonal arrays in relation to MTS have been provided.

Figure 12.2   The Gram-Schmidt Process

The Mahalanobis distance has been used extensively in several areas such as spectrographic applications and agricultural applications. Because it takes correlations between the variables into account, the Mahalanobis distance has proved to be superior to other multidimensional distances such as the Euclidean distance. The Mahalanobis distance is calculated by using the following equation:

$$\text{Mahalanobis distance} = (1/k)\, Z_i C^{-1} Z_i{}^{\mathrm{T}} \qquad (12.1)$$

where Z_i = standardized vector of X_i $(i = 1\ldots k)$,
        C = correlation matrix, and
        k = number of CDEs/variables

The Mahalanobis distance can also be calculated by using the Gram-Schmidt orthogonalization process. The Gram-Schmidt process (GSP) can simply be stated as follows: Given linearly independent vectors $Z_1, Z_2, \ldots,$ Z_k, there exist mutually perpendicular vectors $U_1, U_2, \ldots, U_k$ with the same linear span. This process is described in Figure 12.2.

12.1.1   The Gram Schmidt Orthogonalization Process

Given linearly independent vectors $Z_1, Z_2, \ldots Z_k$, there exist mutually perpendicular vectors $U_1, U_2, \ldots U_k$ with the same linear span (Figure 12.2).

The Gram-Schmidt vectors are constructed sequentially by setting:

$$
\begin{aligned}
U_1 &= Z_1 \\
U_2 &= Z_2 - [(Z'_2 U_1)/(U'_1 U_1)]U_1 \\
&\;\;\vdots \\
U_k &= Z_k - [(Z'_k U_1)/(U'_1 U_1)]U_1 - \ldots - [(Z'_k U_{k-1})/(U'_{k-1} U_{k-1})]U_{k-1}
\end{aligned}
\qquad (12.2)
$$

where $'$ denotes transpose of a vector. When calculating MD using the GSP, standardized values for the variables are used. Therefore, in the preceding set of equations $Z_1, Z_2, \ldots Z_k$ correspond to standardized values. From this set of equations, it is clear that the transformation process depends largely on the first variable.

Calculation of MD using Gram Schmidt's Orthogonalization Process

Suppose we have a sample of size n, and each sample contains observations on k variables. After standardizing the variables, we will have a set of standardized vectors. Let these vectors be as follows:

$$Z_1 = (z_{11}, z_{12}, \ldots, z_{1n})$$
$$Z_2 = (z_{21}, z_{22}, \ldots, z_{2n})$$
$$\vdots$$
$$Z_k = (z_{k1}, z_{k2}, \ldots, z_{kn})$$

After performing GSP, we have orthogonal vectors as follows:

$$U_1 = (u_{11}, u_{12}, \ldots, u_{1n})$$
$$U_2 = (u_{21}, u_{22}, \ldots, u_{2n})$$
$$\vdots$$
$$U_k = (u_{k1}, u_{k2}, \ldots, u_{kn})$$

It easily follows that the mean of vectors $U_1, U_2, \ldots, U_k$ is zero. Let s_1, $s_2, \ldots s_k$ be standard deviations (s.d.s) of $U_1, U_2, \ldots, U_k$, respectively. Since we have a sample of size n, there will be n different MDs. The MD corresponding to the jth observation of the sample is computed using Equation (12.3).

$$MD_j = (1/k)[(u_{1j}^2/s_1^2) + (u_{2j}^2/s_2^2) + \cdots + (u_{kj}^2/s_k^2)] \qquad (12.3)$$

where $j = 1 \ldots n$. The values of MD obtained from Equations (12.1) and (12.3) are exactly the same, and this can be proved easily.

The most important consideration for developing a multivariate measurement system using the Mahalanobis distance is to have a reference point. While it is easier to obtain a reference point for the scale with a single characteristic, it is not so easy to obtain a single reference point when we are dealing with multiple characteristics. Therefore, in MTS, the reference point corresponding to multiple variables is obtained with the help of a group of observations that are as uniform as possible and still enable us to distinguish their different patterns through the MD. These observations are modified in such a way that their center is located at the origin and the corresponding Mahalanobis distances are scaled so as to make the average distance of this group unity. The set of observations used for the reference is often referred to as the *Mahalanobis space* (MS) or *reference group* or *normal group*. Selection of this group is entirely at the discretion of the decision maker conducting the diagnosis. In fraud analytics, this group can be one where there are no incidences of fraud; in a medical diagnosis application, this group can be a set of people without any health problems; and in stock market predictions, this group could correspond to companies having average steady growth in a three-year period. The observations in this group are similar but not the same. Judicious selection of this group is extremely important for accurate diagnosis or predictions.

After developing the scale, the next step is the validation of the scale, which is done with the help of observations that are outside the Mahalanobis space. If the scale is good, the distances of these observations must be consistent with the decision maker's judgment. In other words, if an observation does not belong to the reference group, then it should have a larger distance. To quantify the diagnostics accuracy, we typically use a signal-to-noise (S/N) ratio metric. S/N ratio captures the magnitude of real effects after making some adjustment for uncontrollable variation (noise) by taking into account the correlation between the true or observed information (i.e., input signals) and the output of the diagnostic system (the Mahalanobis distance). In a multivariate context, S/N ratio can simply be defined as the measure of the accuracy of the diagnostics. A typical multidimensional predictive system that is used in MTS can be described using Figure 12.3.

As mentioned, the output or diagnosis accuracy should correlate well with the input signal, and S/N ratios measure this correlation. The diagnostics are conducted based on the information on the variables defining the system, and they should be "accurate" even in the presence of noise factors such as different places of measurement, operating conditions, and so forth.

If the accuracy of the diagnosis is satisfactory, then we identify a useful subset of variables that is sufficient for the measurement scale with acceptable diagnostic accuracy. Experience shows that, in many cases, the

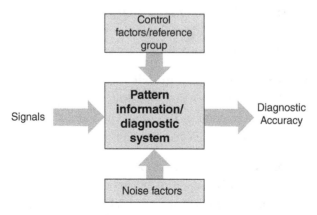

Figure 12.3   Pattern Information or Diagnostic System Used in MTS

accuracy with useful variables is better than that with the original set of variables. However, in some cases, the accuracy with useful variables might be less—which might still be desirable, as it helps reduce the cost of inspection or measurement. In multidimensional systems, the total number of combinations to be examined would be of the order of several thousands; hence, it is not possible to examine all combinations. Here, we propose use of orthogonal arrays (OAs) to reduce the number of combinations to be tested. OAs are developed to estimate the effects of the variables by minimizing the number of combinations to be examined. They have been in use for quite a long time in the field of experimental design. In MTS, the variables are assigned to different columns of an OAs. Based on S/N ratios obtained from different variable combinations, important variables are identified. The future diagnosis is carried out only with these important variables.

12.2   STAGES IN MTS

From the preceding discussion, the basic stages in MTS can be summarized as follows:

Stage I: Develop Measurement Scale
- Select a Mahalanobis space or reference group with suitable variables and observations that are as uniform as possible.
- Use the Mahalanobis space as a base or reference point of the scale.

Stage II: Validate Measurement Scale
- Identify the conditions outside the Mahalanobis space.
- Compute the Mahalanobis distances of these conditions and check whether they are consistent with the decision maker's judgment.

Stage III: Optimize Measurement Scale
- Optimize the scale by identifying the useful set of variables using orthogonal arrays and signal-to-noise ratios.

Stage IV: Conduct Future Diagnosis
- Monitor the conditions using the scale developed with the help of the useful set of variables. Based on the values of Mahalanobis distances, take appropriate corrective actions.

Figure 12.4 shows the different steps in MTS.

From the preceding discussion, it is clear that orthogonal arrays play a prominent role in the third stage of MTS analysis. Each experimental

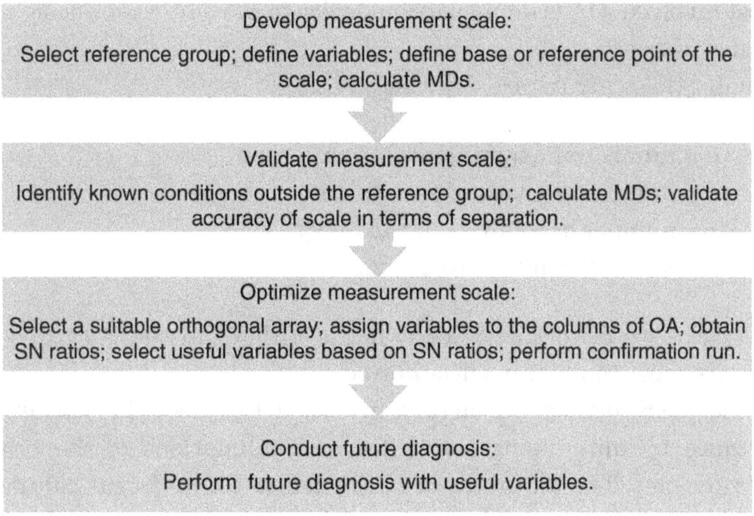

Develop measurement scale:
Select reference group; define variables; define base or reference point of the scale; calculate MDs.

Validate measurement scale:
Identify known conditions outside the reference group; calculate MDs; validate accuracy of scale in terms of separation.

Optimize measurement scale:
Select a suitable orthogonal array; assign variables to the columns of OA; obtain SN ratios; select useful variables based on SN ratios; perform confirmation run.

Conduct future diagnosis:
Perform future diagnosis with useful variables.

Figure 12.4   Steps in MTS

run in the orthogonal array design matrix uses a subset of variables; the resulting S/N ratios of these subsets are calculated using the distances outside of the reference group.

12.3 THE ROLE OF ORTHOGONAL ARRAYS AND SIGNAL-TO-NOISE RATIO IN MULTIVARIATE DIAGNOSIS

In the context of MTS, orthogonal arrays are used to estimate the effects of several factors and the effect of interactions by minimizing the number of experiments, and signal-to-noise ratio is used as a measure of diagnosis accuracy. Use of S/N ratios ensures a high level of prediction with useful variables. S/N ratios are computed for all combinations of the orthogonal array using Mahalanobis distances. S/N ratios are also used to select important variables for future diagnosis. Using S/N ratios as the response, average effects of variables are computed at level 1 (presence) and level 2 (absence). Based on these effects, the importance of variables can be determined. The examples provided in this chapter show how we can make such determinations.

12.3.1 The Role of Orthogonal Arrays

In robust engineering, the main role of OAs is to permit engineers to evaluate a product design with respect to robustness against noise and the cost involved. OA is an inspection device to prevent a poor design from going downstream.

Usually, these arrays are denoted as $L_a(b^c)$

where a = number of experimental runs
   b = number of levels of each factor
   c = number of columns in the array
   L denotes Latin square design

Arrays can have factors with many levels, although two- and three-level factors are most commonly encountered.

In the MTS, orthogonal arrays are used to select the variables of importance by minimizing the different combinations of the original set of variables. The variables are assigned to the different columns of the array. The presence and absence of the variables are considered the levels. Since the variables have only two levels, two-level arrays are used in MTS application. The importance of the variables is judged based on their ability to measure the degree of abnormality on the measurement scale. For each run of an OA, the MDs corresponding to the known abnormal conditions or the conditions outside the MS are computed. We need not consider the MDs corresponding to the reference group because we know that this group is healthy and, based on this group, scale is constructed.

For the purpose of illustration, consider the following example.

Let there be five variables X_1, X_2, X_3, X_4, and X_5. Let us allocate these variables in the first five columns of the $L_8(2^7)$ array, as shown in Table 12.1. In this table, "1" indicates the level corresponding to the presence of a variable and "2" indicates the level corresponding to the absence of a variable. Consider the first three runs of Table 12.1.

1st Run: 1-1-1-1-1

In this run, the MS is constructed with the variable combination X_1-X_2-X_3-X_4-X_5. The correlation matrix is of the order 5×5. The MDs of abnormals are estimated with this matrix.

2nd Run: 1-1-1-2-2

In this run, the MS is constructed with the variable combination X_1-X_2-X_3. The correlation matrix is of the order 3×3. The MDs of abnormals are estimated with this matrix.

Table 12.1   Variable Allocation in $L_8(2^7)$ Array

$L_8(2^7)$ Array							
Column	1	2	3	4	5	6	7
Run/Variable	X_1	X_2	X_3	X_4	X_5		
1	1	1	1	1	1	1	1
2	1	1	1	2	2	2	2
3	1	2	2	1	1	2	2
4	1	2	2	2	2	1	1
5	2	1	2	1	2	1	2
6	2	1	2	2	1	2	1
7	2	2	1	1	2	2	1
8	2	2	1	2	1	1	2

3rd Run: 1-2-2-1-1

In this run, the MS is constructed with the variable combination X_1-X_4-X_5. The correlation matrix is of the order 3×3. The MDs of abnormals are estimated with this matrix.

Based on the MDs of the conditions, outside the MS, corresponding to the runs of an orthogonal array, we can evaluate S/N ratios. Thus, OAs are required for testing the different combinations of the variables to identify the variables of importance based on their ability to measure the conditions outside the MS.

12.3.2   The Role of S/N Ratios in MTS

The S/N ratio tries to capture the magnitude of true information (i.e., signals) after making some adjustment for uncontrollable variation (i.e., noise).

In the case of multivariate diagnosis, the S/N ratio is defined as the measure of the accuracy of the measurement scale for predicting abnormal conditions. S/N ratio is expressed in decibel (dB) units. A higher value for the S/N ratio means lower error of prediction. Note that S/N ratios are calculated using abnormal conditions only, as it is required that the accuracy of the scale be tested based on these conditions.

In multidimensional applications, it is important to identify a useful set of variables that is sufficient to detect the abnormals. It is also important to assess the performance of the given system and the degree of improvement in the performance. In this method, S/N ratios are used to accomplish these objectives.

After obtaining the MDs for the known abnormal conditions corresponding to the various combinations of an OA, S/N ratios are computed for all these combinations to determine the useful set of variables. S/N ratios are important to improve the accuracy of the measurement scale and reduce the cost of diagnosis. The useful set of variables is obtained by evaluating the *gain* in the S/N ratio, which is the difference between the average S/N ratio when the variable is used in an OA and the average S/N ratio when the variable is not used in an OA. If the gain is positive, then the variable is useful.

12.3.3 Types of S/N Ratios

In MTS application, typically the following types of S/N ratios are used:

- Larger-the-better type
- Nominal-the-best type
- Dynamic type

When the true levels of abnormals are not known, the larger-the-better type of S/N ratios is used if all the observations outside the reference group are abnormals. This is because the MDs for abnormals should be higher. If the observations outside the reference group are a mixture of normals and abnormals, then the nominal-the-best type of S/N ratios is used. When the levels of abnormals are known, the dynamic type of S/N ratios is used. In some cases, it is quite difficult to obtain the levels of severity of the abnormals based on the knowledge of the person conducting the diagnosis. In such situations, if we know the abnormals with different degrees of severity (different categories), dynamic S/N ratios can be used by taking the average of the square root of the MDs (working average) in each category as known levels of abnormals.

Equations for S/N Ratios

Larger-the-Better Type

The procedure for calculating S/N ratios corresponding to a run of an OA is as follows:

Let there be t abnormal conditions. Let D_1^2, D_2^2,..., D_t^2 be MDs corresponding to the abnormal situations. The S/N ratio (for the larger-the-better criterion) corresponding to the qth run of an OA is given by the following:

$$\text{S/N ratio} = \eta_q = 10 \log_{10} \left[(1/t) \sum_{i=1}^{t} (1/D_i^2) \right] \qquad (12.4)$$

Nominal-the-Best Type

The procedure for calculating S/N ratios corresponding to a run of an OA is as follows:

Let there be t abnormal conditions. Let D_1^2, D_2^2,..., D_t^2 be MDs corresponding to the abnormal situations. The S/N ratio (nominal-the-better type) corresponding to the qth run of an OA is calculated as follows:

$$T = \text{sum of all } D_i\text{s} = \sum_{i=1}^{t} D_i$$

$$S_m = \text{sum of squares due to mean} = T^2/t$$

$$V_e = \text{mean square error} = \text{variance} = \sum_{i=1}^{t} \frac{(D_i - \bar{D})^2}{(t-1)}$$

where $\bar{D}$ is the average of the D_is

$$\text{S/N ratio} = \eta_q = 10 \log_{10} \left[\frac{1/n(S_m - V_e)}{V_e} \right] \qquad (12.5)$$

Dynamic Type

An examples of the dynamic type is a weather forecasting system and the specific case of rainfall prediction. The procedure for calculating S/N ratios corresponding to a run of an OA is as follows:

Let there be t abnormal conditions. Let D_1^2, D_2^2,..., D_t^2 be the MDs corresponding to the abnormal conditions. Let $M_1, M_2,..., M_t$ be the true levels of severity (rainfall values in the rainfall prediction system example).

For each run of the OA, construct the following ANOVA table:

Source	Degrees of Freedom	Sum of Squares
β	1	S_β
e	$T - 1$	S_e
Total	T	S_T

In the preceding ANOVA table,

$$S_T = \text{total sum of squares} = \sum_{i=1}^{t} D_i^2$$

$$r = \text{sum of squares due to input signal} = \sum_{i=1}^{t} M_i^2$$

$$S_\beta = \text{sum of squares due to slope} = (1/r)\left[\sum_{i=1}^{t} M_i D_i\right]^2$$

$$S_e = \text{error sum of squares} = S_T - S_\beta$$

$$V_e = \text{error variance} = S_e/(t-1)$$

The S/N ratio corresponding to the qth run of OA is given by the following:

$$\text{S/N ratio} = \eta_q = 10 \log_{10}\{(1/r)[S_\beta - V_e]/V_e\} \qquad (12.6)$$

In the case of working average methods, true levels of severity (M) are replaced by the average of the square root of MDs.

12.3.4   Direction of Abnormals

One of the main reasons for using the Mahalanobis distance in multivariate diagnosis is its capability of distinguishing abnormalities from a "healthy" or "normal" group. Sometimes, the abnormal conditions arise out of extremely good situations. Therefore, it is important to identify the direction of the abnormalities to enable the distinction between "good" and "bad" abnormalities to be made. This makes the diagnosis process more effective. If the MD is calculated by using the inverse of the correlation matrix (the MTS method), such distinctions cannot be made. However, this can be accomplished if we use the Gram-Schmidt orthogonalization process to calculate the MD. This section outlines a procedure for identifying the direction of abnormals with suitable equations for different cases. The use of this procedure is demonstrated for a graduate student admission system.

The GSP vectors obtained from Equation (12.2) can be written as:

$$\begin{aligned}
U_1 &= Z_1 \\
U_2 &= Z_2 - c_{2,1}U_1 \\
U_3 &= Z_3 - c_{3,1}U_1 - c_{3,2}U_2 \\
&\vdots \\
U_k &= Z_k - c_{k,1}U_1 - c_{k,2}U_2 \ldots - c_{k,k-1}U_{k-1}
\end{aligned} \qquad (12.7)$$

where $c_{2,1}, c_{2,1}, \ldots, c_{k,k-1}$ are Gram-Schmidt vector coefficients.

First, a discussion of the direction of abnormals is presented in detail for a two-variable case. The same logic is extended for a higher number of variables.

In the case of two variables, the distribution of the points forms an elliptical shape. Since the MS is constructed based on this distribution, for simplicity, we can represent this distribution as the MS. It is a well-known fact that the elliptical shape remains unchanged after orthogonal transformation. Therefore, the distribution corresponding to the GSP vectors will also have an elliptical shape.

We know that the mean of the GSP vectors is located at the zero point. For the two-variable case, the mean of U_1 and U_2 is located at (0,0). All conditions (normal and abnormal) are above or below this point with the exception of the points that match the zero point (mean). Therefore, it is clear that the abnormals are above or below the zero point. Based on the position of the abnormals (above or below zero point) and the value of the MD, we can distinguish between "good" and "bad" abnormals. In the case of two variables, depending on the types of characteristics, we have the following four cases:

1. Both U_1 and U_2: larger-the-better type
2. U_1: smaller-the-better type; U_2: larger-the-better type
3. U_1: larger-the-better type; U_2: smaller-the-better type
4. Both U_1 and U_2: smaller-the-better type

For a two-variable case, the vectors U_1 and U_2 can be written as follows:

$$U_1 = Z_1$$
$$U_2 = Z_2 - c_{2,1}U_1$$

or

$$(u_{11}, u_{12}, \ldots, u_{1n}) = (z_{11}, z_{12}, \ldots, z_{1n})$$
$$(u_{21}, u_{22}, \ldots, u_{2n}) = (z_{21} - c_{2,1}u_{11}, z_{22} - c_{2,1}u_{12}, \ldots, z_{2n} - c_{2,1}u_{1n})$$

For all four of these cases, the rules for identifying the direction of abnormals are described in the following sections.

Case 1: Both U_1 and U_2—Larger-the-Better Type

An example where the characteristics U_1 and U_2 are of the larger-the-better type is a student admission system. In this system, U_1 could be "GPA" (grade point average) and U_2 could be "TOEFL exam score." In this

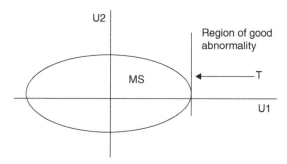

(In this figure, T is threshold and the elliptical
shape represents Mahalanobis space.)

Figure 12.5　Both U_1 and U_2 are Larger-the-Better Type

case, a condition corresponding to very low U_1 and U_2 is an abnormal, and a condition corresponding to very high U_1 and U_2 is also an abnormal.

For the jth condition to be a good-abnormal, the elements of U_1 and U_2 should be above zero (positive) and the corresponding MD should be larger than the threshold (T). These conditions can be mathematically represented as:

1. $u_{1j} > 0$ or $z_{1j} > 0$; $u_{2j} > 0$ or $z_{2j} - c_{2,1} u_{1j} > 0$ or $z_{2j} > c_{2,1} u_{1j}$ and
2. $MD_j > T$

From Equation (12.3), we can write:

$$(1/2)[(u_{1j}^2/s_1^2) + (u_{2j}^2/s_2^2)] > T \text{ or } (u_{1j}^2/s_1^2 + u_{2j}^2/s_2^2) > 2T \quad (12.8)$$

The pictorial representation of these rules is given in Figure 12.5.

For this case, the decision rule can be stated as follows: If elements of U_1 and U_2 corresponding to an abnormal condition are positive and MD is higher than the threshold (T), then the abnormal condition can be classified as "good" abnormality; otherwise, it is a "bad" abnormality.

Case 2: U_1—Smaller-the-Better Type and U_2—Larger-the-Better Type

An example of this situation is the banking system for granting loans. Here, U_1 could be "number of people in a household" and U_2 could be "income level of a family." In this case, a condition corresponding to very high U_1 and very low U_2 is an abnormal, and a condition corresponding to very low U_1 and very high U_2 is also an abnormal.

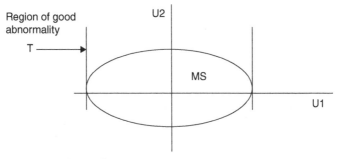

(In this figure, T is threshold and the elliptical
shape represents Mahalanobis space.)

Figure 12.6   U$_1$—Smaller-the-Better Type and U$_2$—Larger-the-Better Type

For the jth condition to be a good-abnormal, the element of U$_1$ should be below zero (negative) and that of U$_2$ should be above zero (positive) and the corresponding MD should be larger than the threshold (T). These conditions can be mathematically represented as follows:

1. $u_{1j} < 0$ or $z_{1j} < 0$; $u_{2j} > 0$ or $z_{2j} - c_{2,1} u_{1j} > 0$ or $z_{2j} > c_{2,1} u_{1j}$ and
2. $MD_j > T$

From Equation (12.3), we can write:

$$(1/2)[(u_{1j}^2/s_1^2) + (u_{2j}^2/s_2^2)] > T \text{ or } (u_{1j}^2/s_1^2 + u_{2j}^2/s_2^2) > 2T \quad (12.9)$$

The pictorial representation of these rules is given in Figure 12.6.

For this case, the decision rule can be stated as follows: If the element of U$_1$ is negative and that of U$_2$ is positive and MD is higher than the threshold (T), then the abnormal condition can be classified as "good" abnormality; otherwise, it is "bad" abnormality.

Case 3: U$_1$—Larger-the-Better Type and U$_2$—Smaller-the-Better Type

An example of this situation is an inspection system, where the characteristic "tensile strength" (U$_1$) is of the larger-the-better type and the characteristic "number of occurrences of a particular defect" (U$_2$) is of the smaller-the-better type. In this case, a condition corresponding to very low U$_1$ and very high U$_2$ is an abnormal, and a condition corresponding to very high U$_1$ and very low U$_2$ is also an abnormal.

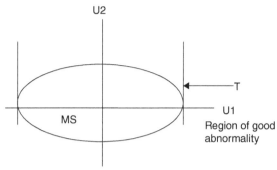

(In this figure, T is threshold and the elliptical
shape represents Mahalanobis space.)

Figure 12.7 U_1—Larger-the-Better Type and U_2—Smaller-the-Better Type

For the jth condition to be a good-abnormal, the element of U_1 should
be above zero (positive) and that of U_2 should be below zero (negative) and
the corresponding MD should be larger than threshold (T). These conditions can be mathematically represented as follows:

1. $u_{1j} > 0$ or $z_{1j} > 0$; $u_{2j} < 0$ or $z_{2j} - c_{2,1} u_{1j} < 0$ or $z_{2j} > c_{2,1} u_{1j}$ and
2. $MD_j > T$

From Equation (12.3), we can write:

$$(1/2)[(u_{1j}^2/s_1^2) + (u_{2j}^2/s_2^2)] > T \text{ or } (u_{1j}^2/s_1^2 + u_{2j}^2/s_2^2) > 2T \qquad (12.10)$$

The pictorial representation of these rules is given in Figure 12.7.

For this case, the decision rule can be stated as follows: If the element
of U_1 is positive and that of U_2 is negative and MD is higher than the
threshold (T), then the corresponding abnormal condition can be classified
as "good" abnormality; otherwise, it is a "bad" abnormality.

Case 4: Both U_1 and U_2 Are Smaller-the-Better Type

An example of a situation where both the characteristics are of the
smaller-the-better type is a printed circuit board inspection system. In
this example, the characteristics "number of occurrences of a particular
defect" (U_1) and "line width reduction after etching process" (U_2) are of
the smaller-the-better type. In this case, a condition corresponding to very
high U_1 and U_2 is an abnormal, and a condition corresponding to very low
U_1 and U_2 is also an abnormal.

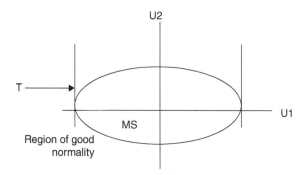

(In this figure, T is threshold and the elliptical
shape represents Mahalanobis space.)

Figure 12.8　Both U_1 and U_2 Are Smaller-the-Better Type

For the jth condition to be a good-abnormal, the elements of U_1 and U_2 should be below zero (negative) and the corresponding MD should be larger than the threshold (T). These conditions can be mathematically represented as follows:

1. $u_{1j} < 0$ or $z_{1j} < 0$; $u_{2j} < 0$ or $z_{2j} - c_{2,1} u_{1j} < 0$ or $z_{2j} < c_{2,1} u_{1j}$ and
2. $MD_j > T$

From Equation (12.3), we can write:

$$(1/2)[(u_{1j}{}^2/s_1{}^2) + (u_{2j}{}^2/s_2{}^2)] > T \text{ or } (u_{1j}{}^2/s_1{}^2 + u_{2j}{}^2/s_2{}^2) > 2T \qquad (12.11)$$

The pictorial representation of these rules is given in Figure 12.8.

For this case, the decision rule can be stated as follows: If the elements of U_1 and U_2 corresponding to an abnormal condition are negative and MD is higher than the threshold (T), then the abnormal condition can be classified as "good" abnormality; otherwise, it is a "bad" abnormality.

Decision Rule for Higher Dimensions

If there are k variables and the sample size is n, the conditions for the jth abnormal to be good are:

$u_{1j} > 0$, if U_1 is larger-the-better type (<0 if U_1 is smaller-the-better type)
$u_{2j} > 0$, if U_2 is larger-the-better type (<0 if U_2 is smaller-the-better type)
$\vdots$
$u_{kj} > 0$, if U_k is larger-the-better type (<0 if U_k is smaller-the-better type)

and

$$(1/k)[(u_{1j}^2/s_1^2) + (u_{2j}^2/s_2^2) + \cdots + (u_{kj}^2/s_k^2)] > T$$

or

$$[(u_{1j}^2/s_1^2) + (u_{2j}^2/s_2^2) + \cdots + (u_{kj}^2/s_k^2)] > kT$$

otherwise, the abnormal condition is bad.

Though this procedure provides guidelines for identifying the direction of abnormals, it is left to the decision maker to decide the type of abnormal conditions. For example, in a student admission system, where the variables are mostly of the higher-the-better type, a student with very high scores on most of the variables can be considered a good-abnormal by the decision maker.

It is important to note that this procedure is applicable only to cases where we have knowledge about the type of variables (such as larger-the-better type or smaller-the-better type).

Graduate Admission System Example

The applicability of this procedure can be demonstrated using the example of a university student admission system. Suppose a student is admitted into the university based on the following three variables:

- Grade point average (GPA): This should be as high as possible on a 4.0 scale.
- GMAT score: This should be as high as possible (maximum score is 1600).
- SAT-Math score: This should be as high as possible (maximum score is 800).

The data corresponding to the reference group along with GSP vectors and MDs are shown in Table 12.2. Since these variables are of the larger-the-better type, this example falls into the first category. There are eight abnormal conditions A1...A8. The abnormal data along with GSP vectors and MDs are given in Table 12.3.

From Table 12.3, it is clear that all of the abnormalities have high MDs. Based on MDs alone, we cannot distinguish between good and bad abnormalities. To make such distinctions, we need to look at GSP vectors.

Table 12.2   Analysis of Reference Group Data

	Original Variables			Gram-Schmidt Variables			
S. No.	X_1 (GPA)	X_2 (SAT)	X_3 (SAT-Math)	U_1	U_2	U_3	MD
1	3.00	1010	670	−0.465	−0.158	0.951	0.537
2	2.90	990	428	−0.714	−0.081	−1.775	1.703
3	3.20	1035	712	0.033	−0.409	1.322	1.028
4	2.80	980	546	−0.963	0.06	−0.355	0.374
5	3.90	1310	677	1.776	−0.062	−0.103	1.061
6	3.20	990	650	0.033	−0.703	0.749	0.807
7	2.80	965	646	−0.963	−0.038	0.854	0.664
8	3.70	1380	715	1.278	0.810	0.144	1.264
9	3.40	1300	645	0.531	0.908	−0.355	1.048
10	3.20	1205	645	0.033	0.702	−0.010	0.534
11	2.60	895	490	−1.461	−0.081	−0.693	0.951
12	3.10	950	555	−0.216	−0.757	−0.205	0.656
13	3.60	1110	520	1.029	−0.747	−1.220	1.679
14	2.70	1045	625	−1.212	0.692	0.367	1.074
15	3.70	1235	690	1.278	−0.138	0.327	0.617

Table 12.3   Analysis of Abnormal Data

	Original Variables			Gram-Schmidt Variables			
S. No.	X_1 (GPA)	X_2 (SAT)	X_3 (SAT-Math)	U_1	U_2	U_3	MD
A_1	2.40	1210	540	−1.959	2.392	−1.105	8.064
A_2	1.80	765	280	−3.453	0.727	−2.566	7.740
A_3	0.90	540	280	−5.695	1.122	−1.676	13.532
A_4	3.60	990	230	1.029	−1.532	−4.194	11.417
A_5	2.10	930	480	−2.706	1.184	−0.836	4.297
A_6	2.60	1140	530	−1.461	1.520	−1.028	3.725
A_7	4.00	1600	800	2.026	1.626	0.361	4.291
A_8	3.90	1580	780	1.776	1.702	0.212	4.210

Assuming the threshold (T) is set at 3.0, A_7 and A_8 can be classified as "good" abnormalities because GSP vectors corresponding to these abnormalities have positive signs and their MDs are higher than threshold. The remaining abnormalities (A_1 to A_6) can be classified as "bad" abnormalities because not all corresponding GSP vectors have positive signs even though their MDs are higher than threshold.

12.4   A MEDICAL DIAGNOSIS EXAMPLE

This example involves a liver disease diagnosis that was carried out by Dr. Kanetaka. The variables considered for the purpose of the diagnosis are as shown in Table 12.4. The healthy group, or reference group, was constructed based on observations of 200 people who did not have any

Table 12.4   Variables in Medical Diagnosis Data

S. No.	Variables	Notation	Notation for Analysis
1	Age		X_1
2	Sex		X_2
3	Total protein in blood	TP	X_3
4	Albumin in blood	Alb	X_4
5	Cholinesterase	ChE	X_5
6	Glutamate O transaminase	GOT	X_6
7	Glutamate P transaminase	GPT	X_7
8	Lactate dehydrogenase	LHD	X_8
9	Alkaline phosphatase	Alp	X_9
10	r-Glutamyl transpeptidase	r-GPT	X_{10}
11	Leucine aminopeptidase	LAP	X_{11}
12	Total cholesterol	TCh	X_{12}
13	Triglyceride	TG	X_{13}
14	Phospholipid	PL	X_{14}
15	Creatinine	Cr	X_{15}
16	Blood urea nitrogen	BUN	X_{16}
17	Uric acid	UA	X_{17}

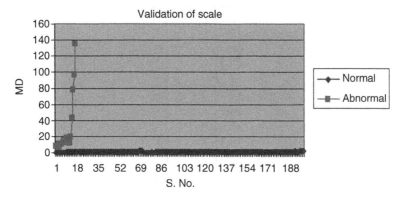

Figure 12.9   Differentiation between Normals and Abnormals
(validation of the scale)

health problems. There were 17 patients with known liver disease problems (these are referred to as abnormal). For this application, different stages of the MTS were applied as described. Figure 12.9 clearly shows the separation between normals and abnormals, indicating the ability of the scale to differentiate between the reference group and the abnormals, which is sufficient to validate the scale.

Next is the optimization phase. In this phase, the useful set of variables was identified using OAs and S/N ratios. Since there are 17 variables and we required a two-level OA, an $L_{32}(2^{31})$ array was selected. $L_{32}(2^{31})$ array is a two-level OA with 32 treatment combinations (runs) and 31 columns. A list of orthogonal arrays is provided in Appendix C. The 17 variables were allocated to the first 17 columns of this array. The MDs corresponding to the 17 abnormal conditions were computed for all 32 combinations of the variables, and dynamic S/N ratios were calculated. The S/N ratios were obtained by using the procedure given in the Section 12.3. The average responses corresponding to the 17 variables are shown in Table 12.5.

In Table 12.5, Level 1: variable is present; Level 2: variable is not present.

From Table 12.5, it is clear that the variables X_4, X_5, X_{10}, X_{12}, X_{13}, X_{14}, X_{15}, and X_{17} have positive gains. That means these variables have higher average responses when they are part of the system (Level 1). Hence, these variables were considered to be useful for a future diagnosis process. The results of the confirmation run showed that the measurement scale (developed with useful variables) can detect the abnormals. This can also be seen from Figure 12.10.

Table 12.5 Average Responses for Dynamic S/N Ratios (in dB units)

Variable	X_1	X_2	X_3	X_4	X_5	X_6	X_7	X_8	X_9	X_{10}	X_{11}	X_{12}	X_{13}	X_{14}	X_{15}	X_{16}	X_{17}
Level 1	−8.18	−8.19	−8.25	−7.95	−7.07	−8.32	−7.98	−8.82	−8.19	−6.36	−8.10	−7.82	−7.56	−7.31	−7.59	−7.98	−7.83
Level 2	−7.74	−7.74	−7.68	−7.98	−8.86	−7.61	−7.95	−7.11	−7.74	−9.57	−7.83	−8.11	−8.37	−8.61	−8.34	−7.95	−8.10
Gain	−0.44	−0.45	−0.57	0.03	1.79	−0.71	−0.02	−1.72	−0.45	3.21	−0.27	0.29	0.80	1.30	0.75	−0.04	0.26

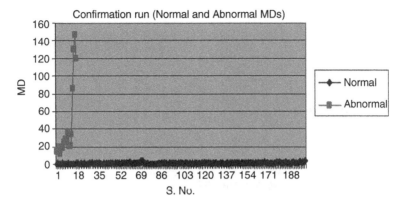

Figure 12.10   Normals and Abnormals after Optimization

It was also found that the average MD of abnormal conditions with useful variables was higher than that with all the variables. This means the insignificant variables will reduce the accuracy of the MD. Since the gain in S/N ratio for X_4 is very small, a combination of the useful variables excluding X_4 is run to check the performance of the system. It was found that abnormals have lower MDs with this combination. Therefore, it was decided to retain X_4 in the set of useful variables.

12.5   CASE STUDY: IMPROVING CLIENT EXPERIENCE

This example concerns a financial institution. Following is a summary of this case.

This study focused on improving the measurement of key indicators of client relationship health. The client health was decided based on 49 variables and classified into green (loyal), yellow (vulnerable), and red (at-risk) groups of clients. Prior to this study, the decisions were made based on the client relationship manager's judgment without having any quantitative method. The method was subjective and not capable of identifying or differentiating specific types of risk from the primary client risk factors. The study's primary goal was to develop a metric that quantitatively determines the healthiness of a client based on the aforementioned factors.

The MTS methodology was applied to quantitatively determine client health. With all 49 variables, the MTS scale was constructed and validated. This is shown in Figure 12.11.

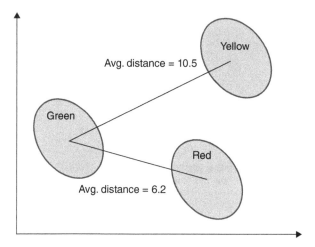

Figure 12.11   Validation of Scale—Distance between Green, Yellow, and Red Clients (with 49 variables)

After performing MTS optimization with an L_{64} OA, the results were as shown in Table 12.6.

After performing S/N ratio analysis and considering other practical constraints, 11 variables were selected as important. With these 11 variables, the performance of the scale was better than that of the scale with 49 variables in terms of separation. This is clear from Figure 12.12.

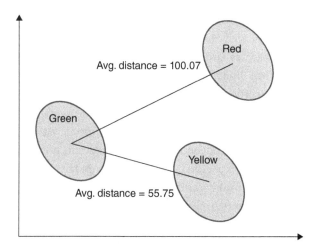

Figure 12.12   Separation between Clients (after Optimization, with 11 Variables)

Table 12.6   MTS Optimization with L_{64} Array

Run #	S/N Ratio	Run #	S/N Ratio	Run #	S/N Ratio
1	0.65	23	0.85	45	0.51
2	1.22	24	0.87	46	0.83
3	0.64	25	0.12	47	0.56
4	0.04	26	0.04	48	0.82
5	1.09	27	0.03	49	0.42
6	1.12	28	0.22	50	−0.36
7	0.47	29	0.82	51	0.03
8	0.60	30	0.85	52	0.11
9	−0.23	31	0.69	53	0.60
10	0.32	32	0.80	54	0.68
11	0.26	33	0.17	55	0.65
12	−0.34	34	−0.20	56	0.75
13	0.67	35	0.03	57	−0.06
14	0.70	36	0.45	58	0.42
15	0.81	37	0.80	59	0.28
16	0.89	38	0.79	60	0.04
17	−0.30	39	0.93	61	0.92
18	−0.30	40	0.91	62	0.82
19	−0.10	41	0.04	63	1.04
20	0.36	42	0.20	64	0.93
21	0.68	43	−0.13		
22	0.77	44	−0.43		

12.5.1   Improvements Made Based on Recommendations from MTS Analysis

A new measurement system was developed by including the 11 attributes from the following:

- Survey
- Volatility within the client
- Volatility within the company

The company was convinced that the performance of the measurement system with these 11 attributes was much more meaningful and objective as compared to traditional subjective evaluations.

12.6 CASE STUDY: UNDERSTANDING THE BEHAVIOR PATTERNS OF DEFAULTING CUSTOMERS

This case study again concerns a financial institution. Following is a summary of this case.

This project is aimed at understanding the behavioral patterns of the customers that are or may be capable of defaulting on a particular loan. It was decided that a set of 10 variables would be used to explain such behavior patterns. The data from the customers who did not default was used to construct the reference group. After collecting data on default and non-default customers, the MTS method was applied to construct and validate the scale with the Mahalanobis distance and correlation matrix. Table 12.7 shows the correlations between the 10 variables used in this study.

Figure 12.13 shows the separation between defaulting customers and the reference group. Based on this figure, we can say that the separation is very good, and we can validate the scale.

After conducting the optimization step, the number of variables was reduced to five (X_4-X_5-X_7-X_8-X_9). With these variables, the separation

Table 12.7   Correlation Matrix

	X_1	X_2	X_3	X_4	X_5	X_6	X_7	X_8	X_9	X_{10}
X_1	1.000	−0.065	0.185	−0.074	0.034	0.072	−0.008	0.040	0.043	−0.200
X_2	−0.065	1.000	0.005	−0.094	−0.152	−0.087	0.009	−0.007	0.082	−0.001
X_3	0.185	0.005	1.000	−0.498	−0.529	−0.132	−0.169	−0.149	0.018	−0.291
X_4	−0.074	−0.094	−0.498	1.000	0.913	0.295	0.009	0.155	−0.030	0.062
X_5	0.034	−0.152	−0.529	0.913	1.000	0.310	0.026	0.141	−0.047	0.081
X_6	0.072	−0.087	−0.132	0.295	0.310	1.000	0.056	−0.063	−0.027	−0.130
X_7	−0.008	0.009	−0.169	0.009	0.026	0.056	1.000	−0.005	0.181	0.047
X_8	0.040	−0.007	−0.149	0.155	0.141	−0.063	−0.005	1.000	−0.010	0.095
X_9	0.043	0.082	0.018	−0.030	−0.047	−0.027	0.181	−0.010	1.000	0.165
X_{10}	−0.200	−0.001	−0.291	0.062	0.081	−0.130	0.047	0.095	0.165	1.000

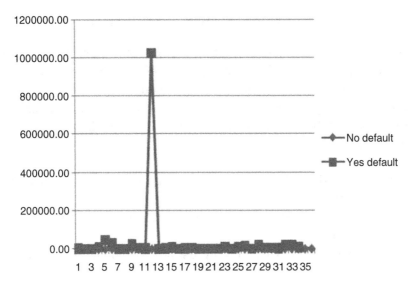

Figure 12.13   MTS Scale Validation

was also quite good. Figure 12.14 shows the separation between the reference group and the defaulting customers optimization.

Since X_4-X_5-X_7-X_8-X_9 are sufficient to distinguish the defaulting customers from the reference group, these variables were used to design strategies for preventing losses attributed to the defaulting customers.

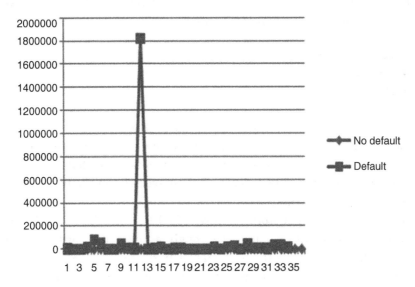

Figure 12.14   Separation with Optimized Scale

12.7   CASE STUDY: MARKETING

This study involves an auto marketing application requiring that customers' buying patterns for different segments of the car market be identified. The objective of this study was to recognize the buying patterns of customers owning a particular model. It was decided that the behavior patterns would be explained using MTS analysis incorporating the following steps:

1. Construct the reference group for a pattern under consideration (base pattern).
2. Consider other patterns as abnormals (conditions outside the reference group).
3. Select the useful variables by using orthogonal arrays and S/N ratios.
4. Use the useful variables for future diagnosis.
5. If there is prior knowledge about the abnormals, then recognize patterns by comparing them with the base pattern.
6. Otherwise, repeat steps 1 through 4 for all other patterns and test the new observation against each to decide which pattern it belongs to.

In this case, the buying patterns were to be identified based on customer survey results. The variables considered for the survey were classified under the following categories:

- Personal views
- Purchase reasons
- Demographics

The customer survey data was obtained from a marketing-related database. After combining the variables in the three categories, 55 variables were considered, covering five car segments. As stated, the purpose of this case study was to identify the buying patterns of the five segments based on the 55 variables.

In some cases, the customers were asked to rank the variables on a scale from 1 to 4, where 1 meant strongly agree and 4 meant strongly disagree. After arranging the 55 variables in the desired order, they were denoted as $X_1, X_2, \ldots, X_{55}$ for the purpose of analysis. Since there were five segments and there was no prior knowledge about these patterns, MTS analysis was performed on all of the segments. For convenience, the five segments are denoted as $S_1, S_2, \ldots, S_5$.

12.7.1 Construction of the Reference Group

For each of the five segments, the reference group was built based on the data set. For example, the reference group for S_1 was constructed by taking observations on 55 variables corresponding to that segment. With these reference groups, the corresponding MDs were calculated.

12.7.2 Validation of the Scale

The second stage in the MTS method is validation. The outside conditions for a given segment were chosen from the other segments. It was found that the abnormals, in all of the cases, had higher MDs; thus, the scale was validated.

12.7.3 Identification of Useful Variables

To identify a useful set from the 55 original variables, the $L_{64}(2^{63})$ orthogonal array (OA) was chosen for each segment analysis. The S/N ratios were computed based on the larger-the-better criterion, because prior information about abnormals was not available.

Table 12.8 provides the list of useful variables corresponding to all five segments. Since for each segment a suitable strategy was to be developed with a manageable number of variables, it was decided to restrict the number of variables per segment to 20. The selection of these variables was done based on the magnitude of gains in the S/N ratio.

With the useful set of variables, confirmation runs were conducted for all five segments. The results of the confirmation indicated that these variables were capable of recognizing the given patterns as effectively as in the case with all 55 variables. Figure 12.15 shows the recognition power of the useful variables in the respective car segments.

Decreasing the number of variables in the optimal system helped to reduce the complexity of the multidimensional systems and develop effective strategies to improve sales.

Table 12.8   Useful Variables Corresponding to the Five Segments

S. No.	S_1	S/N Ratio Gain	S_2	S/N Ratio Gain	S_3	S/N Ratio Gain	S_4	S/N Ratio Gain	S_5	S/N Ratio Gain
1	X_6	0.20	X_{54}	0.60	X_{52}	1.15	X_7	0.50	X_2	0.96
2	X_{23}	0.16	X_7	0.57	X_{54}	0.73	X_{47}	0.29	X_{47}	0.49
3	X_{15}	0.11	X_{52}	0.48	X_{27}	0.27	X_{31}	0.28	X_{55}	0.49
4	X_{18}	0.11	X_{26}	0.36	X_{24}	0.23	X_{41}	0.27	X_7	0.45
5	X_3	0.11	X_{41}	0.30	X_6	0.19	X_{27}	0.25	X_{40}	0.35
6	X_{52}	0.09	X_{47}	0.28	X_{44}	0.18	X_2	0.22	X_{10}	0.33
7	X_{35}	0.09	X_{25}	0.19	X_3	0.15	X_3	0.22	X_3	0.24
8	X_{19}	0.09	X_{27}	0.16	X_{47}	0.15	X_{21}	0.22	X_{25}	0.20
9	X_{40}	0.09	X_{13}	0.14	X_{25}	0.15	X_{24}	0.16	X_{24}	0.17
10	X_{27}	0.09	X_{18}	0.11	X_4	0.13	X_{22}	0.13	X_{21}	0.16
11	X_{14}	0.08	X_8	0.09	X_2	0.13	X_{15}	0.13	X_6	0.15
12	X_{47}	0.08	X_3	0.08	X_{40}	0.12	X_{54}	0.12	X_{26}	0.15
13	X_{22}	0.07	X_{14}	0.08	X_{26}	0.11	X_8	0.12	X_{18}	0.15
14	X_{12}	0.07	X_{24}	0.08	X_{10}	0.10	X_{23}	0.11	X_{54}	0.14
15	X_5	0.06	X_{40}	0.07	X_{14}	0.10	X_{35}	0.11	X_{29}	0.13
16	X_4	0.06	X_{31}	0.05	X_{42}	0.07	X_{52}	0.10	X_{53}	0.09
17	X_{10}	0.06	X_{29}	0.05	X_{55}	0.06	X_{48}	0.08	X_{49}	0.06
18	X_1	0.06	X_{44}	0.02	X_{41}	0.05	X_{40}	0.07	X_{44}	0.06
19	X_{26}	0.05	X_{48}	0.00	X_{35}	0.05	X_{30}	0.06	X_{35}	0.05
20	X_{11}	0.05			X_{31}	0.01	X_{44}	0.04	X_{42}	0.03

12.8   CASE STUDY: GEAR MOTOR ASSEMBLY

This case study was conducted at a document company. The purpose of life testing the 127K27330 gear-motor assembly was to measure all the parameters (or variables) and decide on the reusability of these motors. It is important to identify a suitable measure representing these parameters and based on which a decision on the reusability of a motor can be made. Since all of these parameters may not be necessary to make a decision, it is required that a useful set of parameters be identified to determine whether

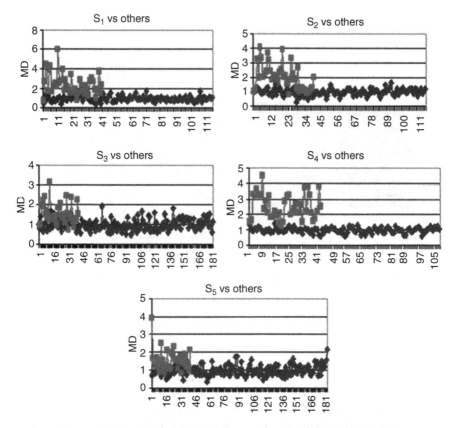

Figure 12.15   Pattern Recognition with a Useful Set of Variables

a used 127K27330 gear-motor assembly would be suitable for reuse. For convenience, the 127K27330 motor is simply referred to as the "motor" in the remainder of this section. This problem can be treated as a diagnosis problem, in which the reusability of a motor was decided based on the value of the Mahalanobis distance. Hence, the MTS method was applied to this problem.

12.8.1   Apparatus

A diagram of the 127K27330 test fixture is shown in Figure 12.16. From left to right, the holding fixture consists of a hand shield, high-resolution encoder, hysteresis brake, customized brake coupling, the motor, and a Destaco clamp. The motor's output coupling engages the brake coupling, which turns the hysteresis brake, which turns the encoder. The Destaco clamp prevents any lateral movement.

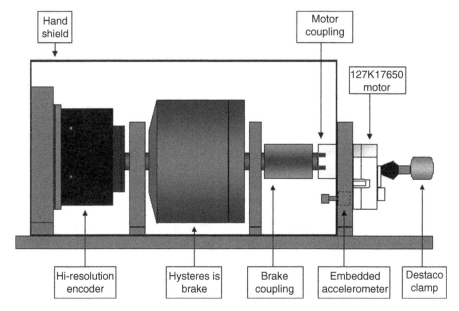

Figure 12.16 127K27330 Test Fixture

12.8.2 Sensors

A PCB accelerometer (Model J352A78, 100 mV/g) was used to measure vibration. This accelerometer was stud mounted in the motor mount plate (see Figure 12.16).A 1-ohm resistor was used for current sensing. A Gurley (Model 8435H, 32,000 pulses/revolution) high-resolution encoder was used to measure motion and speed.

12.8.3 High-Resolution Encoder

Because the speed of the motor is approximately 1.5 rpm, a standard tachometer could not be used, since its output voltage would be negligible. A high-resolution encoder from Gurley (Model 8435H) was used for measuring motor speed. This encoder has a resolution of 32,000 pulses/revolution. A US Digital PC6-84-4 quadrature interpolator was used to increase the resolution of this encoder from 32,000 to 128,000 pulses/revolution.

A LabView example program called Buffered Counting of Events.vi served as the basis for inputting and interpreting the encoder pulse stream.

If, for example, there is an incoming pulse train and it is required that the pulses be counted and the count value accumulated after every 5 milliseconds (ms), here is what needs to be done:

1. Make one of the counters generate a pulse train of 5 ms (200 Hz) and connect the OUT of this counter (no. 1) to the GATE of the next counter (no. 2).
2. Connect the signal to the SOURCE of counter 2.
3. The pulse train generated by counter 1 goes high every 5 ms.

When it goes high for the first time, counter 2 starts counting the signal. It keeps counting until it sees another high at the gate, which would be after 5 ms. At this point, the count value of counter 2 is written to the buffer. Counter 2 is actually still counting. When it sees the next high on the gate, after 5 ms, again the counter value is written to the buffer. Therefore, the buffer would have monotonically increasing values representing the accumulated count of counter 1 after each 5-ms interval. We can do this buffered counting at any interval by changing the 200 Hz (5 ms) to some other value.

To summarize, the output of counter 1 is physically tied to the gate of counter 2. Counter 1 time-stamps the running count of counter 2.

12.8.4   Life Test

The life testing apparatus from the 127K1581 motor test was reused for the 127K27330 life test with a few modifications to the motor baseplate. A QuickBasic program called dc_motor.bas and an optomux/opto22 system provided electronic control. Ten new 127K27330 motors were used for the life test. The parameters were measured at intervals of 10,000 cycles starting from 0 cycles to 120,000 cycles during the life test.

12.8.5   Characterization

After every 10,000 cycles the 10 motors were taken off the test for characterization. The LabView characterization program is called hodaka_ dc_motor.vi. The characterization program ran the motor at three different operating conditions: (1) motor voltage (mv) = 21.6 V, brake voltage (bv) = 4.95 V; (2) mv = 21.6 V, bv = 0 V; (3) mv = 12 V, bv = 4.95 V. These levels were specifically chosen to stress the motor and force a separation between new-motor performance and used-motor performance. The 4.95 V brake voltage corresponded to a 1.96-Nm (276.4-oz-in) load. In these tests, a personal computer, generic SA interface box, and National Instruments AT-MIO-16E-10 board were used for data acquisition.

Of the various parameters measured by hodaka_dc_motor.vi, the following parameters, in the three different operating conditions, were considered to be important:

1. Current
2. Vibration
3. Speed
4. Count—count measurements of counter 2

Some of the parameters could not be considered, because they were fixed while conducting the life test. Since speed measurements were derived from the counts by taking the derivative of the buffered counts, there was no need to consider both of them. Therefore, the parameter count was dropped from the analysis. We were left with nine variables: current (C), vibration (V), and speed (S) in three operating conditions. The variables were denoted as X_1, X_2,..., X_9. The data on these parameters was collected by using hodaka_dc_motor.vi.

After collecting data on these nine variables, the MTS method was used for data analysis.

12.8.6 Construction of the Reference Group or Mahalanobis Space

Motors 1 through 10 were all new when life testing was started. The presumption was that all new motors are good. Therefore, the parameters measured at 0 cycles (corresponding to these motors) were used to construct the Mahalanobis space for the healthy group. When data about the motors was combined, there were numerous observations corresponding to the parameters at 0 cycles. These parameters reached steady state after some point in time. To verify this fact, data on these parameters was plotted on separate graphs. Figure 12.17 shows some of these graphs. From this figure, it is clear that that the parameters attained steady state after some point in time.

To construct the Mahalanobis space (MS), it was not necessary to consider all of the data because the number of observations in the data

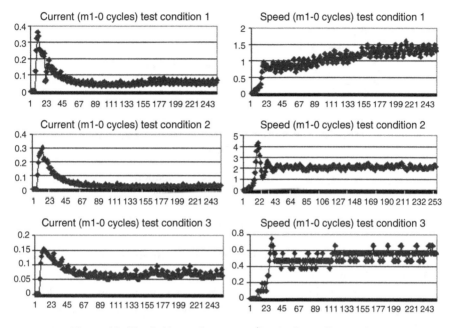

Figure 12.17   Patterns Corresponding to Some Parameters

was large. Therefore, a subset of the original data was used for constructing the MS. The subset selection was done in such a way that it contained an equal number of observations from the steady state and from the transient state. This helped in constructing a uniform MS. Based on this, the MDs corresponding to the observations in the MS were calculated.

12.8.7   Validation of the MTS Scale

After constructing the measurement scale, it was necessary to test the accuracy of the scale by measuring the MDs of some known conditions outside the MS. In this application, parameters measured after 10k, 20k..., 120k cycles were considered conditions outside the MS. Figure 12.18 shows the average MDs corresponding to these cycles. From this figure, we can say that the scale is good because abnormals have higher-value MDs. It is interesting to note that as the number of cycles increases the average MD also goes up, indicating that the motor performance deteriorates with an increase in the number of cycles.

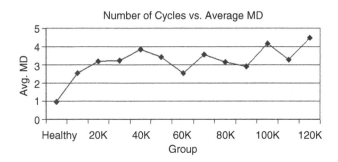

Figure 12.18   MTS Scale Validation

12.8.8   Selection of Useful Variables

In the third stage of the analysis, useful parameters were selected by using orthogonal arrays and S/N ratios. Since there were nine parameters, the $L_{12}(2^{11})$ orthogonal array was used. Since we did not have prior knowledge about the abnormals, the larger-the-better type of S/N ratios was used in both methods. The results of MTS analysis are given in Table 12.9.

In Table 12.9, the variable combination X_1-X_2-X_3-X_5-X_6-X_8-X_9 is considered as a useful combination because the variables in this combination have positive gains.

A confirmation run was conducted for the useful variables in both methods. It was found that from abnormal MDs we could distinguish normals and abnormals. Figure 12.19 shows the difference between the

Table 12.9   S/N Ratio Average Responses and Gains (in dB units)

Variable	Level 1	Level 2	Gain
X_1	6.630	5.960	0.670
X_2	7.250	5.340	1.910
X_3	6.580	6.000	0.580
X_4	5.830	6.750	−0.920
X_5	8.030	4.550	3.480
X_6	6.300	6.290	0.010
X_7	6.110	6.480	−0.370
X_8	8.090	4.500	3.590
X_9	7.070	5.510	1.560

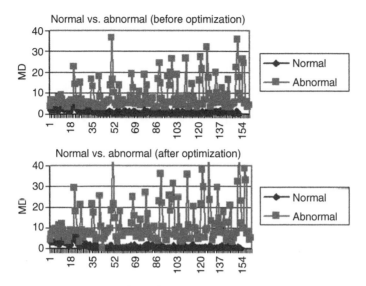

Figure 12.19   MTS Scale Performance Before and After Optimization

original combination and the optimal combination in terms of distinction between normals and abnormals. From this figure, it is clear that the distinction was much better with the optimal combination.

12.9   CONCLUSIONS

From this chapter, we can draw the following conclusions:

- After ensuring high-quality and reliable data, methods such as MTS are very useful in performing diagnostic analytics to derive important insights from the data.
- While doing analysis with multiple CDEs or variables, it is important to consider the correlation effects, since they affect overall information/data quality levels.
- Methods such as MTS are a great value adds to the analytical toolkit, and they can be easily modified to suit the big data context.
- Sometimes, it is important to identify the direction of abnormals in multivariate systems. With the help of the Gram-Schmidt process, we can determine the direction of the abnormalities, which enables a decision maker to take appropriate action. The S/N ratio can also be used as a strategic decision-making tool, since it can be effectively used to develop a good marketing/sales strategy for products in different regions.

Chapter 13

Data Analytics

13.0 INTRODUCTION

In previous chapters, we discussed data quality, how to evaluate data quality, and its impact on business, with some real-world examples. In this chapter, we will briefly discuss the importance of data quality in performing high-quality analytics and making appropriate decisions based on the analytics. We will also discuss the role of data innovation and its relevance in modern industry.

13.1 DATA AND ANALYTICS AS KEY RESOURCES

Harrington (2013) highlights the importance of managing processes, projects, change, knowledge, and resources for organizational excellence. As we know, in this highly regulated environment, there is an ever-growing need to creating and provide safeguards and tools to increase financial transparency and accuracy. This situation has significantly increased the role of data and analytics in business in general. For this reason, data management and analytics capability management have become critical functions in managing overall business and achieving business excellence.

Figure 13.1 shows seven levers of disciplined and effective organization. Besides having good processes, projects, resources, great knowledge, and the ability to change, we need to have the capability to ensure high-quality data and the ability to perform high-quality analytics to survive amid global competition, and these capabilities must be viewed like any other resources. Therefore, it is important to ensure that we have high-quality data across the organization to derive meaningful business outcomes. Because of this, the roles of data management and analytics

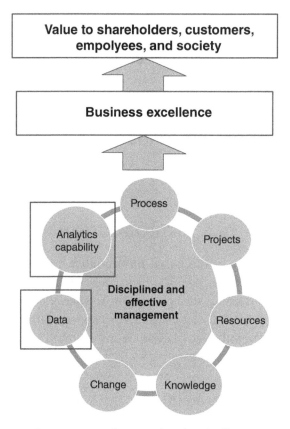

Figure 13.1   Seven Levers of a Disciplined and Effective Organization

management are becoming increasingly important for a disciplined and effective organization.

The importance of having the right kind of data was emphasized by respected statisticians long before the data quality field experienced explosive growth in both industry and academics. R. A. Fisher, a well-known British statistician, said that the first task of a statistician is to conduct the cross-examination of the data for meaningful analysis and interpretation of results. C. R. Rao, a world-renowned Indian statistician, provided a checklist (Rao, 1997) for cross-examination of the data, which is as follows:

- How is the data ascertained and recorded?
- Is the data free from measurement and recording errors? Are measurement concepts well defined? Is there any difference between the observers of the data?

- Are the data genuine? Are there any outliers? Are data from reliable sources?
- What is the size of the data sample? Is it adequate? Is there more than one population from which the data was collected? Are all relevant factors for data identification and classification considered?
- Is there any prior information about the data?

If we carefully look at this checklist, it is clear that the emphasis is given primarily to the data quality and measurement systems that we use for data collection. After we satisfy all data requirements, then we have to think about the type of analytics that we need to perform.

13.1.1   Different Types of Analytics

By data analytics, we mean performing statistical analysis, modeling, and visual analysis to gain new insights that will enable us to make judicious business decisions. In this competitive world, it is important to have new insights through which to understand customer expectations in a much better way. What puts any company ahead of the competition is the ability to execute with efficiency and effectiveness and make smart business decisions based on high-quality analytics. There are different types of analytics, and they can be chosen depending on the purpose. Gartner, Inc. (2012) proposed an analytics ascendency model that shows how the value of analytics increases as we expand the capabilities. Table 13.1 shows different types of analytics, including the types that Gartner proposed. It is important to note that the tools associated with these analytics may overlap, depending on the case we are addressing. A brief description of all these types of analytics is provided next.

Preparatory analytics: This type of analytics can also be called "cross-examination of data" and is useful to evaluate existing data quality levels for variables/CDEs. Techniques such as data quality business rules, data quality rule evaluation, and statistical process control (SPC) are useful in assessing the data quality levels. Detailed descriptions of these techniques appear in earlier chapters of this book.

Descriptive analytics: If we want to know what happened to a particular process, operation, facility, or CDE, we should perform this type of analytics using tools such as data mining, basic profiling, and descriptive statistics. This type of analytics helps us understand the

Table 13.1 Different Types of Analytics

Purpose	Type of Analytics	Tools/Techniques
How good is the data?	Preparatory analytics	Data quality rules, data quality scores, statistical process control, etc.
What happened?	Descriptive analytics	Basic profiling, data mining, descriptive statistics, etc.
Why and when did it happen?	Diagnostic analytics	Control charts, analysis of variance, hypothesis tests, etc.
How did it happen? (root-cause analysis)	Cause-related analytics	Cause-and-effect analysis, failure mode effect analysis, etc.
What will happen?	Predictive analytics	Modeling, regression analysis, etc.
How can we improve?	Prescriptive analytics	Design of experiments, simulations, scenario planning, etc.
How confident can we be?	Reliability-based analytics	Failure analysis, confidence intervals, signal-to-noise ratios, etc.

performance at a given point in time by providing a snapshot with means and standard deviations.

Diagnostic analytics: Diagnostic analytics are performed to determine when, where, why, and how a particular problem has occurred. Techniques such as correlation analysis, hypothesis test, analysis of variance (ANOVA), and control charts are typically used in this type of analytics.

Cause-related analytics: Cause-related analytics are usually performed to identify the causes of the problems or failures. Tools such as a cause-and-effect diagram, cause-and-effect matrix, and failure mode effect analysis (FMEA) are used to perform cause-related analytics.

Predictive analytics: Predictive analytics, as the name suggests, are useful in predicting the behavior of a process, system, or CDE. For this reason, this class of analytics can also be called "what-if" analytics. Techniques such as modeling and regression analysis are useful in performing predictive analytics. Simulation analysis plays an important role here, as it helps to simulate various scenarios and perform what-if analysis.

Prescriptive analytics: Prescriptive analytics are useful in answering questions such as how we can improve the performance. Tools such as designed experiments, simulation analysis, and scenario planning are extremely useful in this class of analytics.

Reliability-based analytics: Reliability-based analytics are typically used in estimating the reliability of a product, process, system, or set of models so that we can be more confident about the results. With reliability-based analytics, we can assign a confidence level and a failure rate for the performance. Failure analysis, confidence intervals, and signal-to-noise ratios are usually used in reliability-based analytics.

It is important to note that the analytics types in Table 13.1 can be used with numerical, text, voice, Web-based, or social media–related data with appropriate transformations/modifications. They can also be used in the context of big data.

13.1.2   Requirements for Executing Analytics

As described, we should select the appropriate set of analytics depending on the purpose. In order to perform the analytics across an organization, the process should start with an "analytics vision," as shown in Figure 13.2. Once we have a clear vision, we can design a suitable strategy for executing analytics. After this step, we should look at the talent and resources that are available for performing the analytics. If there are gaps, we should start acquiring great talent and appropriate resources as part of the investment strategy for analytics.

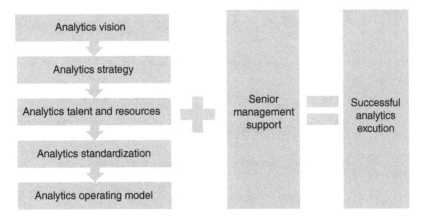

Figure 13.2   Successful Analytics Execution

When planning to expand the use of analytics across the organization, it is important to have a standardized approach along with an operating model for successful execution. Standardized approach helps us to use appropriate type of analytics in a given scenario although the tools may vary from application to application. The operating model comes in handy when we want to know how to deploy different types of analytics, associated methodologies, and interpretation of results etc.

Referring to Figure 13.2, it is needless to say that the most important requirement for analytics execution is senior management support. No other requirements can be fulfilled without the commitment from senior management. After satisfying analytics requirements, the next stage is to define a process for execution. Section 13.1.3 outlines such a process.

13.1.3   Process of Executing Analytics

The first step in this process is to define the problem (as shown in Figure 13.3) and understand the purpose. Then we need to collect relevant data and ensure high data quality. After the data quality has been ensured, we must decide what type analytics we need to employ, using the questions presented in Table 13.1 as a guide for the decision making. Based on the data and the constraints we have to deal with, we can build suitable frameworks or models. In the next step, we need to validate

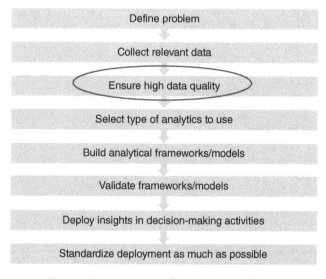

Figure 13.3   Process of Executing Analytics

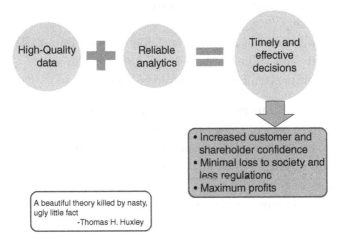

Figure 13.4   Importance of the Combination of High-Quality Data and Analytics

these frameworks or models by including data that was not part of the model-building activity. After this validation step, we should have a plan to deploy these insights in decision-making activities. Note that we need to standardize the method of deploying the insights as much as possible.

In Figure 13.3, the "Ensure High Data Quality" step is highlighted because high-quality data is absolutely required to run sound analytics and achieve meaningful business outcomes. Oftentimes, analytics fail because of poor-quality data, and the loss associated with poor-quality data can be quite significant. As shown in Figure 13.4, the combination of high-quality data and reliable analytics will result in increased levels of customer, regulatory, and shareholder confidence by minimizing societal loss with maximum profits.

13.2   DATA INNOVATION

The amount of data in this world is growing exponentially. Organizations across the globe are producing trillions of bytes of data. This includes data from products, customers, operations, and technology from a variety of industries such as banking, healthcare, manufacturing, and retail. The data can come from various sources including systems, data processors, mobile phones, and social media such as LinkedIn and Facebook, and it can be numeric, discrete, or in the form of texts, e-mails, voice conversations, or online chats.

Processing such large sets of data to derive meaningful insights and achieve meaningful business outcomes to maximize profits is a challenge.

Various types of analytics play an important role in this kind of data processing exercise.

The systematic use of analytics with high-quality data to derive meaningful insights and value can be termed *data innovation*.

The data innovation function should be able to:

- Partner with businesses to generate new analytical insights from innovative uses of cross-unit and cross-functional data
- Provide risk, market, and macro and micro insights
- Provide intelligence about the customers, their suppliers, and the network of relationships
- Optimize business opportunities to improve the performance and efficiency of processes

The probability of increasing the level of innovation depends on the amounts of data acquired and the ability to process it. Therefore, big data analytics play an important role in data innovation.

13.2.1 Big Data

If we have a collection of large and complex data sets in a variety of forms such as numerical, text, social media, mobile media, and voice from variety of sources and it is beyond the capability of the usual database tools and data processing applications to capture, store, manage, and analyze, then such a collection of data sets is called *big data*. If data can be thought of as clay with which to make good bricks for an organization, then big data can be thought of as the various minerals that go into making that clay. The quality and reliability of the bricks depends on the mineral content of the clay, as the success of an organization depends on the quality of the data that its processes are based on.

Big data creates value for the organization in several different ways, and it can be viewed as a key strategic asset for competition and growth. The advantages of big data can be summarized as follows:

- It helps an organization build a data culture that will enable it to make effective and well-informed decisions by increasing transparency.

- It helps an organization better understand variability or noise across various systems, data sources, and data elements. This, in turn, enhances product performance and increases the efficiency and effectiveness of the organization's processes.
- It helps an organization understand the behavior patterns of its customers in various segments and design suitable strategies to satisfy their needs.
- It helps an organization create new products, processes, and technologies, and thereby drive an innovation culture across the enterprise.

13.2.2   Big Data Analytics

The goal of big data analytics is to aid organizations in processing large amounts of data so as to make better business decisions and maximize profits. There should be dedicated resources to run big data analytics with all kinds of data (structured or unstructured).

Processing of big data requires high-end technologies with the ability to perform analytics quickly and efficiently. Big data technologies include NoSQL databases, Hadoop, and MapReduce. The types of analytics described in Table 13.1 are also useful in the context of big data. However, some adjustments to the tools may be required when dealing with a combination of structured and unstructured data.

Techniques such as A/B testing, correlations and association analysis, cluster analysis, factor analysis, data fusion and genetic algorithms, machine learning and fuzzy logic techniques, artificial neural networks, regression analysis, principal component analysis, discrimination and classification analysis, test of additional information (Rao's test), decision trees, Euclidian distance, Mahalanobis distance, Taguchi methods, time series analysis, and simulations are extremely useful for big data processing. Brief descriptions of some of the multivariate techniques are provided in the following sections.

Principal Component Analysis

Principal component analysis (PCA) aims at explaining the variance-covariance structure through fewer linear combinations of original variables. These linear combinations are called the *principal components*. Johnson and Wichern (1992) provide a clear discussion of PCA. The principal components depend entirely on the covariance or correlation matrix. Their development does not require a multivariate normality assumption.

Let the standardized random vector $Z^T = [Z_1, Z_2, ..., Z_p]$ have the correlation matrix C with eigen values $\lambda_1 \geq \lambda_2 \geq ... \geq \lambda_p \geq 0$, where T denotes the transpose of the vector.

Consider the following linear combinations:

$$Y_1 = l_1^T Z = l_{11}Z_1 + l_{21}Z_2 + \cdots + l_{p1}X_p$$
$$Y_2 = l_2^T Z = l_{12}Z_1 + l_{22}Z_2 + \cdots + l_{p2}X_p \qquad (13.1)$$
$$Y_p = l_p^T Z = l_{1p}Z_1 + l_{2p}Z_2 + \cdots + l_{pp}X_p$$

We can write the following:

$$V(Y_i) = l_i^T C l_i \text{ and } \text{Cov}(Y_i Y_k) = l_i^T C l_k, \text{ where } i,k = 1, 2, ..., p$$

The principal components are those uncorrelated linear combinations $Y_1, Y_2, ..., Y_p$ whose variances $(V(Y_i))$ are as large possible.

We can also prove that the total variance $= {}_i\Sigma V(X_i) = \lambda_1 + \lambda_2 + \cdots + \lambda_p = {}_i\Sigma V(Y_i); i = 1, ..., p$.

The proportion of total variance due to the kth principal component $= \lambda_k/(\lambda_1 + \lambda_2 + \cdots + \lambda_p)$.

Note that the principle components can be constructed either by covariance matrix or correlation matrix depending upon the measurement units of the variables.

Discrimination and Classification Method

The discrimination and classification method is intended for separating the distinct sets of objects (or observations) and allocating new objects to previously defined groups. The objectives of the discrimination and classification method are:

1. To describe the differential features of objects or observations from several known groups (populations). In this method, "discriminants" are found in such a way that the groups are separated as much as possible.
2. To classify objects (observations) into two or more labeled classes. The emphasis is on deriving a rule that can be used to optimally assign a new object to the labeled classes.

An extensive discussion of this method is provided in Johnson and Wichern (1992).

Fisher's Discriminant Function

Fisher actually arrived at the linear classification statistic by transforming the multivariate observations X to univariate observations Y such that the Ys derived from populations A and B were separated as much as possible. Fisher suggested taking linear combinations of X to obtain Ys because they are simple enough functions of X to be handled easily.

Let there be two populations A and B. The linear discrimination function Y is calculated as:

$$Y = L^T X, \text{ where } L^T = (m_A - m_B)\, C^{-1}{}_{\text{pooled}} \qquad (13.2)$$

where m_A = mean of A

$\quad m_B$ = mean of B

$\quad\quad$ T = transpose of a vector

$\quad\quad$ X = new observation

$\quad C_{\text{pooled}}$ = pooled covariance matrix

$\quad C_{\text{pooled}} = [1/(N_1 + N_2 - 2)][(N_1 - 1)C_1 + (N_2 - 1)C_2]$

$\quad\quad$ C_1 = covariance matrix corresponding to the first group

$\quad\quad$ C_2 = covariance matrix corresponding to the second group

$\quad\quad$ N_1 = sample size of the first group

$\quad\quad$ N_2 = sample size of the second group

Cutoff point (m) is calculated as $m = (1/2)(m_A - m_B)C^{-1}{}_{\text{pooled}} (m_A + m_B)$.

The classification rule then becomes:

If $L^T X > m$, classify X as population A.
If $L^T X < m$, classify X as population B.

Use of Mahalanobis Distance

An observation is classified into a group if the Mahalanobis distance (squared distance) of observation to the group center (mean) is the minimum. An assumption is made that covariance matrices are equal for all groups. There is a unique part of the squared distance formula for each group, and that is called the *linear discriminant function* for that group. For any observation, the group with the smallest squared distance has the largest linear discriminant function, and the observation is then classified into this group.

The maximum separation in the samples is given by:

$$D^2 = (m_A - m_B)^T C^{-1}{}_{\text{pooled}}(m_A - m_B) \qquad (13.3)$$

When there are more than two populations, considering prior probabilities and cost of misclassification, we can institute the following decision rule:

- Calculate the Mahalanobis distance (D_i^2) associated with the observation X corresponding to a population i as: $D_i^2 = (X - m_i)^T C^{-1}_{pooled} (X - m_i)$; where, m_i = Mean of population i and C_{pooled} = pooled covariance matrix.
- When there are k populations, assign X to group i ($I = 1, ..., k$), if $D_i^2 = \min (D_1^2, D_2^2, D_3^2 ... D_k^2)$.

The Mahalanobis distance can also be written as:

$$D_i^2 = -2[m_i^T C^{-1}_{pooled} X - 0.5 m_i^T C^{-1}_{pooled} m_i] + X^T C^{-1}_{pooled} X \quad (13.4)$$

In Equation (13.4), the term in square brackets is a linear function of X, and is called the linear discriminant function for group i. For a given X, the group with the smallest squared distance has the largest linear discriminant function. So this gives us another rule for classifying an observation. According to this rule, assign X to a group having the largest discriminant function.

Stepwise Regression

Stepwise regression is widely used for the selection of variables in multidimensional systems. The procedure iteratively constructs a sequence of regression models by adding and removing variables at each step. The method requires a specified value of the F-statistic for addition and deletion of the variables in the iterations. The method needs several iterations, if the number of variables is high. A discussion of stepwise regression is given in Montgomery and Peck (1982).

The basic method of stepwise regression is to calculate an F-statistic for each variable in the model. If the model contains $X_1, ..., X_p$, then the F-statistic for X_i is given as:

$$F = (\text{SSE } [X_1, ..., X_{i-1}, X_{i+1} ... X_p] - \text{SSE } [X_1, ..., ... X_p])/$$
$$(\text{MSE}[X_1, ..., X_{i-1}, X_{i+1} ... X_p]) \quad (13.5)$$

The F-statistic in Equation (13.5) has 1 and $n - p - 1$ degrees of freedom. In this equation, SSE indicates the sum of squares due to errors.

If the F-value for any variable is less than F_{out} (specified value) to remove, the variable with the smallest F-value is removed from the model. The regression equation is calculated for this smaller model, and the procedure proceeds to a new step.

If no variable can be removed, the procedure attempts to add a variable. An F-statistic is calculated for each variable not yet in the model. Suppose the model, at this stage, contains $X_1, ..., X_p$. Then the F-statistic for a new variable, X_{p+1} is:

$$F = (SSE[X_1, ..., X_p] - SSE[X_1, ..., X_p, X_{p+1}])/$$
$$(MSE[X_1, ..., X_{i-1}, X_{i+1} ... X_p, X_{p+1}]) \qquad (13.6)$$

The variable with the largest F-value is then added, provided its F-value is larger than F_{in} (specified value) to enter. Adding this variable is equivalent to choosing the variable that most effectively reduces the SSE. When no more variables can be entered into or removed from the model, the stepwise procedure ends.

Test of Additional Information (Rao's Test)

The test of additional information proposed by Dr. C. R. Rao is also used to identify a set of useful variables. This test is known as *Rao's test*. In Rao's test, which uses Fischer's linear discrimination function, the test of significance is carried out for a subset of the total number of variables. If the F-ratio is not high, then we can discard the subset of variables. For this test procedure please refer to Rao (1973).

The test statistic is calculated using the following equation:

$$F = [(N_1 + N_2 - p - q)/(p - q)] \times [(N_1 \times N_2 \times (D_p{}^2 - D_q{}^2)]/$$
$$[(N_1 + N_2)(N_1 + N_2 - 2) + N_1 N_2 D_q{}^2] \qquad (13.7)$$

where $D_p{}^2$ = distance with p (all) characteristics
$D_q{}^2$ = distance with a subset q, of p characteristics
N_1 = sample size of the first group
N_2 = sample size of the second group

The distances (D^2) are calculated with the help of the following equation on the basis of mean vectors of both the groups.

$$D^2 = (X_n - X_a)^T C^{-1}{}_{pooled}(X_n - X_a) \qquad (13.8)$$

where X_n = mean vector of normal group
          X_a = mean vector of abnormal group
      C^{-1}_{pooled} = inverse of pooled covariance matrix
      C_{pooled} = $[1/(N_1 + N_2 - 2)][(N_1 - 1)C_1 + (N_2 - 1)C_2]$
          C_1 = covariance matrix corresponding to p variables
          C_2 = covariance matrix corresponding to q (a subset of p) variables

The F-statistic in Equation (13.7) has degrees of freedom $(p - q)$ and $(N_1 + N_2 - p - q)$. A high F-ratio indicates that the variables in the subset provide additional information about the discriminant analysis. Before conducting this test, identification of a subset of variables based on certain criteria is required.

Multiple Regression Analysis

In multiple regression (MR), the objective is to estimate the characteristic Y, which is a function of the variables $X_1, X_2, \ldots, X_k$. If multiple regression is used for the purpose of classification, a decision regarding an observation $(X_1, X_2, \ldots, X_k)$ can be taken based on the value of Y. The multiple regression fit will be of the form:

$$Y_i = \beta_0 + \beta_1 X_{i1} + \beta_2 X_{i2} + \cdots + \beta_k X_{ik} + \varepsilon_I \tag{13.9}$$

where $I = 1, \ldots, n$ (n is the sample size)

The constants (β) are estimated by the method of least squares. The error terms (ε_i) are assumed to have the following properties:

1. $E(\varepsilon_i) = 0$
2. $V(\varepsilon_i) = \sigma^2$ (constant)
3. $\text{Cov}(\varepsilon_j, \varepsilon_k) = 0, j \# k$

A discussion of multiple regression is provided in Montgomery and Peck (1982).

Multivariate Process Control

When p process variables are being measured simultaneously, multivariate process control charts are used to monitor the process performance over a period of time. There are several types of these charts, such as multivariate Shewhart charts and multivariate Cusum charts. These charts operate just like univariate charts, in which corrective actions are taken whenever the process is out of the control limits.

Artificial Neural Networks

Artificial neural networks (ANNs) have been used for pattern recognition, learning, classification, generalization, and interpretation of noisy inputs. An ANN can be considered a structure (network) composed of interconnected units (artificial neurons). Each unit has an input/output (I/O) characteristic and implements a local computation or function. The output of any unit is determined by its I/O characteristic, its interconnection to other units, and (possibly) external inputs. An ANN does not constitute one network, but a diverse family of networks.

In this section, we discuss the feed-forward (backpropagation) method because this method is commonly used for identifying different patterns. The feed-forward algorithm is one of the methods of backpropagation. The backpropagation method is widely used in the pattern recognition field of classification. Given inputs and outputs, this method develops a specific nonlinear mapping, which is helpful in diagnostic applications.

The Feed-Forward (Backpropagation) Method

This method is used primarily for supervised learning in a feed-forward multiplayer perceptron (MLP). Specifically, the backpropagation method is used for training MLPs. Backpropagation is one of the most widely used learning processes in neural networks, and it was first developed by Werbos in 1974. Training MLPs with backpropagation algorithms results in a nonlinear mapping or an associated task. Thus, given two sets of data—that is, input/output pairs—the MLP can have its synaptic weights adjusted by the backpropagation algorithm to develop a specific nonlinear mapping. The MLP, with fixed weights after the training process, can provide an association task for classification, pattern recognition, diagnosis, and so forth. During the training phase of the MLP, the synaptic weights are adjusted to minimize the disparity between the actual and the desired outputs of the MLP averaged overall input patterns.

The standard backpropagation algorithm for training of the MLP network is based on the steepest descent gradient approach applied to minimization of an energy function representing the instantaneous error.

Standard Backpropagation Algorithm

1. Initialize the network synaptic weights to small random values.
2. From the set of training input/output pairs, present input patterns and calculate the network response.
3. Compare the desired network response with the actual output of the network, then all the local errors can be computed.
4. Update the weights of the network.
5. Until the network reaches a predetermined level of accuracy in producing the adequate response for all the training patterns, continue steps 2 through 4.

13.2.3   Big Data Analytics Operating Model

In order to successfully execute big data analytics, we need to have a highly effective end-to-end operational model. The main constituents of this model are shown in Figure 13.5.

The first component, management and governance, is important since this navigates the subsequent activities with regard to big data analytics. This includes drivers such as steering committees, program management aspects, project and change management aspects, compliance with organization requirements, compliance with infrastructure requirements, and road maps/how-to-guides.

The data strategy component is useful in understanding the data and planning how to use it so as to acquire better insights and make meaningful

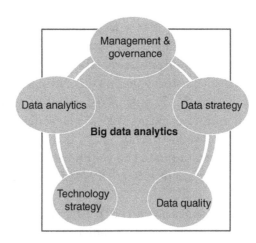

Figure 13.5   Big Data Analytics Operating Model

decisions. The data quality component should work closely with the data strategy group and help in cleaning the data and making sure that the data is fit for the intended purpose.

The data analytics component should work closely with both the data strategy and the data processing groups to make sure there is a common understanding of the data and that the data is of high quality. This component should have the capability of managing new and innovative ideas and executing them through analytical frameworks, models, or algorithms. The technology strategy component is extremely critical in executing sound big data analytics. This should include having a big data infrastructure such as a Hadoop platform and tools related to application development, knowledge management, and analytical support.

It is important to have the support and commitment of senior management in order to execute big data analytics, as the effectiveness of these components depends on such support.

13.2.4   Big Data Analytics Projects: Examples

Following is a list of sample big data analytics projects with descriptions.

Target's customer prediction analysis (Duhigg, Charles. 2012): A good example of a big data analytics project is predicting customer buying patterns based on all the relevant information collected when a "guest ID" and a Target Visa debit card are used. With the guest ID the name, address, and tender can be captured, and with the Target Visa debit card the information can be tied to the customer's store purchases. Using this information, and with some additional processing, the behavior patterns of the customers can be predicted.

Prediction of behavior patterns of defaulting customers: A financial company uses both structured and unstructured data (actual transactions, e-mail messages, phone conversations, and social media information) to predict the behavior patterns of defaulting customers so they can present strategies for these customers on an individual basis and minimize losses due to defaults.

IBM's Watson and *Jeopardy* (IBM Website): IBM's use of its capabilities to change the way information was employed to do business and make decisions is a good example of big data analytics execution. To accomplish this, IBM focused on three capabilities: natural language processing, hypothesis generation, and evidence-based learning. IBM developed a computer system by the name Watson to compete in *Jeopardy* and won. This system was developed based on big data analytics.

Identification of potential internal fraud cases: Several companies are leveraging big data analytics to generate new models for monitoring and identifying potential internal fraud cases.

Network analysis: Many companies are using big data analytics to develop insights through network flows by looking at the entire supply chain and identify opportunities with existing and new clients.

13.3   CONCLUSIONS

The conclusions drawn from this chapter can be summarized as follows:

- For running high-quality big data analytics and for data innovation, it is extremely important to have high-quality data. Therefore, preparatory analytics and cross-examination of data play a significant role.
- Data management and analytics capability management have become critical functions in overall management of a business and for achieving business excellence. They should be viewed in the same way as other resources such as people, facilities, and raw materials.
- Different types of analytics exist, so the appropriate type for the intended purpose and business requirements should be selected.
- An effective operating model for executing big data analytics is necessary and should incorporate the following components: management and governance, data strategy, data quality, and technology. The successful deployment of these components depends on the level of support and commitment from senior management.
- Good data coupled with big data techniques are key for organizational success because they provide very important insights that assist in making sound decisions.

Chapter 14

Building a Data Quality Practices Center

14.0 INTRODUCTION

Thus far, we have discussed building an effective DQ program and the methods, frameworks, and approaches that are essential for executing the program. In order to build these capabilities throughout a company, it is necessary to establish a strong DQ practices center (DQPC). The DQPC will have the operational capability to provide services, tools, and governance to deliver tangible insights and business value from the data. In this chapter, we describe the building of such a center with the required capabilities.

14.1 BUILDING A DQPC

The target state objective for any data quality program should be to create a fully functional data quality practices center (DQPC). The DQPC will have the required capabilities and will offer services to assist various business functions and business units. The fundamental building blocks identified for the DQPC are shown in Figure 14.1, and they should be kept in mind throughout the evolution of the DQ program.

As shown in Figure 14.1, the DQPC will have four important components: enablers, governance, monitoring and improvements, and analytical insights. A brief description of each component is provided as follows.

> **Enablers:** This component is responsible for delivering DQ services such as standardizing the DQ toolset, supporting metadata, and conducting various DQ assessment activities, besides providing required DQ resources and expertise to accelerate DQ adoption.

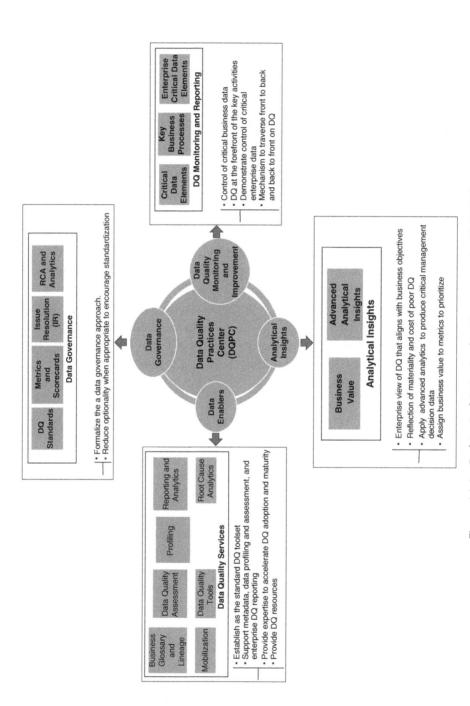

Figure 14.1   End-to-End Data Quality Management with DQPC

Governance: The primary responsibilities of this component include formalizing the data governance structure with focus on the standardization of various processes and analyses.

Monitoring and improvements: This component includes control of CDE data including enterprise CDEs (if a CDE intersects more than one business process and is used in multiple applications, then it is referred to as an *enterprise CDE*) and associated business processes.

Analytical insights: This component is responsible for conducting advanced analytics to produce data that can be used in various critical decision activities and computing business values associated with data quality.

The information provided in the previous chapters of this book will help companies come closer to achieving cohesive and enterprise-wide data quality capability. Companies can derive enormous benefits from identifying common enterprise problems and tracking them upstream to find the common root causes.

14.2   CONCLUSIONS

We can summarize the conclusions of this chapter as follows:

- This chapter highlights the importance of building out data quality capabilities with the end objective of creating a data quality practices center. Companies can derive significant benefits from having a centralized DQPC, as it helps to identify common enterprise problems and solve them through a systematic and standardized approach.

- Data quality needs to be managed throughout the enterprise with the help of a DQPC because data usage occurs simultaneously in many different business processes and common root causes can affect many users.

Appendix A

EQUATIONS FOR SIGNAL-TO-NOISE (S/N) RATIOS

Nondynamic S/N Ratios

- Nominal-the-Best
- Smaller-the-Better
- Larger-the-Better

Nominal-the-Best Type (Type I)

Let data points be $y_1 \quad y_2 \ldots\ldots\ldots y_n$

Nominal-the-Best Type (Type II)

Let data points be $y_1 \quad y_2 \ldots\ldots\ldots y_n$

$$S/N = \eta_{dB} = 10\text{Log}\left[\frac{\frac{1}{n}(S_m - V_e)}{V_e}\right] = 10\text{Log}\left[\frac{\frac{1}{n}\left(\frac{T^2}{n} - \sigma_{n-1}^2\right)}{\sigma_{n-1}^2}\right]$$

$$= 10\text{Log}\left[\frac{\frac{T^2}{n^2}}{\sigma_{n-1}^2}\right]$$

$$= 10\text{Log}\left[\frac{\bar{y}^2}{\sigma_{n-1}^2}\right]$$

We can also show the nominal-the-best S/N ratio as:

$$S/N = \eta_{dB} = 10\text{Log}\left[\frac{1}{V_e}\right] = 10\text{Log}\left[\frac{1}{\sigma_{n-1}^2}\right]$$

In this equation, the error variance (V_e) is an unbiased estimate of σ^2.

Note: The higher the S/N ratio becomes, the smaller the variability is. Maximizing this S/N ratio is equivalent to minimizing standard deviation or variation.

Smaller-the-Better Type

Let data points be $y_1 \quad y_2 \ldots\ldots y_n$

$$S/N = \eta_{dB} = 10 Log \left[\frac{1}{\frac{1}{n}\sum_{i=1}^{n} y_i^2} \right] = 10 Log \left[\frac{1}{\bar{y}^2 + \sigma^2} \right]$$

Note: Maximizing this S/N ratio minimizes the mean and standard deviation.

Larger-the-Better Type

Let data points be $y_1 \quad y_2 \ldots\ldots y_n$

$$S/N = \eta_{dB} = 10 Log \left[\frac{1}{\frac{1}{n}\sum_{i=1}^{n} \frac{1}{y_i^2}} \right] = -10 Log \left(\frac{1}{n}\sum_{i=1}^{n} \frac{1}{y_i^2} \right)$$

Maximizing this S/N maximizes the mean and minimizes standard deviation.

Dynamic S/N Ratios

Data set from outer array (sample size, $n = 16$).

	M_1	M_2	M_3	M_4
N_1Q_1	Y_1	Y_2	Y_3	Y_4
N_1Q_2	Y_5	Y_6	Y_7	Y_8
N_1Q_1	Y_9	Y_{10}	Y_{11}	Y_{12}
N_2Q_2	Y_{13}	Y_{14}	Y_{15}	Y_{16}
Total	Y_1	Y_2	Y_3	Y_4

n = # of data points, sample size = 16
$r = M_1^2 + M_2^2 + M_3^2 + M_4^2$
r_0 = # of data in $M_i = 4$

Y_i = Totle sum of data from M_i

Total sum of squares = $S_T = \sum_{i=1}^{n} y_i^2$

Sum of squares due to slope (β),

$$S_\beta = \frac{1}{r \times r_0} [Y_1 M_1 + Y_2 M_2 + Y_3 M_3 + Y_4 M_4]^2$$

Error sum of squares, $S_e = S_T - S_\beta$

Also, error variance, $V_e = \dfrac{S_e}{n-1}$

$$\text{S/N} = \eta_{dB} = 10\text{Log} \left[\frac{\dfrac{1}{r \times r_0}(S_\beta - V_e)}{V_e} \right]$$

Note: $\dfrac{1}{r \times r_0}(S_\beta - V_e)$ is an unbiased estimate of β^2

V_e is an unbiased estimate of mean square.

$$\beta = \sqrt{\frac{1}{r \times r_0}(S_\beta - V_e)} \cong \frac{1}{r \times r_0}(Y_1 M_1 + Y_2 M_2 + Y_3 M_3 + Y_4 M_4)$$

Appendix B

MATRIX THEORY: RELATED TOPICS

What Is a Matrix?

A matrix is an array of elements arranged in rows and columns. Matrix manipulations play a significant role in multivariate analysis, or pattern analysis.

If matrix A has m rows and n columns, then we say that matrix A is of size $m \times n$. An example of 3×4 matrix is shown as follows:

$$A = \begin{bmatrix} a_{11} & a_{12} & a_{13} & a_{14} \\ a_{21} & a_{22} & a_{23} & a_{24} \\ a_{31} & a_{32} & a_{33} & a_{34} \end{bmatrix}$$

Transpose of a Matrix

If the rows and columns of matrix A are interchanged, the resultant matrix is called the *transpose* of matrix A and is denoted by A^T or A'. If A is of size $m \times n$, then A^T is of size $n \times m$. The transpose of A is a 3×4 matrix and is shown as follows:

$$A^T \text{ or } A' = \begin{bmatrix} a_{11} & a_{21} & a_{31} \\ a_{12} & a_{22} & a_{32} \\ a_{13} & a_{23} & a_{33} \\ a_{14} & a_{24} & a_{34} \end{bmatrix}$$

Square Matrix

If the number of rows and the number of columns of a matrix are the same, then that matrix is called a *square* matrix.

Determinant of a Matrix

The determinant is a characteristic number associated with a square matrix. The importance of the determinant can be realized when solving a system of linear equations using matrix algebra. The solution to the system of equations contains the inverse matrix term, which is obtained by dividing the adjoint matrix by the determinant. If the determinant is zero, then the solution does not exist.

Let us consider a 2×2 matrix, as follows:

$$A = \begin{bmatrix} a_{11} & a_{12} \\ a_{21} & a_{22} \end{bmatrix}$$

The determinant of this matrix is $a_{11}a_{22} - a_{12}a_{21}$.

Now let us consider a 3×3 matrix, as follows:

$$A = \begin{bmatrix} a_{11} & a_{12} & a_{13} \\ a_{21} & a_{22} & a_{23} \\ a_{31} & a_{32} & a_{33} \end{bmatrix}$$

The determinant of A can be calculated as:

$$\det. A = a_{11}A_{11} + a_{12}A_{12} + a_{13}A_{13}$$

Where $A_{11} = (a_{22}a_{33} - a_{23}a_{32})$, $A_{12} = -(a_{21}a_{33} - a_{23}a_{31})$, and $A_{13} = (a_{21}a_{32} - a_{22}a_{31})$ are called *cofactors* of the elements a_{11}, a_{12}, and a_{13} of matrix A, respectively. The cofactors can be computed from submatrices obtained by deleting the rows and columns passing through the respective elements. Along a row or a column, the cofactors will have alternate plus and minus signs, with the first cofactor having a positive sign.

The preceding equation for the determinant is obtained by using the elements of the first row and their cofactors. The same value for the determinant can be obtained by using other rows or any column of the matrix with corresponding cofactors. In general, the determinant of a $n \times n$ square matrix can be written as:

$$\det. A = a_{i1}A_{i1} + a_{i2}A_{i2} + \cdots + a_{in}A_{in} \text{ along any row } i, \text{ where } I = 1,2, \ldots ,n$$

or

$$\det. A = a_{1j}A_{1j} + a_{2j}A_{2j} + \cdots + a_{nj}A_{nj} \text{ along any column } j, \text{ where } j = 1,2, \ldots ,n$$

Cofactor

From the preceding discussion, it is clear that the cofactor of A_{ij} of an element a_{ij} is the factor remaining after the element a_{ij} is factored out. The method of computing the cofactors was explained for a 3×3 matrix. Along a row or a column, the cofactors will have alternate signs of positive and negative, with the first cofactor having a positive sign.

Adjoint Matrix of a Square Matrix

The adjoint of a square matrix A is obtained by replacing each element of A with its own cofactor and transposing the result.

Let us again consider a 3×3 matrix, as shown here:

$$A = \begin{bmatrix} a_{11} & a_{12} & a_{13} \\ a_{21} & a_{22} & a_{23} \\ a_{31} & a_{32} & a_{33} \end{bmatrix}$$

The cofactor matrix containing cofactors (A_{ij}) of the elements of the preceding matrix can be written as:

$$A = \begin{bmatrix} A_{11} & A_{12} & A_{13} \\ A_{21} & A_{22} & A_{23} \\ A_{31} & A_{32} & A_{33} \end{bmatrix}$$

The adjoint of matrix A, which is obtained by transposing the cofactor matrix, can be written as:

$$\text{adj.}\, A = \begin{bmatrix} A_{11} & A_{21} & A_{31} \\ A_{12} & A_{22} & A_{32} \\ A_{13} & A_{23} & A_{33} \end{bmatrix}$$

Inverse Matrix

The inverse of matrix A (denoted as A^{-1}) can be obtained by dividing the elements of its adjoint by the determinant. Note that $A\, A^{-1} = A^{-1}\, A = I$, where I is an identity matrix with all on-diagonal elements as 1 and off-diagonal elements as 0.

Singular and Nonsingular Matrices

If the determinant of a square matrix is zero, then it is called a *singular* matrix. Otherwise, the matrix is known as *nonsingular.*

Some Other Definitions

Correlation coefficient: The measure of linear association between the variables X1 and X2. This value lies between −1 and +1.

Correlation matrix: The matrix that gives correlation coefficients between the variables.

Standardized distance: Distance of an observation from the mean in terms of standard deviations.

Standardized variables: Variables obtained after subtracting the mean from the original variables and dividing the subtracted quantity by the standard deviation.

Degrees of freedom: The number of independent parameters associated with an entity. These entities could be a matrix experiment, or a factor, or a sum of squares.

Normal distribution: The most commonly used distribution in statistics. This distribution is also known as a *Gaussian distribution*. It is a bell-shaped curve and is symmetric about the mean. The distribution is specified by two parameters: mean and standard deviation.

Appendix C

SOME USEFUL ORTHOGONAL ARRAYS

The orthogonal array is denoted as $L_a(b^c)$ where:
- L = Latin square
- a = Number of test trials
- b = Number of levels for each column
- c = Number of columns in the array

Two-Level Orthogonal Arrays

$L_4(2^3)$ Orthogonal Array

No.	1	2	3
1	1	1	1
2	1	2	2
3	2	1	2
4	2	2	1

$L_8(2^7)$ Orthogonal Array

No.	1	2	3	4	5	6	7
1	1	1	1	1	1	1	1
2	1	1	1	2	2	2	2
3	1	2	2	1	1	2	2
4	1	2	2	2	2	1	1
5	2	1	2	1	2	1	2
6	2	1	2	2	1	2	1
7	2	2	1	1	2	2	1
8	2	2	1	2	1	1	2

L₁₂(2¹¹) Orthogonal Array

No.	1	2	3	4	5	6	7	8	9	10	11
1	1	1	1	1	1	1	1	1	1	1	1
2	1	1	1	1	1	2	2	2	2	2	2
3	1	1	2	2	2	1	1	1	2	2	2
4	1	2	1	2	2	1	2	2	1	1	2
5	1	2	2	1	2	2	1	2	1	2	1
6	1	2	2	2	1	2	2	1	2	1	1
7	2	1	2	2	1	1	2	2	1	2	1
8	2	1	2	1	2	2	2	1	1	1	2
9	2	1	1	2	2	2	1	2	2	1	1
10	2	2	2	1	1	1	1	2	2	1	2
11	2	2	1	2	1	2	1	1	1	2	2
12	2	2	1	1	2	1	2	1	2	2	1

This is a special orthogonal array where interactions are distributed to all columns, more or less uniformly.

Conclusions regarding main effects are more robust against confounding of interactions.

L₁₆(2¹⁵) Orthogonal Array

No.	1	2	3	4	5	6	7	8	9	10	11	12	13	14	15
1	1	1	1	1	1	1	1	1	1	1	1	1	1	1	1
2	1	1	1	1	1	1	1	2	2	2	2	2	2	2	2
3	1	1	1	2	2	2	2	1	1	1	1	2	2	2	2
4	1	1	1	2	2	2	2	2	2	2	2	1	1	1	1
5	1	2	2	1	1	2	2	1	1	2	2	1	1	2	2
6	1	2	2	1	1	2	2	2	2	1	1	2	2	1	1
7	1	2	2	2	2	1	1	1	1	2	2	2	2	1	1
8	1	2	2	2	2	1	1	2	2	1	1	1	1	2	2
9	2	1	2	1	2	1	2	1	2	1	2	1	2	1	2
10	2	1	2	1	2	1	2	2	1	2	1	2	1	2	1
11	2	1	2	2	1	2	1	1	2	1	2	2	1	2	1
12	2	1	2	2	1	2	1	2	1	2	1	1	2	1	2
13	2	2	1	1	2	2	1	1	2	2	1	1	2	2	1
14	2	2	1	1	2	2	1	2	1	1	2	2	1	1	2
15	2	2	1	2	1	1	2	1	2	2	1	2	1	1	2
16	2	2	1	2	1	1	2	2	1	1	2	1	2	2	1

$L_{32}(2^{31})$ Orthogonal Array

No.	1	2	3	4	5	6	7	8	9	10	11	12	13	14	15	16	17	18	19	20	21	22	23	24	25	26	27	28	29	30	31
1	1	1	1	1	1	1	1	1	1	1	1	1	1	1	1	1	1	1	1	1	1	1	1	1	1	1	1	1	1	1	1
2	1	1	1	1	1	1	1	1	1	1	1	1	1	1	1	2	2	2	2	2	2	2	2	2	2	2	2	2	2	2	2
3	1	1	1	1	1	1	1	2	2	2	2	2	2	2	2	1	1	1	1	1	1	1	1	2	2	2	2	2	2	2	2
4	1	1	1	1	1	1	1	2	2	2	2	2	2	2	2	2	2	2	2	2	2	2	2	1	1	1	1	1	1	1	1
5	1	1	1	2	2	2	2	1	1	1	1	2	2	2	2	1	1	1	1	2	2	2	2	1	1	1	1	2	2	2	2
6	1	1	1	2	2	2	2	1	1	1	1	2	2	2	2	2	2	2	2	1	1	1	1	2	2	2	2	1	1	1	1
7	1	1	1	2	2	2	2	2	2	2	2	1	1	1	1	1	1	1	1	2	2	2	2	2	2	2	2	1	1	1	1
8	1	1	1	2	2	2	2	2	2	2	2	1	1	1	1	2	2	2	2	1	1	1	1	1	1	1	1	2	2	2	2
9	1	2	2	1	1	2	2	1	1	2	2	1	1	2	2	1	1	2	2	1	1	2	2	1	1	2	2	1	1	2	2
10	1	2	2	1	1	2	2	1	1	2	2	1	1	2	2	2	2	1	1	2	2	1	1	2	2	1	1	2	2	1	1
11	1	2	2	1	1	2	2	2	2	1	1	2	2	1	1	1	1	2	2	1	1	2	2	2	2	1	1	2	2	1	1
12	1	2	2	1	1	2	2	2	2	1	1	2	2	1	1	2	2	1	1	2	2	1	1	1	1	2	2	1	1	2	2
13	1	2	2	2	2	1	1	1	1	2	2	2	2	1	1	1	1	2	2	2	2	1	1	1	1	2	2	2	2	1	1
14	1	2	2	2	2	1	1	1	1	2	2	2	2	1	1	2	2	1	1	1	1	2	2	2	2	1	1	1	1	2	2
15	1	2	2	2	2	1	1	2	2	1	1	1	1	2	2	1	1	2	2	2	2	1	1	2	2	1	1	1	1	2	2
16	1	2	2	2	2	1	1	2	2	1	1	1	1	2	2	2	2	1	1	1	1	2	2	1	1	2	2	2	2	1	1
17	2	1	2	1	2	1	2	1	2	1	2	1	2	1	2	1	2	1	2	1	2	1	2	1	2	1	2	1	2	1	2
18	2	1	2	1	2	1	2	1	2	1	2	1	2	1	2	2	1	2	1	2	1	2	1	2	1	2	1	2	1	2	1
19	2	1	2	1	2	1	2	2	1	2	1	2	1	2	1	1	2	1	2	1	2	1	2	2	1	2	1	2	1	2	1
20	2	1	2	1	2	1	2	2	1	2	1	2	1	2	1	2	1	2	1	2	1	2	1	1	2	1	2	1	2	1	2

(continued)

223

$L_{32}(2^{31})$ Orthogonal Array (*continued*)

No.	1	2	3	4	5	6	7	8	9	10	11	12	13	14	15	16	17	18	19	20	21	22	23	24	25	26	27	28	29	30	31
21	2	1	2	2	1	2	1	1	2	1	2	2	1	2	1	1	2	1	2	2	1	2	1	1	2	1	2	2	1	2	1
22	2	1	2	2	1	2	1	1	2	1	2	2	1	2	1	2	1	2	1	1	2	1	2	2	1	2	1	1	2	1	2
23	2	1	2	2	1	2	1	2	1	2	1	1	2	1	2	1	2	1	2	2	1	2	1	2	1	2	1	1	2	1	2
24	2	1	2	2	1	2	1	2	1	2	1	1	2	1	2	2	1	2	1	1	2	1	2	1	2	1	2	2	1	2	1
25	2	2	1	1	2	2	1	1	2	2	1	1	2	2	1	1	2	2	1	1	2	2	1	1	2	2	1	1	2	2	1
26	2	2	1	1	2	2	1	1	2	2	1	1	2	2	1	2	1	1	2	2	1	1	2	2	1	1	2	2	1	1	2
27	2	2	1	1	2	2	1	2	1	1	2	2	1	1	2	1	2	2	1	1	2	2	1	2	1	1	2	2	1	1	2
28	2	2	1	1	2	2	1	2	1	1	2	2	1	1	2	2	1	1	2	2	1	1	2	1	2	2	1	1	2	2	1
29	2	2	1	2	1	1	2	1	2	2	1	2	1	1	2	1	2	2	1	2	1	1	2	1	2	2	1	2	1	1	2
30	2	2	1	2	1	1	2	1	2	2	1	2	1	1	2	2	1	1	2	1	2	2	1	2	1	1	2	1	2	2	1
31	2	2	1	2	1	1	2	2	1	1	2	1	2	2	1	1	2	2	1	2	1	1	2	2	1	1	2	1	2	2	1
32	2	2	1	2	1	1	2	2	1	1	2	1	2	2	1	2	1	1	2	1	2	2	1	1	2	2	1	2	1	1	2

$L_{64}(2^{63})$ Orthogonal Array

Run/Expt. no.	1	2	3	4	5	6	7	8	9	10	11	12	13	14	15	16	17	18	19	20	21	22	23	24	25	26	27	28	29	30	31
1	1	1	1	1	1	1	1	1	1	1	1	1	1	1	1	1	1	1	1	1	1	1	1	1	1	1	1	1	1	1	1
2	1	1	1	1	1	1	1	1	1	1	1	1	1	1	1	1	1	1	1	1	1	1	1	1	1	1	1	1	1	1	1
3	1	1	1	1	1	1	1	1	1	1	1	1	1	1	1	2	2	2	2	2	2	2	2	2	2	2	2	2	2	2	2
4	1	1	1	1	1	1	1	1	1	1	1	1	1	1	1	2	2	2	2	2	2	2	2	2	2	2	2	2	2	2	2
5	1	1	1	1	1	1	1	2	2	2	2	2	2	2	2	1	1	1	1	1	1	1	1	2	2	2	2	2	2	2	2
6	1	1	1	1	1	1	1	2	2	2	2	2	2	2	2	1	1	1	1	1	1	1	1	2	2	2	2	2	2	2	2
7	1	1	1	1	1	1	1	2	2	2	2	2	2	2	2	2	2	2	2	2	2	2	2	1	1	1	1	1	1	1	1
8	1	1	1	1	1	1	1	2	2	2	2	2	2	2	2	2	2	2	2	2	2	2	2	1	1	1	1	1	1	1	1
9	1	1	1	2	2	2	2	1	1	1	1	2	2	2	2	1	1	1	1	2	2	2	2	1	1	1	1	2	2	2	2
10	1	1	1	2	2	2	2	1	1	1	1	2	2	2	2	1	1	1	1	2	2	2	2	1	1	1	1	2	2	2	2
11	1	1	1	2	2	2	2	1	1	1	1	2	2	2	2	2	2	2	2	1	1	1	1	2	2	2	2	1	1	1	1
12	1	1	1	2	2	2	2	1	1	1	1	2	2	2	2	2	2	2	2	1	1	1	1	2	2	2	2	1	1	1	1
13	1	1	1	2	2	2	2	2	2	2	2	1	1	1	1	1	1	1	1	2	2	2	2	2	2	2	2	1	1	1	1
14	1	1	1	2	2	2	2	2	2	2	2	1	1	1	1	1	1	1	1	2	2	2	2	2	2	2	2	1	1	1	1
15	1	1	1	2	2	2	2	2	2	2	2	1	1	1	1	2	2	2	2	1	1	1	1	1	1	1	1	2	2	2	2
16	1	1	1	2	2	2	2	2	2	2	2	1	1	1	1	2	2	2	2	1	1	1	1	1	1	1	1	2	2	2	2
17	1	2	2	1	1	2	2	1	1	2	2	1	1	2	2	1	1	2	2	1	1	2	2	1	1	2	2	1	1	2	2
18	1	2	2	1	1	2	2	1	1	2	2	1	1	2	2	1	1	2	2	1	1	2	2	1	1	2	2	1	1	2	2
19	1	2	2	1	1	2	2	1	1	2	2	1	1	2	2	2	2	1	1	2	2	1	1	2	2	1	1	2	2	1	1
20	1	2	2	1	1	2	2	1	1	2	2	1	1	2	2	2	2	1	1	2	2	1	1	2	2	1	1	2	2	1	1
21	1	2	2	1	1	2	2	2	2	1	1	2	2	1	1	1	1	2	2	1	1	2	2	2	2	1	1	2	2	1	1

(continued)

225

L$_{64}$(2^{63}) Orthogonal Array (continued)

Run/Expt. no.	1	2	3	4	5	6	7	8	9	10	11	12	13	14	15	16	17	18	19	20	21	22	23	24	25	26	27	28	29	30	31
22	1	2	2	1	1	2	2	2	2	1	1	2	2	1	1	1	1	2	2	1	1	2	2	2	2	1	1	2	2	1	1
23	1	2	2	1	1	2	2	2	2	1	1	2	2	1	1	2	2	1	1	2	2	1	1	1	1	2	2	1	1	2	2
24	1	2	2	1	1	2	2	2	2	1	1	2	2	1	1	2	2	1	1	2	2	1	1	1	1	2	2	1	1	2	2
25	1	2	2	2	2	1	1	1	1	2	2	2	2	1	1	1	1	2	2	2	2	1	1	1	1	2	2	2	2	1	1
26	1	2	2	2	2	1	1	1	1	2	2	2	2	1	1	1	1	2	2	2	2	1	1	1	1	2	2	2	2	1	1
27	1	2	2	2	2	1	1	1	1	2	2	2	2	1	1	2	2	1	1	1	1	2	2	2	2	1	1	1	1	2	2
28	1	2	2	2	2	1	1	1	1	2	2	2	2	1	1	2	2	1	1	1	1	2	2	2	2	1	1	1	1	2	2
29	1	2	2	2	2	1	1	2	2	1	1	1	1	2	2	1	1	2	2	2	2	1	1	2	2	1	1	1	1	2	2
30	1	2	2	2	2	1	1	2	2	1	1	1	1	2	2	1	1	2	2	2	2	1	1	2	2	1	1	1	1	2	2
31	1	2	2	2	2	1	1	2	2	1	1	1	1	2	2	2	2	1	1	1	1	2	2	1	1	2	2	2	2	1	1
32	1	2	2	2	2	1	1	2	2	1	1	1	1	2	2	2	2	1	1	1	1	2	2	1	1	2	2	2	2	1	1
33	2	1	2	1	2	1	2	1	2	1	2	1	2	1	2	1	2	1	2	1	2	1	2	1	2	1	2	1	2	1	2
34	2	1	2	1	2	1	2	1	2	1	2	1	2	1	2	1	2	1	2	1	2	1	2	1	2	1	2	1	2	1	2
35	2	1	2	1	2	1	2	1	2	1	2	1	2	1	2	2	1	2	1	2	1	2	1	2	1	2	1	2	1	2	1
36	2	1	2	1	2	1	2	1	2	1	2	1	2	1	2	2	1	2	1	2	1	2	1	2	1	2	1	2	1	2	1
37	2	1	2	1	2	1	2	2	1	2	1	2	1	2	1	1	2	1	2	1	2	1	2	2	1	2	1	2	1	2	1
38	2	1	2	1	2	1	2	2	1	2	1	2	1	2	1	1	2	1	2	1	2	1	2	2	1	2	1	2	1	2	1
39	2	1	2	1	2	1	2	2	1	2	1	2	1	2	1	2	1	2	1	2	1	2	1	1	2	1	2	1	2	1	2
40	2	1	2	1	2	1	2	2	1	2	1	2	1	2	1	2	1	2	1	2	1	2	1	1	2	1	2	1	2	1	2
41	2	1	2	2	1	2	1	1	2	1	2	2	1	2	1	1	2	1	2	2	1	2	1	1	2	1	2	2	1	2	1
42	2	1	2	2	1	2	1	1	2	1	2	2	1	2	1	1	2	1	2	2	1	2	1	1	2	1	2	2	1	2	1

	43	44	45	46	47	48	49	50	51	52	53	54	55	56	57	58	59	60	61	62	63	64
	2	2	2	2	1	1	1	1	2	2	2	2	1	1	2	2	1	1	1	1	2	2
	1	1	1	2	2	2	2	2	1	1	1	1	2	2	1	1	2	2	2	2	1	1
	2	2	2	2	1	1	2	2	1	1	1	1	2	2	1	1	2	2	2	2	1	1
	1	1	1	1	2	2	1	1	2	2	2	2	1	1	2	2	1	1	1	1	2	2
	1	1	1	2	2	1	1	2	2	2	2	1	1	1	1	2	2	2	2	1	1	1
	2	2	2	2	1	1	2	2	1	1	1	1	2	2	2	2	1	1	1	1	2	2
	1	1	1	1	2	2	2	1	1	1	1	2	2	2	2	1	1	1	1	2	2	
	2	2	2	2	1	1	1	1	2	2	2	2	1	1	1	1	2	2	2	2	1	1
	2	2	1	1	2	2	1	1	2	2	1	1	2	2	2	2	1	1	2	2	1	1
	1	1	2	2	1	1	2	2	1	1	2	2	1	1	1	1	2	2	1	1	2	2
	2	2	1	1	2	2	2	2	1	1	1	2	2	1	1	1	2	2	1	1	2	2
	1	1	2	2	1	1	1	1	2	2	1	1	2	2	2	1	1	1	2	2	1	1
	1	1	2	2	1	1	1	2	2	1	1	2	2	1	1	2	2	1	1	2	2	
	2	2	1	1	2	2	2	2	1	1	2	2	1	1	2	2	1	1	2	2	1	1
	1	1	2	2	1	1	2	2	1	1	2	2	1	1	2	2	1	1	2	2	1	1
	2	2	1	1	2	2	1	1	2	2	1	1	2	2	1	1	2	2	1	1	2	2
	1	1	2	2	2	1	1	1	1	2	2	2	2	2	2	1	1	1	1	1	1	
	2	2	1	1	1	1	2	2	2	2	1	1	1	1	1	1	2	2	2	2	2	2
	1	1	2	2	2	2	2	2	1	1	1	1	1	1	1	2	2	2	2			
	2	2	1	1	1	1	1	1	2	2	2	2	2	2	2	1	1	1	1			
	2	2	1	1	1	1	1	1	1	2	2	2	1	1	1	1	2	2	2			
	1	1	2	2	2	2	2	2	1	1	1	1	2	2	2	2	1	1	1			
	2	2	1	1	1	1	2	2	2	1	1	1	1	2	2	2	1	1	1			
	1	1	2	2	2	2	1	1	1	2	2	2	1	1	1	2	2	2	2			
	2	2	2	2	2	2	2	2	1	1	1	1	2	2	2	2	2	2	2			
	2	2	2	2	2	2	2	2	2	2	2	1	1	1	1	1	1	1	1			
	1	1	1	1	1	2	2	2	2	2	2	1	1	1	1	1	1	1	1			
	2	2	2	2	2	1	1	1	1	1	2	2	2	2	2	2	2	2	2			
	2	2	2	2	2	1	1	1	1	1	1	1	1	1	1	1	1	1	1			
	2	1	1	1	1	2	2	2	2	2	2	2	2	2	2	2	2	2	2			
	2	2	2	2	2	2	2	2	2	2	2	2	2	2	2	2	2	2	2			

L$_{64}$(2^{63}) Orthogonal Array (*continued*)

Run/Expt. no.	32	33	34	35	36	37	38	39	40	41	42	43	44	45	46	47	48	49	50	51	52	53	54	55	56	57	58	59	60	61	62	63
1	1	1	1	1	1	1	1	1	1	1	1	1	1	1	1	1	1	1	1	1	1	1	1	1	1	1	1	1	1	1	1	1
2	2	2	2	2	2	2	2	2	2	2	2	2	2	2	2	2	2	2	2	2	2	2	2	2	2	2	2	2	2	2	2	2
3	1	1	2	2	2	2	2	2	1	1	1	1	2	2	1	1	2	2	2	2	2	2	2	2	2	2	2	2	2	2	2	2
4	2	2	2	2	2	2	2	2	2	2	2	2	1	2	2	2	1	1	1	1	1	1	1	1	1	1	1	1	1	1	1	1
5	1	1	1	1	1	1	1	1	2	2	2	2	1	2	2	2	2	2	2	2	2	2	1	1	2	2	1	1	1	2	1	2
6	2	1	2	2	2	2	2	2	1	1	1	1	1	2	2	1	2	2	2	2	2	2	2	2	1	1	2	2	2	1	2	1
7	1	2	1	1	2	1	2	1	2	2	2	2	2	2	1	2	2	2	2	2	2	2	1	1	1	1	1	1	1	1	1	1
8	2	1	2	2	2	2	2	2	1	1	1	1	2	2	1	2	2	2	2	2	2	2	2	2	2	2	2	2	2	2	2	2
9	1	2	2	1	2	2	1	2	2	2	2	1	2	2	2	1	2	2	2	2	1	1	2	2	1	2	2	2	2	2	2	2
10	2	1	2	2	2	2	2	2	1	1	1	1	2	2	1	2	2	2	2	2	2	1	2	1	2	1	2	1	1	1	1	1
11	1	2	1	1	2	1	1	1	2	2	2	2	1	1	2	1	1	1	1	1	1	1	1	1	1	1	1	2	2	1	1	1
12	2	1	2	2	2	2	2	2	1	1	1	1	2	2	1	2	2	2	2	2	2	2	2	2	2	2	2	2	2	2	2	2
13	1	2	1	1	2	1	1	1	2	2	2	2	1	1	2	1	1	1	1	1	1	1	1	1	1	1	1	1	1	2	2	1
14	2	2	2	2	2	2	2	2	2	2	2	2	2	2	2	2	2	2	2	2	2	2	2	2	2	2	2	2	2	2	2	2
15	1	1	1	1	1	1	1	1	1	1	1	1	1	1	1	1	1	1	1	1	1	1	1	1	1	1	1	1	1	1	1	1
16	2	2	2	2	2	2	2	2	2	2	2	2	2	2	2	2	2	2	2	2	2	2	2	2	2	2	2	2	2	2	2	2
17	1	1	1	1	1	1	1	1	1	1	1	1	1	1	1	1	1	1	1	1	1	1	1	1	1	1	1	1	1	1	1	1
18	2	2	2	2	2	2	2	2	2	2	2	2	2	2	2	2	2	2	2	2	2	2	2	2	2	2	2	2	2	2	2	2
19	1	1	1	1	1	1	1	1	1	1	1	1	1	1	1	1	1	1	1	1	1	1	1	1	1	1	1	1	1	1	1	1
20	2	2	2	2	2	2	2	2	2	2	2	2	2	2	2	2	2	2	2	2	2	2	2	2	2	2	2	2	2	2	2	2
21	1	1	1	1	1	1	1	1	1	1	1	1	1	1	1	1	1	1	1	1	1	1	1	1	1	1	1	1	1	2	1	1

228

22	23	24	25	26	27	28	29	30	31	32	33	34	35	36	37	38	39	40	41	42	43	44	45
2	2	1	1	2	2	1	2	1	1	2	2	1	1	2	1	2	2	1	1	2	2	1	2
2	2	1	1	2	2	1	2	1	1	2	1	2	2	1	2	1	1	2	2	1	1	2	1
1	1	2	2	1	1	2	1	2	2	1	2	1	1	2	1	2	2	1	1	2	2	1	2
1	2	1	1	2	2	1	1	2	1	2	2	1	2	1	2	2	1	1	1	2	2	1	1
2	2	1	2	1	1	1	2	1	2	2	1	2	1	1	2	1	2	1	2	1	2	1	1

L$_{64}$(2^{63}) Orthogonal Array (*continued*)

Run/Expt. no.	32	33	34	35	36	37	38	39	40	41	42	43	44	45	46	47	48	49	50	51	52	53	54	55	56	57	58	59	60	61	62	63
46	2	1	2	1	1	2	2	1	1	2	2	1	2	1	2	1	2	1	2	1	1	2	1	2	1	2	1	2	2	1	2	1
47	1	2	1	2	2	1	1	2	2	1	1	2	1	2	1	2	2	1	2	1	1	2	2	1	2	1	1	2	2	1	2	1
48	2	1	2	1	1	2	2	1	1	2	2	1	2	1	2	1	1	2	1	2	2	1	2	1	2	1	2	1	1	2	1	2
49	1	2	2	1	1	2	2	1	2	1	1	2	2	1	2	1	2	1	2	1	2	1	2	1	1	2	1	2	1	2	1	2
50	2	1	1	2	2	1	1	2	1	2	2	1	1	2	1	2	1	2	1	2	1	2	1	2	2	1	2	1	2	1	2	1
51	1	2	2	1	1	2	2	1	2	1	1	2	2	1	2	1	2	1	2	1	2	1	2	1	1	2	1	2	1	2	1	2
52	2	1	1	2	2	1	1	2	1	2	2	1	1	2	1	2	2	1	2	1	1	2	1	2	2	1	2	1	2	1	2	1
53	1	2	2	1	2	1	1	2	2	1	2	1	1	2	1	2	1	2	1	2	2	1	1	2	2	1	2	1	1	2	2	1
54	2	1	1	2	1	2	2	1	1	2	1	2	2	1	2	1	2	1	2	1	1	2	2	1	1	2	1	2	2	1	1	2
55	1	2	2	1	2	1	1	2	2	1	2	1	1	2	1	2	1	2	1	2	2	1	1	2	2	1	2	1	1	2	2	1
56	2	1	1	2	1	2	2	1	1	2	1	2	2	1	2	1	2	1	2	1	1	2	2	1	1	2	1	2	2	1	1	2
57	1	2	2	1	2	1	1	2	2	1	2	1	1	2	2	1	1	2	1	2	1	2	2	1	2	1	1	2	2	1	1	2
58	2	1	1	2	1	2	2	1	1	2	1	2	2	1	1	2	2	1	2	1	2	1	1	2	1	2	2	1	1	2	2	1
59	1	2	2	1	2	1	1	2	2	1	2	1	1	2	2	1	1	2	1	2	1	2	2	1	2	1	1	2	2	1	1	2
60	2	1	1	2	1	2	2	1	1	2	1	2	2	1	1	2	2	1	2	1	2	1	1	2	1	2	2	1	1	2	2	1
61	1	2	2	1	2	1	1	2	2	1	2	1	1	2	2	1	1	2	1	2	1	2	2	1	2	1	1	2	2	1	1	2
62	2	1	1	2	1	2	2	1	1	2	1	2	2	1	1	2	2	1	2	1	2	1	1	2	1	2	2	1	1	2	1	2
63	1	2	2	1	2	1	1	2	2	1	2	1	1	2	2	1	1	2	1	2	1	2	2	1	2	1	1	2	2	1	2	1
64	2	1	2	1	1	2	2	1	2	1	2	1	2	1	1	2	2	1	2	1	2	1	2	1	2	1	2	1	2	1	2	1

230

$L_{128}(2^{127})$ Orthogonal Array

Run/Expt. no.	1	2	3	4	5	6	7	8	9	10	11	12	13	14	15	16	17	18	19	20	21	22	23	24	25	26	27	28	29	30	31
1	1	1	1	1	1	1	1	1	1	1	1	1	1	1	1	1	1	1	1	1	1	1	1	1	1	1	1	1	1	1	1
2	1	1	1	1	1	1	1	1	1	1	1	1	1	1	1	1	1	1	1	1	1	1	1	1	1	1	1	1	1	1	1
3	1	1	1	1	1	1	1	1	1	1	1	1	1	1	1	1	1	1	1	1	1	1	1	1	1	1	1	1	1	1	1
4	1	1	1	1	1	1	1	1	1	1	1	1	1	1	1	1	1	1	1	1	1	1	1	1	1	1	1	1	1	1	1
5	1	1	1	1	1	1	1	1	1	1	1	1	1	1	1	2	2	2	2	2	2	2	2	2	2	2	2	2	2	2	2
6	1	1	1	1	1	1	1	1	1	1	1	1	1	1	1	2	2	2	2	2	2	2	2	2	2	2	2	2	2	2	2
7	1	1	1	1	1	1	1	1	1	1	1	1	1	1	1	2	2	2	2	2	2	2	2	2	2	2	2	2	2	2	2
8	1	1	1	1	1	1	1	1	1	1	1	1	1	1	1	2	2	2	2	2	2	2	2	2	2	2	2	2	2	2	2
9	1	1	1	1	1	1	1	2	2	2	2	2	2	2	2	1	1	1	1	1	1	1	1	2	2	2	2	2	2	2	2
10	1	1	1	1	1	1	1	2	2	2	2	2	2	2	2	1	1	1	1	1	1	1	1	2	2	2	2	2	2	2	2
11	1	1	1	1	1	1	1	2	2	2	2	2	2	2	2	1	1	1	1	1	1	1	1	2	2	2	2	2	2	2	2
12	1	1	1	1	1	1	1	2	2	2	2	2	2	2	2	1	1	1	1	1	1	1	1	2	2	2	2	2	2	2	2
13	1	1	1	1	1	1	1	2	2	2	2	2	2	2	2	2	2	2	2	2	2	2	2	1	1	1	1	1	1	1	1
14	1	1	1	1	1	1	1	2	2	2	2	2	2	2	2	2	2	2	2	2	2	2	2	1	1	1	1	1	1	1	1
15	1	1	1	1	1	1	1	2	2	2	2	2	2	2	2	2	2	2	2	2	2	2	2	1	1	1	1	1	1	1	1
16	1	1	1	1	1	1	1	2	2	2	2	2	2	2	2	2	2	2	2	2	2	2	2	1	1	1	1	1	1	1	1
17	1	1	1	2	2	2	2	1	1	1	1	2	2	2	2	1	1	1	1	2	2	2	2	1	1	1	1	2	2	2	2
18	1	1	1	2	2	2	2	1	1	1	1	2	2	2	2	1	1	1	1	2	2	2	2	1	1	1	1	2	2	2	2
19	1	1	1	2	2	2	2	1	1	1	1	2	2	2	2	1	1	1	1	2	2	2	2	1	1	1	1	2	2	2	2
20	1	1	1	2	2	2	2	1	1	1	1	2	2	2	2	1	1	1	1	2	2	2	2	1	1	1	1	2	2	2	2
21	1	1	1	2	2	2	2	1	1	1	1	2	2	2	2	2	2	2	2	1	1	1	1	2	2	2	2	1	1	1	1

(continued)

L$_{128}$(2^{127}) Orthogonal Array (*continued*)

Run/Expt. no.	1	2	3	4	5	6	7	8	9	10	11	12	13	14	15	16	17	18	19	20	21	22	23	24	25	26	27	28	29	30	31
22	1	1	1	2	2	2	2	1	1	1	1	2	2	2	2	2	2	2	2	1	1	1	1	2	2	2	2	1	1	1	1
23	1	1	1	2	2	2	2	1	1	1	1	2	2	2	2	2	2	2	2	1	1	1	1	2	2	2	2	1	1	1	1
24	1	1	1	2	2	2	2	1	1	1	1	2	2	2	2	2	2	2	2	1	1	1	1	2	2	2	2	1	1	1	1
25	1	1	1	2	2	2	2	2	2	2	2	1	1	1	1	1	1	1	1	2	2	2	2	2	2	2	2	1	1	1	1
26	1	1	1	2	2	2	2	2	2	2	2	1	1	1	1	1	1	1	1	2	2	2	2	2	2	2	2	1	1	1	1
27	1	1	1	2	2	2	2	2	2	2	2	1	1	1	1	1	1	1	1	2	2	2	2	2	2	2	2	1	1	1	1
28	1	1	1	2	2	2	2	2	2	2	2	1	1	1	1	1	1	1	1	2	2	2	2	2	2	2	2	1	1	1	1
29	1	1	1	2	2	2	2	2	2	2	2	1	1	1	1	2	2	2	2	1	1	1	1	1	1	1	1	2	2	2	2
30	1	1	1	2	2	2	2	2	2	2	2	1	1	1	1	2	2	2	2	1	1	1	1	1	1	1	1	2	2	2	2
31	1	1	1	2	2	2	2	2	2	2	2	1	1	1	1	2	2	2	2	1	1	1	1	1	1	1	1	2	2	2	2
32	1	1	1	2	2	2	2	2	2	2	2	1	1	1	1	2	2	2	2	1	1	1	1	1	1	1	1	2	2	2	2
33	1	2	2	1	1	2	2	1	1	2	2	1	1	2	2	1	1	2	2	1	1	2	2	1	1	2	2	1	1	2	2
34	1	2	2	1	1	2	2	1	1	2	2	1	1	2	2	1	1	2	2	1	1	2	2	1	1	2	2	1	1	2	2
35	1	2	2	1	1	2	2	1	1	2	2	1	1	2	2	1	1	2	2	1	1	2	2	1	1	2	2	1	1	2	2
36	1	2	2	1	1	2	2	1	1	2	2	1	1	2	2	1	1	2	2	1	1	2	2	1	1	2	2	1	1	2	2
37	1	2	2	1	1	2	2	1	1	2	2	1	1	2	2	2	2	1	1	2	2	1	1	2	2	1	1	2	2	1	1
38	1	2	2	1	1	2	2	1	1	2	2	1	1	2	2	2	2	1	1	2	2	1	1	2	2	1	1	2	2	1	1
39	1	2	2	1	1	2	2	1	1	2	2	1	1	2	2	2	2	1	1	2	2	1	1	2	2	1	1	2	2	1	1
40	1	2	2	1	1	2	2	1	1	2	2	1	1	2	2	2	2	1	1	2	2	1	1	2	2	1	1	2	2	1	1
41	1	2	2	1	1	2	2	2	2	1	1	2	2	1	1	1	1	2	2	1	1	2	2	2	2	1	1	2	2	1	1
42	1	2	2	1	1	2	2	2	2	1	1	2	2	1	1	1	1	2	2	1	1	2	2	2	2	1	1	2	2	1	1

(continued)

	43	44	45	46	47	48	49	50	51	52	53	54	55	56	57	58	59	60	61	62	63	64	65	66
	1	1	2	2	2	2	1	1	1	1	2	2	2	2	2	2	2	2	1	1	1	1	2	2
	1	1	2	2	2	2	1	1	1	1	2	2	2	2	2	2	2	2	1	1	1	1	1	1
	2	2	1	1	1	1	2	2	2	2	1	1	1	1	1	1	1	2	2	2	2	2	2	2
	2	2	1	1	1	1	2	2	2	2	1	1	1	1	1	1	1	2	2	2	2	2	1	1
	1	1	2	2	2	2	2	2	2	2	1	1	1	1	1	1	2	2	2	2	2	2	2	2
	1	1	2	2	2	2	2	2	2	2	1	1	1	1	1	1	2	2	2	2	2	1	1	1
	2	2	1	1	1	1	1	1	1	1	2	2	2	2	2	2	2	1	1	1	1	1	2	2
	2	2	1	1	1	1	1	1	1	1	2	2	2	2	2	2	2	1	1	1	1	1	1	1
	2	2	1	1	1	1	2	2	2	1	2	2	2	1	1	1	1	2	2	2	2	2	2	2
	2	2	1	1	1	1	2	2	2	1	2	2	2	1	1	1	1	2	2	2	2	1	1	1
	1	1	2	2	2	2	1	1	1	1	2	2	2	2	1	1	1	1	2	2	2	2	2	2
	1	1	2	2	2	2	1	1	1	1	2	2	2	2	1	1	1	1	2	2	2	2	1	1
	2	2	1	1	1	2	2	2	2	1	1	1	1	2	2	2	2	1	1	1	1	2	2	2
	2	2	1	1	1	2	2	2	2	1	1	1	1	2	2	2	2	1	1	1	1	1	1	1
	1	1	1	1	1	1	1	1	1	1	2	2	2	2	2	2	2	2	2	2	2	2	2	2
	1	1	1	1	1	1	1	1	1	1	2	2	2	2	2	2	2	2	1	1	1	1	1	1
	2	2	2	2	2	2	2	2	2	2	2	2	2	1	1	1	1	1	1	1	1	1	2	2
	2	2	2	2	2	2	2	2	2	2	2	2	2	1	1	1	1	1	1	1	1	1	1	1
	1	1	1	1	1	1	2	2	2	2	2	2	2	2	1	1	1	1	1	1	1	1	2	2
	1	1	1	1	1	1	2	2	2	2	2	2	2	2	1	1	1	1	1	1	1	1	1	1
	2	2	2	2	2	2	1	1	1	1	1	1	1	2	2	2	2	2	2	2	2	2	2	2
	2	2	2	2	2	2	1	1	1	1	1	1	1	2	2	2	2	2	2	2	2	1	1	1
	2	2	2	2	2	1	1	1	1	1	1	1	1	1	2	2	2	2	2	2	2	2	2	2
	2	2	2	2	2	1	1	1	1	1	1	1	1	1	2	2	2	2	2	2	2	1	1	1
	2	2	2	2	2	1	1	1	1	1	1	1	1	1	1	1	1	1	1	1	1	1	2	2
	1	1	1	1	1	1	2	2	2	2	2	2	2	2	2	2	2	2	2	2	2	2	2	2
	1	1	1	1	1	1	2	2	2	2	2	2	2	2	2	2	2	2	2	2	1	1	1	1
	2	2	2	2	2	2	2	2	2	2	2	2	2	2	2	2	2	2	2	2	2	2	2	2
	2	2	2	2	2	1	1	1	1	1	1	1	1	2	2	2	2	2	2	2	2	1	1	1
	2	2	2	2	2	1	1	1	1	1	1	1	1	1	1	1	1	1	1	1	1	1	2	2
	1	1	1	1	1	1	1	1	1	1	1	1	1	1	1	1	1	1	1	1	1	1	2	2

L$_{128}$(2^{127}) Orthogonal Array (continued)

Run/ Expt. no.	1	2	3	4	5	6	7	8	9	10	11	12	13	14	15	16	17	18	19	20	21	22	23	24	25	26	27	28	29	30	31
67	2	1	2	1	2	1	2	1	2	1	2	1	2	1	2	1	2	1	2	1	2	1	2	1	2	1	2	1	2	1	2
68	2	1	2	1	2	1	2	1	2	1	2	1	2	1	2	1	2	1	2	1	2	1	2	1	2	1	2	1	2	1	2
69	2	1	2	1	2	1	2	1	2	1	2	1	2	1	2	2	1	2	1	2	1	2	1	2	1	2	1	2	1	2	1
70	2	1	2	1	2	1	2	1	2	1	2	1	2	1	2	2	1	2	1	2	1	2	1	2	1	2	1	2	1	2	1
71	2	1	2	1	2	1	2	1	2	1	2	1	2	1	2	2	1	2	1	2	1	2	1	2	1	2	1	2	1	2	1
72	2	1	2	1	2	1	2	2	1	2	1	2	1	2	1	2	1	2	1	2	1	2	2	1	2	1	2	1	2	1	1
73	2	1	2	1	2	1	2	2	1	2	1	2	1	2	1	2	1	2	1	2	1	2	2	1	2	1	2	1	2	1	1
74	2	1	2	1	2	1	2	2	1	2	1	2	1	2	1	1	2	1	2	1	2	1	2	2	1	2	1	2	1	2	1
75	2	1	2	1	2	1	2	2	1	2	1	2	1	2	1	1	2	1	2	1	2	1	2	2	1	2	1	2	1	2	1
76	2	1	2	1	2	1	2	2	1	2	1	2	1	2	1	1	2	1	2	1	2	1	2	2	1	2	1	2	1	2	1
77	2	1	2	1	2	1	2	2	1	2	1	2	1	2	1	2	1	2	1	2	1	2	1	1	2	1	2	1	2	1	2
78	2	1	2	1	2	1	2	2	1	2	1	2	1	2	1	2	1	2	1	2	1	2	1	1	2	1	2	1	2	1	2
79	2	1	2	1	2	1	2	2	1	2	1	2	1	2	1	2	1	2	1	2	1	2	1	1	2	1	2	1	2	1	2
80	2	1	2	1	2	1	2	2	1	2	1	2	1	2	1	2	1	2	1	2	1	2	1	1	2	1	2	1	2	1	2
81	2	1	2	2	1	2	1	1	2	1	2	1	2	2	1	1	2	1	2	2	1	1	2	1	2	2	1	1	2	2	1
82	2	1	2	2	1	2	1	1	2	1	2	2	1	2	1	2	1	2	1	2	1	1	2	2	1	1	2	1	2	2	1
83	2	1	2	2	1	2	1	1	2	1	2	2	1	2	1	2	1	2	1	2	1	2	1	2	1	2	1	2	1	2	1
84	2	1	2	2	1	2	1	1	2	1	2	2	1	2	1	2	1	2	1	2	1	2	1	2	1	2	1	2	1	2	1
85	2	1	2	2	1	2	1	1	2	1	2	2	1	2	1	1	2	1	2	1	2	2	1	2	2	1	1	1	2	1	2
86	2	1	2	2	1	2	1	1	2	1	2	2	1	2	1	1	2	1	2	1	2	2	1	2	2	1	1	1	2	1	2
87	2	1	2	2	1	2	1	1	2	1	2	2	1	2	1	2	1	2	1	2	1	2	1	2	1	2	1	2	1	2	2

234

(continued)

	88	89	90	91	92	93	94	95	96	97	98	99	100	101	102	103	104	105	106	107	108	109	110	111
	2	2	2	2	2	1	1	1	1	1	1	1	1	2	2	2	2	2	2	2	2	1	1	1
	1	1	1	1	1	2	2	2	2	2	2	2	2	1	1	1	1	1	1	1	1	2	2	2
	2	1	2	2	2	1	1	1	1	2	2	2	2	1	1	1	1	1	1	1	1	2	2	2
	1	1	1	1	1	2	2	2	2	1	1	1	1	2	2	2	2	2	2	2	2	1	1	1
	1	1	1	1	1	2	2	2	2	1	1	1	1	2	2	2	2	2	2	2	2	1	1	1
	2	2	2	2	2	1	1	1	2	2	2	2	1	1	1	1	1	1	1	2	2	2		
	1	2	1	1	1	2	2	2	2	2	2	2	1	1	1	1	1	1	1	2	2	2		
	2	2	2	2	2	1	1	1	1	1	1	1	2	2	2	2	2	2	2	1	1	1		
	2	1	1	1	2	2	2	2	1	1	1	1	2	2	2	1	1	1	1	2	2	2		
	1	2	2	2	1	1	1	1	2	2	2	2	1	1	1	2	2	2	2	1	1	1		
	2	1	1	1	2	2	2	2	2	2	2	1	1	1	1	2	2	2	2	1	1	1		
	1	2	2	2	1	1	1	1	2	2	2	2	1	1	1	2	2	2	2	2	2	2		
	1	2	2	2	2	1	1	1	1	1	2	2	2	1	1	1	1	2	2	2	2	2		
	2	1	1	1	2	2	2	2	2	2	1	1	1	2	2	2	1	1	1	2	2	2		
	1	2	2	2	1	1	1	1	2	2	2	1	1	1	1	2	2	2	1	1	1			
	2	1	1	1	2	2	2	1	1	1	1	2	2	2	2	1	1	1	2	2	2	2		
	1	2	2	2	2	2	1	1	1	1	1	1	1	2	2	2	2	2	2	2	2	2		
	2	1	1	1	1	1	2	2	2	2	2	2	2	1	1	1	1	1	1	1	1	1		
	1	2	2	2	2	2	2	2	2	2	2	2	1	1	1	1	1	1	1	1	1	1		
	2	1	1	1	1	1	1	1	1	1	1	1	2	2	2	2	2	2	2	2	2	2		
	2	1	1	1	1	1	1	1	1	1	1	1	2	2	2	2	2	2	2	2	2	2		
	1	2	2	2	2	2	2	2	2	2	2	1	1	1	1	1	1	1	1	1	1	1		
	2	1	1	1	1	1	1	1	2	2	2	2	2	2	1	1	1	1	1	1	1	1		
	1	2	2	2	2	2	2	1	1	1	1	2	2	2	2	2	2	2						
	2	1	1	1	1	1	1	1	1	1	1	1	1	1	1	1	1	1	1	1	1	1		
	2	2	2	2	2	2	2	2	2	2	2	2	2	2	2	2	2	2	2	2	2	2		
	1	1	1	1	1	1	1	1	2	2	2	2	2	2	2	2	2	2	2	2	2	2		
	2	2	2	2	2	2	2	1	1	1	1	1	1	1	1	1	1	1	1	1	1	1		
	2	2	2	2	2	2	2	1	1	1	1	1	1	1	1	1	1	1	1	1	1	1		
	1	1	1	1	1	1	1	2	2	2	2	2	2	2	2	2	2	2	2	2	2	2		
	2	2	2	2	2	2	2	2	2	2	2	2	2	2	2	2	2	2	2	2	2	2		

$L_{128}(2^{127})$ Orthogonal Array (*continued*)

Run/Expt. no.	1	2	3	4	5	6	7	8	9	10	11	12	13	14	15	16	17	18	19	20	21	22	23	24	25	26	27	28	29	30	31
112	2	2	1	1	2	2	1	2	1	1	2	2	1	1	2	2	1	1	2	2	1	1	2	1	2	2	1	1	2	2	1
113	2	2	1	2	1	1	2	1	2	2	1	2	1	1	2	1	2	2	1	2	1	1	2	1	2	2	1	2	1	1	2
114	2	2	1	2	1	1	2	1	2	2	1	2	1	1	2	1	2	2	1	2	1	1	2	1	2	2	1	2	1	1	2
115	2	2	1	2	1	1	2	1	2	2	1	2	1	1	2	1	2	2	1	2	1	1	2	1	2	2	1	2	1	1	2
116	2	2	1	2	1	1	2	1	2	2	1	2	1	1	2	1	2	2	1	2	1	1	2	1	2	2	1	2	1	1	2
117	2	2	1	2	1	1	2	1	2	2	1	2	1	1	2	2	1	1	2	1	2	2	1	2	1	1	2	1	2	2	1
118	2	2	1	2	1	1	2	1	2	2	1	2	1	1	2	2	1	1	2	1	2	2	1	2	1	1	2	1	2	2	1
119	2	2	1	2	1	1	2	1	2	2	1	2	1	1	2	2	1	1	2	1	2	2	1	2	1	1	2	1	2	2	1
120	2	2	1	2	1	1	2	1	2	2	1	2	1	1	2	2	1	1	2	1	2	2	1	2	1	1	2	1	2	2	1
121	2	2	1	2	1	1	2	2	1	1	2	1	2	2	1	1	2	2	1	2	1	1	2	2	1	1	2	1	2	2	1
122	2	2	1	2	1	1	2	2	1	1	2	1	2	2	1	1	2	2	1	2	1	1	2	2	1	1	2	1	2	2	1
123	2	2	1	2	1	1	2	2	1	1	2	1	2	2	1	1	2	2	1	2	1	1	2	2	1	1	2	1	2	2	1
124	2	2	1	2	1	1	2	2	1	1	2	1	2	2	1	1	2	2	1	2	1	1	2	2	1	1	2	1	2	2	1
125	2	2	1	2	1	1	2	2	1	1	2	1	2	2	1	2	1	1	2	1	2	2	1	1	2	2	1	2	1	1	2
126	2	2	1	2	1	1	2	2	1	1	2	1	2	2	1	2	1	1	2	1	2	2	1	1	2	2	1	2	1	1	2
127	2	2	1	2	1	1	2	2	1	1	2	1	2	2	1	2	1	1	2	1	2	2	1	1	2	2	1	2	1	1	2
128	2	2	1	2	1	1	2	2	1	1	2	1	2	2	1	2	1	1	2	1	2	2	1	1	2	2	1	2	1	1	2

L₁₂₈(2¹²⁷) Orthogonal Array (*continued*)

Run/ Expt. no.	32	33	34	35	36	37	38	39	40	41	42	43	44	45	46	47	48	49	50	51	52	53	54	55	56	57	58	59	60	61	62
1	1	1	1	1	1	1	1	1	1	1	1	1	1	1	1	1	1	1	1	1	1	1	1	1	1	1	1	1	1	1	1
2	1	1	1	1	1	1	1	1	1	1	1	1	1	1	1	1	1	1	1	1	1	1	1	1	1	1	1	1	1	1	1
3	2	2	2	2	2	2	2	2	2	2	2	2	2	2	2	2	2	2	2	2	2	2	2	2	2	2	2	2	2	2	2
4	2	2	2	2	2	2	2	2	2	2	2	2	2	2	2	2	2	2	2	2	2	2	2	2	2	2	2	2	2	2	2
5	1	1	1	1	1	1	1	1	1	1	1	1	1	1	1	1	1	1	1	1	1	1	1	1	1	1	1	1	1	1	1
6	1	1	1	1	1	1	1	1	1	1	1	1	1	1	1	1	1	1	1	1	1	1	1	1	1	1	1	1	1	1	1
7	2	2	2	2	2	2	2	2	2	2	2	2	2	2	2	2	2	2	2	2	2	2	2	2	2	2	2	2	2	2	2
8	2	2	2	2	2	2	2	2	2	2	2	2	2	2	2	2	2	2	2	2	2	2	2	2	2	2	2	2	2	2	2
9	1	1	1	1	1	1	1	1	1	1	1	1	1	1	1	1	1	1	1	1	1	1	1	1	1	1	1	1	1	1	1
10	1	1	1	1	1	1	1	1	1	1	1	1	1	1	1	1	1	1	1	1	1	1	1	1	1	1	1	1	1	1	1
11	2	2	2	2	2	2	2	2	2	2	2	2	2	2	2	2	2	2	2	2	2	2	2	2	2	2	2	2	2	2	2
12	2	2	2	2	2	2	2	2	2	2	2	2	2	2	2	2	2	2	2	2	2	2	2	2	2	2	2	2	2	2	2
13	1	1	1	1	1	1	1	1	1	1	1	1	1	1	1	1	1	1	1	1	1	1	1	1	1	1	1	1	1	1	1
14	1	1	1	1	2	2	2	2	1	1	1	1	2	2	2	2	1	1	1	1	2	2	2	2	1	1	1	1	2	2	2
15	2	2	2	2	2	2	2	2	1	1	1	1	2	2	2	2	2	2	2	2	2	2	2	2	1	1	1	1	2	2	2
16	2	2	2	2	2	2	2	2	1	1	1	1	2	2	2	2	2	2	2	2	2	2	2	2	1	1	1	1	2	2	2
17	1	1	1	1	2	2	2	2	2	2	2	2	1	1	1	1	1	1	1	1	2	2	2	2	2	2	1	1	2	2	2
18	1	1	1	1	2	2	2	2	2	2	2	2	1	1	1	1	1	1	1	1	2	2	2	2	2	2	1	1	2	2	2
19	2	2	2	2	1	1	1	1	2	2	2	2	2	2	2	2	2	2	2	2	1	1	1	1	2	2	2	2	2	2	2
20	2	2	2	2	1	1	1	1	2	2	2	2	2	2	2	2	2	2	2	2	1	1	1	1	2	2	2	2	1	1	1
21	1	1	1	1	2	2	2	2	1	1	1	1	2	2	2	2	1	1	1	1	2	2	2	2	2	2	2	2	1	1	1

(continued)

Run/ Expt. no.	32	33	34	35	36	37	38	39	40	41	42	43	44	45	46	47	48	49	50	51	52	53	54	55	56	57	58	59	60	61	62
22	1	1	1	1	2	2	2	2	1	1	1	1	2	2	2	2	2	2	2	2	1	1	1	1	2	2	2	2	1	1	1
23	2	2	2	2	1	1	1	1	2	2	2	2	1	1	1	1	1	1	1	1	2	2	2	2	1	1	1	1	2	2	2
24	2	2	2	2	1	1	1	1	2	2	2	2	1	1	1	1	1	1	1	1	2	2	2	2	1	1	1	1	2	2	2
25	1	1	1	1	2	2	2	2	1	1	1	1	2	2	2	2	2	2	2	2	1	1	1	1	2	2	2	2	1	1	1
26	1	1	1	1	2	2	2	2	1	1	1	1	2	2	2	2	1	1	1	1	2	2	2	2	1	1	1	1	1	1	1
27	1	2	2	1	2	2	2	1	1	1	1	1	2	2	2	2	2	2	2	2	1	1	1	1	2	2	2	1	2	2	2
28	2	2	2	2	2	2	2	2	1	1	1	1	2	2	2	2	2	2	2	2	2	2	2	2	2	2	2	1	2	2	2
29	2	2	2	2	1	1	1	1	2	2	2	2	1	1	1	1	2	2	2	2	1	1	1	1	1	1	1	1	2	2	2
30	1	1	1	1	2	2	2	2	1	1	1	1	1	1	1	1	2	2	2	2	1	1	1	1	1	1	1	1	2	2	2
31	2	2	2	2	1	1	1	1	2	2	2	2	2	2	2	2	1	1	1	1	2	2	2	2	2	2	2	2	1	1	2
32	2	2	2	2	2	2	2	2	1	1	1	1	2	2	2	2	1	1	1	1	2	2	2	2	2	2	2	2	1	1	2
33	1	1	1	1	1	1	1	1	2	2	2	2	1	1	1	1	2	2	2	2	1	1	1	1	1	1	1	1	1	1	1
34	1	1	1	1	2	2	2	2	1	1	1	1	2	2	2	2	1	1	1	1	2	2	2	2	1	1	1	1	2	2	2
35	2	2	2	2	2	2	2	2	2	2	2	2	2	2	2	2	2	2	2	2	2	2	2	2	2	2	2	2	2	2	2
36	2	2	2	2	2	2	2	2	2	2	2	2	1	1	1	1	2	2	2	2	1	1	1	1	2	2	2	2	1	1	1
37	1	1	1	1	1	1	1	1	1	1	1	1	1	1	1	1	1	1	1	1	1	1	1	1	2	2	2	2	2	2	2
38	1	1	1	1	2	2	2	2	2	2	2	2	2	2	2	2	1	1	1	1	1	1	1	1	2	2	2	2	1	1	2
39	2	2	2	2	2	2	2	2	2	2	2	2	2	2	2	2	2	2	2	2	2	2	2	2	1	1	1	1	2	2	2
40	2	2	2	2	1	1	1	1	2	2	2	2	2	2	2	2	1	1	1	1	2	2	2	2	2	2	2	2	1	1	2
41	1	1	2	2	1	1	2	2	2	2	1	1	2	2	1	1	1	1	2	2	1	1	2	2	2	2	1	1	2	2	1
42	1	1	2	2	1	1	2	2	2	2	1	1	2	2	1	1	1	1	2	2	1	1	2	2	2	2	1	1	2	2	1

(continued)

	43	44	45	46	47	48	49	50	51	52	53	54	55	56	57	58	59	60	61	62	63	64	65	66
	2	2	2	2	1	1	1	1	2	2	2	2	1	1	2	2	1	1	1	1	2	2	1	1
	1	1	1	1	2	2	2	2	1	1	1	1	2	2	1	1	2	2	2	2	1	1	2	2
	1	1	1	1	2	2	2	2	1	1	1	1	2	2	2	2	1	1	1	1	1	1	1	1
	2	2	2	2	1	1	2	2	1	1	1	1	2	2	2	2	1	1	2	2	1	1	2	2
	2	2	2	2	1	1	2	2	1	1	1	1	2	2	2	2	1	1	1	1	1	1	1	1
	1	1	1	1	2	2	1	1	2	2	2	2	1	1	2	2	1	1	1	1	2	2	2	2
	1	1	1	1	2	2	1	1	2	2	2	2	1	1	2	2	1	1	1	1	2	2	1	1
	2	1	1	1	2	2	1	1	2	2	2	2	1	1	1	1	2	2	2	2	1	1	2	2
	2	2	2	2	1	1	2	2	1	1	1	1	2	2	2	2	1	1	1	1	2	2	2	2
	2	2	2	2	1	1	2	2	1	1	1	1	2	2	2	2	1	1	1	1	2	2	1	1
	1	1	1	1	2	2	2	2	1	1	1	1	2	2	2	2	1	1	1	1	2	2	2	2
	2	1	1	1	2	2	2	2	1	1	1	1	2	2	2	2	1	1	1	1	2	2	1	1
	2	2	2	1	1	1	1	1	2	2	2	2	1	1	2	2	2	2	1	1	1	1	2	2
	2	2	2	1	1	1	1	1	2	2	2	2	1	1	2	2	2	2	1	1	1	1	1	1
	2	2	1	1	2	2	2	1	1	2	2	1	1	2	2	1	1	2	2	1	1	2	2	2
	2	2	1	1	2	2	2	1	1	2	2	1	1	2	2	1	1	2	2	1	1	1	1	1
	1	1	2	2	1	1	2	2	1	1	2	2	1	1	2	2	1	1	2	2	1	1	2	2
	1	1	2	2	1	1	2	2	1	1	2	2	1	1	2	2	1	1	2	2	1	1	1	1
	2	2	1	1	2	2	2	1	1	2	2	1	1	2	2	1	1	2	2	1	1	2	2	2
	2	2	1	1	2	2	2	1	1	2	2	1	1	2	2	1	1	2	2	1	1	1	1	1
	1	1	2	2	1	1	1	2	2	1	1	2	2	1	1	2	2	1	1	2	2	2	2	2
	2	1	1	2	2	1	1	2	2	1	1	2	2	1	1	2	2	1	1	2	2	1	1	1
	2	2	1	1	2	2	2	1	1	2	2	1	1	2	2	1	1	2	2	1	1	2	2	2
	2	2	1	1	2	2	2	1	1	2	2	1	1	2	2	1	1	2	2	1	1	1	1	1

$L_{128}(2^{127})$ Orthogonal Array (*continued*)

Run/Expt. no.	32	33	34	35	36	37	38	39	40	41	42	43	44	45	46	47	48	49	50	51	52	53	54	55	56	57	58	59	60	61	62
67	2	1	2	1	2	1	2	1	2	1	2	1	2	1	2	1	2	1	2	1	2	1	2	1	2	1	2	1	2	1	2
68	2	1	2	1	2	1	2	1	2	1	2	1	2	1	2	1	2	1	2	1	2	1	2	1	2	1	2	1	2	1	2
69	1	2	1	2	1	2	1	2	1	2	1	2	1	2	1	2	2	1	2	1	2	1	2	1	2	1	2	1	2	1	2
70	1	2	1	2	1	2	1	2	1	2	1	2	1	2	1	2	2	1	2	1	2	1	2	1	2	1	2	1	2	1	2
71	2	1	2	1	2	1	2	1	2	1	2	1	2	1	2	1	1	2	1	2	1	2	1	2	1	2	1	2	1	2	1
72	2	1	2	1	2	1	2	1	2	1	2	1	2	1	2	1	1	2	1	2	1	2	1	2	1	2	1	2	1	2	1
73	1	2	1	2	1	2	1	2	2	1	2	1	2	1	2	1	1	2	1	2	1	2	1	2	2	1	2	1	2	1	2
74	1	2	1	2	1	2	1	2	2	1	2	1	2	1	2	1	1	2	1	2	1	2	1	2	2	1	2	1	2	1	2
75	2	1	2	1	2	1	2	1	1	2	1	2	1	2	1	2	2	1	2	1	2	1	2	1	1	2	1	2	1	2	1
76	2	1	2	1	2	1	2	1	1	2	1	2	1	2	1	2	2	1	2	1	2	1	2	1	1	2	1	2	1	2	1
77	1	2	1	2	1	2	1	2	2	1	2	1	2	1	2	1	2	1	2	1	2	1	2	1	1	2	1	2	1	2	1
78	1	2	1	2	1	2	1	2	2	1	2	1	2	1	2	1	2	1	2	1	2	1	2	1	1	2	1	2	1	2	1
79	2	1	2	1	2	1	2	1	1	2	1	2	1	2	1	2	1	2	1	2	1	2	1	2	2	1	2	1	2	1	2
80	2	1	2	1	2	1	2	1	1	2	1	2	1	2	1	2	1	2	1	2	1	2	1	2	2	1	2	1	2	1	2
81	1	2	1	2	2	1	2	1	1	2	1	2	2	1	2	1	1	2	1	2	2	1	2	1	1	2	1	2	2	1	2
82	1	2	1	2	2	1	2	1	1	2	1	2	2	1	2	1	1	2	1	2	2	1	2	1	1	2	1	2	2	1	2
83	2	1	2	1	1	2	1	2	2	1	2	1	1	2	1	2	2	1	2	1	1	2	1	2	2	1	2	1	1	2	1
84	2	1	2	1	1	2	1	2	2	1	2	1	1	2	1	2	2	1	2	1	1	2	1	2	2	1	2	1	1	2	1
85	1	2	1	2	2	1	2	1	1	2	1	2	2	1	2	1	2	1	2	1	1	2	1	2	2	1	2	1	1	2	1
86	1	2	1	2	2	1	2	1	1	2	1	2	2	1	2	1	2	1	2	1	1	2	1	2	2	1	2	1	1	2	1
87	2	1	2	1	1	2	1	2	2	1	2	1	1	2	1	2	1	2	1	2	2	1	2	1	1	2	1	2	2	1	2

88	2	1	2	1	1	2	1	2	2	1	2	1	1	2	1	2	1	2	1	2	2	1	2	1	1	2	1	2	2	1	2
89	1	2	1	2	2	1	2	1	2	1	2	1	1	2	1	2	1	2	1	2	2	1	2	1	2	1	2	1	1	2	1
90	1	2	1	2	2	1	2	1	2	1	2	1	1	2	1	2	1	2	1	2	2	1	2	1	2	1	2	1	1	2	1
91	2	1	2	1	1	2	1	2	1	2	1	2	2	1	2	1	2	1	2	1	1	2	1	2	1	2	1	2	2	1	2
92	2	1	2	1	1	2	1	2	1	2	1	2	2	1	2	1	2	1	2	1	1	2	1	2	1	2	1	2	2	1	2
93	1	2	1	2	2	1	2	1	2	1	2	1	1	2	1	2	2	1	2	1	1	2	1	2	1	2	1	2	2	1	2
94	1	2	1	2	2	1	2	1	2	1	2	1	1	2	1	2	2	1	2	1	1	2	1	2	1	2	1	2	2	1	2
95	2	1	2	1	1	2	1	2	1	2	1	2	2	1	2	1	1	2	1	2	2	1	2	1	2	1	2	1	1	2	1
96	2	1	2	1	1	2	1	2	1	2	1	2	2	1	2	1	1	2	1	2	2	1	2	1	2	1	2	1	1	2	1
97	1	2	2	1	1	2	2	1	1	2	2	1	1	2	2	1	1	2	2	1	1	2	2	1	1	2	2	1	1	2	2
98	1	2	2	1	1	2	2	1	1	2	2	1	1	2	2	1	1	2	2	1	1	2	2	1	1	2	2	1	1	2	2
99	2	1	1	2	2	1	1	2	2	1	1	2	2	1	1	2	2	1	1	2	2	1	1	2	2	1	1	2	2	1	1
100	2	1	1	2	2	1	1	2	2	1	1	2	2	1	1	2	2	1	1	2	2	1	1	2	2	1	1	2	2	1	1
101	1	2	2	1	1	2	2	1	1	2	2	1	1	2	2	1	2	1	1	2	2	1	1	2	2	1	1	2	2	1	1
102	1	2	2	1	1	2	2	1	1	2	2	1	1	2	2	1	2	1	1	2	2	1	1	2	2	1	1	2	2	1	1
103	2	1	1	2	2	1	1	2	2	1	1	2	2	1	1	2	1	2	2	1	1	2	2	1	1	2	2	1	1	2	2
104	2	1	1	2	2	1	1	2	2	1	1	2	2	1	1	2	1	2	2	1	1	2	2	1	1	2	2	1	1	2	2
105	1	2	2	1	1	2	2	1	2	1	1	2	2	1	1	2	1	2	2	1	1	2	2	1	2	1	1	2	2	1	1
106	1	2	2	1	1	2	2	1	2	1	1	2	2	1	1	2	1	2	2	1	1	2	2	1	2	1	1	2	2	1	1
107	2	1	1	2	2	1	1	2	1	2	2	1	1	2	2	1	2	1	1	2	2	1	1	2	1	2	2	1	1	2	2
108	2	1	1	2	2	1	1	2	1	2	2	1	1	2	2	1	2	1	1	2	2	1	1	2	1	2	2	1	1	2	2
109	1	2	2	1	1	2	2	1	2	1	1	2	2	1	1	2	2	1	1	2	2	1	1	2	1	2	2	1	1	2	2
110	1	2	2	1	1	2	2	1	2	1	1	2	2	1	1	2	2	1	1	2	2	1	1	2	1	2	2	1	1	2	2
111	2	1	1	2	2	1	1	2	1	2	2	1	1	2	2	1	1	2	2	1	1	2	2	1	2	1	1	2	2	1	1

(continued)

L₁₂₈(2¹²⁷) Orthogonal Array (continued)

Run/Expt. no.	32	33	34	35	36	37	38	39	40	41	42	43	44	45	46	47	48	49	50	51	52	53	54	55	56	57	58	59	60	61	62
112	2	1	1	2	2	1	1	2	2	2	2	1	1	2	2	1	1	2	2	1	1	2	2	1	2	1	1	2	2	1	1
113	1	2	2	1	2	1	1	2	1	2	2	1	2	1	1	2	1	2	2	1	2	1	1	2	1	2	2	1	2	1	1
114	1	2	2	1	2	1	1	2	1	2	2	1	2	1	1	2	2	1	2	1	2	1	1	2	1	2	2	1	2	1	1
115	2	1	1	2	1	2	2	1	2	1	1	2	1	2	2	1	2	1	1	2	2	1	2	1	2	1	1	2	1	2	2
116	2	1	1	2	2	1	2	1	2	1	1	2	1	2	2	1	1	2	1	2	2	1	2	1	2	1	1	2	1	2	2
117	1	2	2	1	1	2	1	2	1	2	2	1	1	2	2	1	2	1	2	1	2	1	2	1	1	2	1	2	1	2	2
118	1	2	2	1	1	2	1	2	1	2	2	1	2	1	1	2	2	1	2	1	2	1	2	1	2	1	1	2	1	2	2
119	2	1	1	2	1	2	2	1	2	1	1	2	1	2	2	1	1	2	1	2	1	2	2	1	1	2	2	1	2	1	1
120	2	1	1	2	1	2	2	1	2	1	1	2	1	2	2	1	1	2	2	1	1	2	1	2	2	1	2	1	1	2	1
121	1	2	2	1	2	1	1	2	1	2	2	1	1	2	2	1	2	1	2	1	1	2	1	2	2	1	2	1	2	1	2
122	1	2	2	1	2	1	1	2	1	2	2	1	1	2	2	1	2	1	2	1	1	2	1	2	1	2	2	1	2	1	2
123	2	1	1	2	1	2	2	1	2	1	1	2	1	2	1	2	2	1	1	2	2	1	2	1	1	2	2	1	2	1	1
124	2	1	1	2	1	2	2	1	1	2	2	1	2	1	1	2	2	1	1	2	2	1	2	1	1	2	2	1	2	1	1
125	1	2	2	1	2	1	1	2	2	1	1	2	2	1	2	1	1	2	1	2	2	1	2	1	1	2	1	2	2	1	2
126	1	2	2	1	2	1	1	2	2	1	1	2	1	2	2	1	1	2	1	2	2	1	1	2	2	1	1	2	2	1	2
127	2	1	1	2	1	2	2	1	1	2	2	1	2	1	1	2	2	1	2	1	1	2	1	2	2	1	1	2	1	2	2
128	2	1	1	2	1	2	2	1	1	2	2	1	2	1	1	2	1	2	2	1	1	2	1	2	2	1	1	2	1	2	2

L$_{128}$(2^{127}) Orthogonal Array (*continued*)

Run/ Expt. no.	63	64	65	66	67	68	69	70	71	72	73	74	75	76	77	78	79	80	81	82	83	84	85	86	87	88	89	90	91	92	93
1	1	1	1	1	1	1	1	1	1	1	1	1	1	1	1	1	1	1	1	1	1	1	1	1	1	1	1	1	1	1	1
2	1	2	2	2	2	2	2	2	2	2	2	2	2	2	2	2	2	2	2	2	2	2	2	2	2	2	2	2	2	2	2
3	2	1	1	1	1	1	1	2	1	1	2	1	2	1	1	1	1	1	1	1	1	1	1	1	2	1	1	1	1	1	1
4	2	2	2	2	2	2	2	2	2	2	1	2	2	2	2	2	2	2	2	2	2	2	2	2	2	2	2	2	2	2	2
5	2	2	1	1	1	2	1	2	1	1	2	1	2	1	1	1	1	2	2	2	1	2	2	2	2	2	1	2	2	2	2
6	2	2	2	2	2	2	2	2	2	2	1	2	2	2	2	2	2	2	2	2	2	2	1	2	1	1	2	1	1	1	2
7	1	2	1	1	1	1	1	2	1	1	2	1	2	1	1	1	2	1	1	1	1	1	2	1	2	2	1	2	2	2	2
8	1	1	1	1	1	1	1	2	2	2	1	2	1	2	2	2	1	2	2	2	1	2	1	2	1	1	2	1	1	1	1
9	1	2	2	2	2	2	2	1	2	2	2	1	2	2	2	2	2	2	2	2	1	2	2	2	2	2	1	2	2	2	2
10	2	2	2	2	2	2	2	2	1	1	1	2	1	1	1	1	1	1	1	1	2	1	1	1	1	1	2	1	1	1	1
11	2	1	1	1	1	1	1	2	2	2	1	2	1	2	2	2	1	2	2	2	2	2	2	2	1	1	1	1	1	1	2
12	1	2	2	2	2	2	2	1	1	1	2	1	2	1	1	1	2	1	1	1	1	1	1	1	2	2	1	2	2	2	1
13	1	1	1	1	1	1	1	2	1	1	2	1	2	1	1	1	2	1	1	1	1	1	2	1	1	1	2	1	1	1	1
14	1	1	2	2	2	2	2	1	1	1	1	2	1	1	1	1	1	1	1	1	2	1	2	1	2	2	1	2	2	2	2
15	2	2	1	2	2	2	2	2	2	2	1	2	1	2	2	2	2	2	2	2	1	2	2	2	1	1	2	1	1	1	1
16	2	1	1	1	1	1	1	2	2	2	2	1	2	2	2	2	2	2	2	2	2	2	1	2	1	1	2	1	1	1	2
17	2	2	1	2	2	2	2	2	1	1	2	1	2	1	1	1	2	1	1	1	1	1	2	1	2	2	1	2	2	2	2
18	2	2	1	2	2	2	2	2	2	2	2	1	2	2	2	2	2	2	2	2	1	2	1	2	2	2	2	2	2	2	1
19	1	1	1	1	1	1	1	1	1	1	1	2	1	1	1	1	1	1	1	1	2	1	2	1	2	2	1	2	1	1	2
20	1	2	2	2	2	2	2	1	1	1	1	2	1	1	1	1	2	2	2	2	2	2	1	2	1	1	2	2	2	2	1
21	1	1	1	2	2	2	2	2	2	2	2	1	2	2	2	2	2	2	2	2	2	2	1	2	1	1	2	2	2	2	1

(continued)

L$_{128}$(2^{127}) Orthogonal Array (*continued*)

Run/Expt. no.	63	64	65	66	67	68	69	70	71	72	73	74	75	76	77	78	79	80	81	82	83	84	85	86	87	88	89	90	91	92	93
22	1	2	2	2	2	1	1	1	1	2	2	2	2	1	1	1	1	1	1	1	1	2	2	2	2	1	1	1	1	2	2
23	2	1	1	1	1	2	2	2	2	1	1	1	1	2	2	2	2	2	2	2	2	1	1	1	1	2	2	2	2	1	1
24	2	2	2	2	2	1	1	1	1	2	2	2	2	1	1	1	1	1	1	1	1	2	2	2	2	1	1	1	1	2	2
25	1	1	1	1	1	2	2	2	2	1	1	1	1	2	2	2	2	2	2	2	2	1	1	1	1	2	2	2	2	1	1
26	1	2	2	2	2	1	1	1	1	2	2	2	2	1	1	1	1	2	2	2	2	1	1	1	1	2	2	2	2	1	1
27	2	2	2	2	2	1	1	1	1	2	2	2	2	1	1	1	1	2	2	2	2	1	1	1	1	2	2	2	2	1	1
28	2	2	2	2	2	1	1	1	1	2	2	2	2	1	1	1	1	1	1	1	1	2	2	2	2	1	1	1	1	2	2
29	2	2	2	2	2	1	1	1	1	2	2	2	2	1	1	1	1	1	1	1	1	2	2	2	2	1	1	1	1	2	2
30	2	2	2	2	2	1	1	1	1	2	2	2	2	1	1	1	1	2	2	2	2	1	1	1	1	2	2	2	2	1	1
31	1	1	1	1	1	2	2	2	2	1	1	1	1	2	2	2	2	1	1	1	1	2	2	2	2	1	1	1	1	2	2
32	2	2	2	2	2	1	1	1	1	2	2	2	2	1	1	1	1	1	1	1	1	2	2	2	2	1	1	1	1	2	2
33	2	2	2	2	2	1	1	1	1	2	2	2	2	1	1	1	1	2	2	2	2	1	1	1	1	2	2	2	2	1	1
34	2	1	1	1	1	2	2	2	2	1	1	1	1	2	2	2	2	2	2	2	2	1	1	1	1	2	2	2	2	1	1
35	1	2	2	2	2	1	1	1	1	2	2	2	2	1	1	1	1	2	2	2	2	1	1	1	1	2	2	2	2	1	1
36	1	1	1	1	1	2	2	2	2	1	1	1	1	2	2	2	2	1	1	1	1	2	2	2	2	1	1	1	1	2	2
37	1	1	1	1	1	2	2	2	2	1	1	1	1	2	2	2	2	1	1	1	1	2	2	2	2	1	1	1	1	2	2
38	1	2	2	2	2	1	1	1	1	2	2	2	2	1	1	1	1	1	1	1	1	2	2	2	2	1	1	1	1	2	2
39	2	2	2	2	2	1	1	1	1	2	2	2	2	1	1	1	1	2	2	2	2	1	1	1	1	2	2	2	2	1	1
40	2	2	2	2	2	1	1	1	1	2	2	2	2	2	2	2	2	1	1	1	1	2	2	2	2	1	1	1	1	2	2
41	1	1	1	1	1	2	2	2	2	1	1	1	1	2	2	2	2	1	1	1	1	1	1	1	1	2	2	2	2	1	1
42	1	2	2	2	2	1	1	1	1	2	2	2	2	1	1	1	1	2	2	2	2	1	1	1	1	2	2	2	2	1	1

(continued)

	43	44	45	46	47	48	49	50	51	52	53	54	55	56	57	58	59	60	61	62	63	64	65	66
	2	1	1	2	1	2	2	1	2	1	1	2	1	2	1	2	1	2	2	1	2	1	2	1
	2	1	1	2	1	2	2	1	2	1	1	2	1	2	1	2	1	2	2	1	1	2		
	1	2	2	1	2	1	2	1	2	1	1	2	1	2	1	2	2	1	2	1	2	1		
	1	2	2	1	2	1	2	1	2	1	1	2	1	2	1	2	1	2	2	1	2	1	1	2
	2	1	1	2	1	2	1	2	1	2	2	1	2	1	2	1	1	2	1	2	2	1		
	2	1	1	2	1	2	1	2	1	2	2	1	2	1	2	1	2	1	1	2	1	2	1	2
	2	1	1	2	1	2	1	2	1	2	2	1	2	1	1	2	1	2	2	1	2	1	2	1
	2	1	1	2	1	2	1	2	1	2	2	1	2	1	1	2	1	2	2	1	2	1	1	2
	1	2	2	1	2	1	2	1	2	1	2	2	1	2	1	2	1	2	2	1	2	2	1	
	1	2	2	1	2	1	2	1	2	1	2	2	1	2	1	1	2	1	2	1	2	1	2	
	2	1	1	2	1	2	1	2	1	2	1	2	2	1	2	1	2	1	2	2	1		
	2	1	1	2	1	2	2	1	2	1	2	1	2	1	2	1	1	2	1	2	1	2		
	1	2	2	1	2	1	1	2	1	2	2	1	2	1	1	2	1	2	2	1	2	1	2	1
	1	2	2	1	2	1	2	1	2	2	1	2	1	1	2	1	2	2	1	2	1	1	2	
	1	2	1	2	1	2	1	2	1	1	2	1	2	2	1	2	1	2	1	2	1	2	1	
	1	2	1	2	1	2	1	2	1	2	1	2	2	1	2	1	2	1	2	1	1	2		
	2	1	2	1	2	1	2	1	2	1	2	1	1	2	1	2	1	2	1	2	2	1		
	2	1	2	1	2	1	2	1	2	1	2	1	1	2	1	2	1	2	1	2	1	2		
	1	2	1	2	1	2	2	1	2	1	2	1	2	1	2	1	2	1	2	2	1		
	1	2	1	2	1	2	2	1	2	1	2	1	1	2	1	2	1	2	1	2	1	2		
	2	1	2	1	2	1	1	2	1	2	1	2	1	2	2	1	2	1	2	1	2	1		
	2	1	2	1	2	1	1	2	1	2	1	2	1	2	2	1	2	1	2	1	1	2		
	2	1	2	1	2	1	1	2	1	2	1	2	1	2	1	2	1	2	1	2	2	1		
	2	1	2	1	2	1	2	1	2	1	2	1	2	1	2	1	2	1	2	1	2			
	1	2	1	2	1	2	2	1	2	1	2	1	2	1	2	1	2	1	2	1	2	1		
	1	2	1	2	1	2	2	1	2	1	2	1	2	1	2	1	2	1	2	1	1	2		
	2	1	2	1	2	1	2	1	2	1	2	1	2	1	2	1	2	1	2	1	2	1		
	2	1	2	1	2	1	2	1	2	1	2	1	2	1	2	1	2	1	2	1	1	2		
	1	2	1	2	1	2	1	2	1	2	1	2	1	2	1	2	1	2	1	2	2	1		
	1	2	1	2	1	2	1	2	1	2	1	2	1	2	1	2	1	2	1	2	1	2		
	2	2	2	2	1	1	1	1	2	2	2	2	1	1	2	2	1	1	1	1	2	2	2	2

245

$L_{128}(2^{127})$ Orthogonal Array (*continued*)

Run/Expt. no.	63	64	65	66	67	68	69	70	71	72	73	74	75	76	77	78	79	80	81	82	83	84	85	86	87	88	89	90	91	92	93
67	1	1	2	1	2	1	2	1	2	1	2	1	2	2	2	1	2	2	2	1	2	1	2	1	2	1	2	2	2	1	2
68	1	2	1	2	1	2	1	2	1	2	1	2	1	1	1	2	1	1	1	2	1	2	1	2	1	2	1	1	1	2	1
69	1	1	2	1	2	1	2	1	2	1	2	1	2	2	2	1	2	2	2	1	2	1	2	1	2	1	2	2	2	1	2
70	1	2	1	2	1	2	1	2	1	2	1	2	1	1	1	2	1	1	1	2	1	2	1	2	1	2	1	1	1	2	1
71	2	1	2	1	2	1	2	1	2	1	2	1	2	2	2	1	2	2	2	1	2	1	2	1	2	1	2	2	2	1	2
72	2	2	1	2	1	2	1	2	1	2	1	2	1	1	1	2	1	1	1	2	1	2	1	2	1	2	1	1	1	2	1
73	1	1	2	1	2	1	2	1	2	1	2	1	2	2	2	1	2	2	2	1	2	1	2	1	2	1	2	2	2	1	2
74	1	2	1	2	1	2	1	2	1	2	1	2	1	1	1	2	1	1	1	2	1	2	1	2	1	2	1	1	1	2	1
75	2	1	2	1	2	1	2	1	2	1	2	1	2	2	2	1	2	2	2	1	2	1	2	1	2	1	2	2	2	1	2
76	2	2	1	2	1	2	1	2	1	2	1	2	1	1	1	2	1	1	1	2	1	2	1	2	1	2	1	1	1	2	1
77	2	1	2	1	2	1	2	1	2	1	2	1	2	2	2	1	2	2	2	1	2	1	2	1	2	1	2	2	2	1	2
78	2	2	1	2	1	2	1	2	1	2	1	2	1	1	1	2	1	1	1	2	1	2	1	2	1	2	1	1	1	2	1
79	1	1	2	1	2	1	2	1	2	1	2	1	2	2	2	1	2	2	2	1	2	1	2	1	2	1	2	2	2	1	2
80	1	2	1	2	1	2	1	2	1	2	1	2	1	1	1	2	1	1	1	2	1	2	1	2	1	2	1	1	1	2	1
81	1	1	2	1	2	1	2	1	2	1	2	1	2	2	2	1	2	2	2	1	2	1	2	1	2	1	2	2	2	1	2
82	1	2	1	2	1	2	1	2	1	2	1	2	1	1	1	2	1	1	1	2	1	2	1	2	1	2	1	1	1	2	1
83	2	1	2	1	2	1	2	1	2	1	2	1	2	2	2	1	2	2	2	1	2	1	2	1	2	1	2	2	2	1	2
84	2	2	1	2	1	2	1	2	1	2	1	2	1	1	1	2	1	1	1	2	1	2	1	2	1	2	1	1	1	2	1
85	2	1	2	1	2	1	2	1	2	1	2	1	2	2	2	1	2	2	2	1	2	1	2	1	2	1	2	2	2	1	2
86	2	2	1	2	1	2	1	2	1	2	1	2	1	1	1	2	1	1	1	2	1	2	1	2	1	2	1	1	1	2	1
87	1	1	2	1	2	1	2	1	2	1	2	1	2	2	2	1	2	2	2	1	2	1	2	1	2	1	2	2	2	1	2

88	89	90	91	92	93	94	95	96	97	98	99	100	101	102	103	104	105	106	107	108	109	110	111
1	2	1	2	1	1	2	1	2	2	1	2	1	1	2	1	2	1	2	1	2	2	1	2
2	1	2	1	2	2	1	2	1	1	2	1	2	2	1	2	1	2	1	2	1	1	2	1
2	1	2	1	2	2	1	2	1	1	2	1	2	2	1	2	1	2	1	2	1	1	2	1
1	2	1	2	1	1	2	1	2	2	1	2	1	1	2	1	2	1	2	1	2	2	1	2
2	1	2	1	2	2	1	2	1	1	2	1	2	1	2	1	2	1	2	1	2	2	1	2
1	2	1	2	1	1	2	1	2	1	2	1	2	2	1	2	1	2	1	2	1	1	2	1
1	2	1	2	1	1	2	1	2	2	1	2	1	1	2	1	2	1	2	1	2	2	1	2
2	2	1	2	1	1	2	1	2	2	1	2	1	1	2	1	2	2	1	2	1	1	2	1
2	1	2	1	2	2	1	2	1	2	1	2	1	2	1	2	1	2	1	2	1	1	2	1
2	2	1	2	1	1	2	1	2	1	2	1	2	2	1	2	1	1	2	1	2	2	1	2
2	2	1	2	1	1	2	1	2	2	1	2	1	2	1	2	1	1	2	1	2	2	1	2
1	1	2	1	2	2	1	2	1	2	1	2	1	1	2	1	2	2	1	2	1	1	2	1
2	2	1	2	1	1	2	1	2	1	2	1	2	1	1	2	1	2	2	1	2	1	2	1
1	1	2	1	2	2	1	2	1	1	2	1	2	2	1	2	1	2	2	1	2	1	1	2
2	2	1	2	1	2	1	2	1	2	1	2	1	2	1	2	1	2	1	2	1	2	1	2
1	1	2	1	2	1	2	1	2	2	1	2	1	2	1	2	1	1	2	1	2	1	2	1
2	2	1	2	1	2	1	2	1	2	1	2	1	2	1	2	1	1	2	1	2	1	2	1
1	1	2	1	2	1	2	1	2	1	2	1	2	2	1	2	1	2	1	2	1	2	1	2
2	1	2	1	2	1	2	1	2	1	2	1	2	1	2	2	1	2	1	2	1	2	1	2
2	2	1	2	1	2	1	2	1	1	2	1	2	1	2	2	1	2	1	2	1	2	1	1
2	1	2	1	2	1	2	1	2	2	1	2	1	2	1	2	1	2	1	2	1	2	1	1
1	2	2	1	2	1	2	1	2	1	2	1	2	1	2	1	2	1	2	1	2	1	2	2
2	1	2	1	2	1	2	1	2	2	1	2	1	2	1	2	1	2	1	2	1	2	1	2
1	2	1	2	1	2	1	2	1	1	2	1	2	1	2	1	2	1	2	1	2	1	2	1
2	1	2	1	2	1	2	1	1	2	1	2	1	2	1	2	1	2	1	2	1	2	1	1
2	1	2	1	2	1	2	1	2	2	1	2	1	2	1	2	1	2	1	2	1	2	1	2
1	2	1	2	1	2	1	2	1	1	2	1	2	1	2	1	2	1	2	1	2	1	2	2
2	1	2	1	2	1	2	1	1	2	1	2	1	2	1	2	1	2	1	2	1	2	1	1
1	2	1	2	1	2	1	2	2	1	2	1	2	1	2	1	2	1	2	1	2	1	2	1
2	1	2	1	2	1	2	1	2	1	2	1	2	1	2	1	2	1	2	1	1	2	1	2

(continued)

L$_{128}$(2^{127}) Orthogonal Array (*continued*)

Run/ Expt. no.	63	64	65	66	67	68	69	70	71	72	73	74	75	76	77	78	79	80	81	82	83	84	85	86	87	88	89	90	91	92	93
112	2	2	1	1	2	2	1	1	2	2	2	2	1	1	2	2	1	1	2	2	1	1	2	2	1	2	1	1	2	2	1
113	2	1	2	2	1	2	1	1	2	2	2	2	1	2	1	1	2	1	2	2	1	2	1	1	2	1	2	2	1	2	1
114	2	2	1	1	2	1	2	2	1	1	2	2	1	1	2	2	1	2	1	1	2	2	1	2	1	2	1	1	2	1	2
115	1	1	2	2	1	2	1	1	2	1	2	2	1	2	1	1	2	1	2	2	1	2	1	1	2	1	2	2	1	2	1
116	1	2	1	1	2	2	1	2	1	2	2	2	1	2	1	2	1	2	1	1	2	2	1	2	1	2	1	1	2	1	2
117	1	1	2	2	1	2	1	2	1	1	2	2	1	2	1	1	2	2	1	1	2	2	1	2	1	2	1	1	2	1	2
118	1	2	1	1	2	1	2	1	2	2	2	2	1	2	1	2	1	1	2	2	1	2	1	1	2	2	1	2	1	2	1
119	1	1	2	2	1	2	1	2	1	1	2	2	1	2	1	1	2	2	1	1	2	2	1	2	1	2	1	1	2	1	2
120	2	2	1	1	2	1	2	1	2	2	2	2	1	2	1	2	1	1	2	2	1	2	1	2	1	2	1	2	1	2	1
121	2	1	2	2	1	2	1	2	1	1	2	2	1	2	1	1	2	2	1	1	2	2	1	2	1	2	1	1	2	1	2
122	1	1	2	2	1	2	1	1	2	1	2	2	1	2	1	1	2	1	2	2	1	2	1	1	2	1	2	2	1	2	1
123	2	2	1	1	2	1	2	1	2	2	2	2	1	2	1	2	1	1	2	2	1	2	1	2	1	2	1	2	1	2	1
124	2	1	2	2	1	2	1	2	1	1	2	2	1	2	1	1	2	2	1	1	2	2	1	2	1	2	1	1	2	1	2
125	2	2	1	1	2	1	2	1	2	2	2	2	1	2	1	2	1	1	2	2	1	2	1	2	1	2	1	2	1	2	1
126	2	1	2	2	1	2	1	2	1	1	2	2	1	2	1	1	2	2	1	1	2	2	1	2	1	2	1	1	2	1	2
127	1	1	2	2	1	2	1	1	2	1	2	2	1	2	1	1	2	1	2	2	1	2	1	1	2	1	2	2	1	2	1
128	1	2	1	1	2	1	2	2	1	1	2	2	1	1	2	2	1	2	1	1	2	2	1	2	1	2	1	1	2	1	2

L$_{128}$(2^{127}) Orthogonal Array (continued)

Run/Expt. no.	94	95	96	97	98	99	100	101	102	103	104	105	106	107	108	109	110	111	112	113	114	115	116	117	118	119	120	121	122	123	124	125	126	127
1	1	1	1	1	1	1	1	1	1	1	1	1	1	1	1	1	1	1	1	1	1	1	1	1	1	1	1	1	1	1	1	1	1	1
2	2	2	2	2	2	2	2	2	2	2	2	2	2	2	2	2	2	2	2	2	2	2	2	2	2	2	2	2	2	2	2	2	2	2
3	1	1	2	2	2	2	2	2	1	1	2	2	2	2	2	2	2	2	2	2	1	2	2	2	2	2	2	2	2	2	2	2	2	2
4	2	2	1	1	1	1	1	1	1	1	1	1	1	1	1	1	1	1	1	1	1	1	1	1	1	1	1	1	1	1	1	1	1	1
5	2	2	1	1	1	1	1	1	2	2	2	2	2	2	1	1	2	2	2	2	1	2	1	2	2	2	2	2	2	2	1	2	2	2
6	1	1	2	2	1	1	1	1	2	2	2	2	2	2	2	2	2	1	1	1	1	1	1	1	1	1	1	1	1	1	2	2	2	1
7	2	2	2	2	2	2	2	2	1	1	2	2	2	2	2	2	2	2	1	1	1	1	1	1	1	1	1	1	1	1	1	1	1	1
8	1	1	2	2	2	2	2	2	1	1	1	1	1	1	1	1	2	2	2	2	2	2	2	2	2	2	2	2	2	2	1	1	1	1
9	2	2	1	1	1	1	1	1	2	2	2	2	2	2	2	2	2	2	2	2	2	2	1	1	1	1	1	1	1	1	2	2	2	2
10	1	1	2	2	2	2	2	2	2	2	2	2	2	2	1	1	1	1	2	2	2	2	2	2	2	2	2	2	2	2	2	2	2	2
11	2	2	2	2	2	2	2	2	1	1	1	1	1	1	1	1	1	1	1	1	1	1	2	2	2	2	1	1	1	1	1	1	1	1
12	1	1	2	2	2	2	2	2	1	1	1	1	1	1	1	1	1	1	2	2	2	2	2	2	2	2	1	1	1	1	1	1	1	1
13	2	2	1	1	1	1	1	1	2	2	2	2	2	2	2	2	2	2	1	1	1	1	1	1	1	2	2	2	2	2	2	2	2	2
14	1	1	2	2	2	2	2	2	1	1	1	1	2	2	2	2	1	1	1	1	1	1	1	1	2	1	1	1	1	1	2	2	2	2
15	2	2	1	1	2	2	2	2	2	2	2	2	2	2	2	2	2	2	2	2	2	2	1	2	1	2	1	1	1	1	2	2	2	2
16	2	1	1	1	1	1	1	1	2	2	2	2	2	2	2	2	2	2	2	2	2	2	2	2	2	2	2	2	2	2	2	2	2	2
17	2	2	2	2	1	1	2	2	2	2	2	2	2	2	2	2	2	2	2	2	2	2	1	1	1	2	2	2	2	1	1	1	1	1
18	1	1	2	2	1	1	1	1	1	1	1	1	1	1	2	2	2	2	2	2	2	2	2	2	2	2	1	1	1	2	1	1	1	1
19	2	2	2	2	2	2	2	2	2	2	2	2	2	2	1	1	1	1	1	1	2	2	2	2	2	2	2	2	2	2	2	2	2	1
20	1	1	1	1	1	1	2	2	2	2	1	1	1	1	2	2	2	2	1	1	1	1	2	2	2	2	2	2	1	1	1	2	2	2

(continued)

249

L$_{128}$(2^{127}) Orthogonal Array (*continued*)

Run/Expt. no.	94	95	96	97	98	99	100	101	102	103	104	105	106	107	108	109	110	111	112	113	114	115	116	117	118	119	120	121	122	123	124	125	126	127
21	1	1	2	1	1	1	2	2	2	2	1	1	1	1	2	2	2	2	2	2	2	2	1	1	1	1	2	2	2	2	1	1	1	1
22	2	2	2	2	2	1	1	1	1	1	2	2	2	2	1	1	1	1	1	1	1	1	2	2	2	2	1	1	1	1	2	2	2	2
23	1	1	1	1	2	2	1	1	1	1	2	2	2	2	1	1	1	1	1	1	1	1	2	2	2	2	1	1	1	1	2	2	2	2
24	2	2	2	2	1	1	2	2	2	2	1	1	1	1	2	2	2	2	2	2	2	2	1	1	1	1	2	2	2	2	1	1	1	1
25	1	2	1	1	1	1	2	2	2	2	1	1	1	1	2	2	2	2	1	1	1	1	2	2	2	2	1	1	1	1	1	1	1	1
26	2	1	2	1	1	1	1	1	1	1	2	2	2	2	1	1	1	1	2	2	2	2	1	1	1	1	2	2	2	2	2	2	2	2
27	1	2	2	2	2	1	1	1	1	1	2	2	2	2	1	1	1	1	2	2	2	2	1	1	1	1	2	2	2	2	2	2	2	2
28	2	1	1	1	2	2	2	2	2	2	1	1	1	1	2	2	2	2	1	1	1	1	2	2	2	2	1	1	1	1	1	1	1	1
29	2	2	1	1	1	1	2	2	2	2	1	1	1	1	2	2	2	2	2	2	2	2	1	1	1	1	2	2	2	2	1	1	1	1
30	1	1	2	2	2	1	1	1	1	1	2	2	2	2	1	1	1	1	1	1	1	1	2	2	2	2	1	1	1	1	2	2	2	2
31	2	2	2	2	1	2	2	2	2	2	1	1	1	1	2	2	2	2	1	1	1	1	2	2	2	2	1	1	1	1	2	2	2	2
32	1	1	1	1	2	1	1	1	1	1	2	2	2	2	1	1	1	1	2	2	2	2	1	1	1	1	2	2	2	2	1	1	1	1
33	2	1	2	2	2	1	2	2	2	2	1	1	1	1	2	2	2	2	2	2	2	2	1	1	1	1	2	2	2	2	2	2	2	2
34	1	2	1	1	1	2	1	1	1	1	2	2	2	2	1	1	1	1	1	1	1	1	2	2	2	2	1	1	1	1	1	1	1	1
35	2	1	2	2	1	2	2	2	2	2	1	1	1	1	2	2	2	2	2	2	2	2	1	1	1	1	2	2	2	2	1	1	1	1
36	1	2	1	1	2	1	1	1	1	1	2	2	2	2	1	1	1	1	1	1	1	1	2	2	2	2	1	1	1	1	2	2	2	2
37	1	1	1	1	1	2	2	2	2	2	1	1	1	1	2	2	2	2	2	2	2	2	1	1	1	1	2	2	2	2	2	2	2	2
38	2	2	2	2	2	1	1	1	1	1	2	2	2	2	1	1	1	1	1	1	1	1	2	2	2	2	1	1	1	1	1	1	1	1
39	1	1	1	1	1	2	2	2	2	2	1	1	1	1	2	2	2	2	1	1	1	1	2	2	2	2	1	1	1	1	2	2	2	2
40	2	2	2	2	2	1	1	1	1	1	2	2	2	2	1	1	1	1	2	2	2	2	1	1	1	1	2	2	2	2	1	1	1	1
41	1	1	1	1	1	1	1	1	1	1	2	2	2	2	2	2	2	2	2	2	2	2	1	1	1	1	2	2	2	2	2	2	2	2

250

42	43	44	45	46	47	48	49	50	51	52	53	54	55	56	57	58	59	60	61	62	63	64	65	66
2	2	1	1	2	1	1	2	1	2	2	1	2	1	1	2	2	1	1	2	1	2	2	1	2
2	2	1	2	1	1	2	1	2	2	1	2	1	1	2	2	1	1	2	1	2	2	1	1	2
1	1	2	1	2	2	1	2	1	1	2	1	2	2	1	1	2	1	2	1	1	2	2	1	1
1	1	2	1	2	2	1	2	1	1	2	1	2	2	1	1	2	2	1	1	1	2	1	2	
2	2	1	2	1	1	2	2	1	1	2	1	2	2	1	1	2	2	1	1	2	2	1		
2	2	1	2	1	1	2	2	1	1	2	1	2	2	1	1	2	2	1	1	2	2	1	2	
1	1	2	1	2	2	1	1	2	2	1	2	1	1	2	2	1	1	2	1	2	2	1	2	1
1	1	2	1	2	2	1	1	2	2	1	2	1	1	2	2	1	1	2	1	2	2	1	1	2
1	1	2	1	2	2	1	1	2	2	1	2	1	1	2	1	2	2	1	2	1	1	2	2	1
1	1	2	1	2	2	1	1	2	1	2	1	1	2	1	2	2	1	2	1	1	2	1	2	
2	2	1	2	1	1	2	2	1	1	2	1	2	2	1	2	1	1	2	1	2	2	1	2	1
2	2	1	2	1	2	2	1	1	2	1	2	2	1	2	1	1	2	1	2	2	1	1	2	
1	1	2	1	2	2	1	2	1	1	2	2	1	2	1	1	2	1	2	2	1	1	2	1	
1	1	2	1	2	2	1	2	1	1	2	2	1	2	1	1	2	1	2	2	1	1	1	2	
2	2	1	2	1	1	2	1	2	2	1	2	1	1	2	1	2	2	1	2	1	1	2	2	1
2	2	1	2	1	1	2	1	2	2	1	2	1	1	2	1	2	2	1	2	1	1	2	2	1
2	2	1	1	2	1	1	2	2	1	1	2	2	1	2	1	1	2	2	1	1	2	2	1	
2	2	1	1	2	1	1	2	2	1	2	1	1	2	2	1	2	1	1	2	2	1	1	2	
1	1	2	2	1	1	2	2	1	1	2	2	1	1	2	1	2	2	1	2	1	1	2	1	
1	1	2	2	1	1	2	2	1	1	2	2	1	1	2	1	2	2	1	1	2	1	1	2	
2	2	1	1	2	1	2	1	1	2	2	1	1	2	1	2	2	1	1	2	2	1	2	1	
2	2	1	1	2	1	2	1	1	2	2	1	2	1	2	2	1	1	2	2	1	1	2		
1	1	2	2	1	1	2	1	2	2	1	1	2	2	1	2	1	1	2	2	1	1	2	2	1
1	1	2	2	1	1	2	1	2	2	1	1	2	2	1	2	1	1	2	2	1	1	2	1	2
1	1	2	2	1	1	2	1	2	2	1	1	2	2	1	2	1	1	2	2	1	2	1	1	
1	2	1	2	2	1	1	2	1	2	2	1	2	1	1	2	2	1	1	2	2	1	2		
2	2	1	1	2	2	1	2	1	1	2	2	1	1	2	2	1	1	2	2	1	2	1		
2	2	1	1	2	2	1	2	1	1	2	2	1	1	2	2	1	1	2	2	1	1	2		
1	1	2	2	1	1	2	2	1	2	1	1	2	2	1	1	2	2	1	1	2	2	1		
1	1	2	2	1	1	2	2	1	2	1	1	2	2	1	1	2	2	1	1	2	1	1	2	
2	2	1	1	2	2	1	1	2	2	1	1	2	2	1	1	2	2	1	1	2	2	1	2	1
2	2	1	1	2	2	1	1	2	2	1	1	2	2	1	1	2	2	1	1	2	2	1	1	2
2	1	2	2	1	2	1	1	2	1	2	2	1	2	1	2	1	1	2	1	2	2	1	2	
2	1	2	2	1	2	1	1	2	1	2	2	1	2	1	2	1	1	2	1	2	2	1	1	2

L$_{128}$(2^{127}) Orthogonal Array (*continued*)

Run/ Expt. no.	94	95	96	97	98	99	100	101	102	103	104	105	106	107	108	109	110	111	112	113	114	115	116	117	118	119	120	121	122	123	124	125	126	127
67	1	2	2	1	2	1	2	1	2	1	2	1	2	1	2	1	2	1	2	1	2	1	2	1	2	1	2	1	2	1	2	1	2	1
68	2	1	1	2	1	2	1	2	1	2	1	2	1	2	1	2	1	2	1	2	1	2	1	2	1	2	1	2	1	2	1	2	1	2
69	2	1	2	2	1	2	1	2	1	2	1	2	1	2	1	2	1	2	1	2	1	2	1	2	1	2	1	2	1	2	1	2	1	2
70	1	2	2	1	2	1	2	1	2	1	2	1	2	1	2	1	2	1	2	1	2	1	2	1	2	1	2	1	2	1	2	1	2	1
71	2	1	1	2	1	2	1	2	1	2	1	2	1	2	1	2	1	2	1	2	1	2	1	2	1	2	1	2	1	2	1	2	1	2
72	1	2	1	2	1	2	1	2	1	2	1	2	1	2	1	2	1	2	1	2	1	2	1	2	1	2	1	2	1	2	1	2	1	2
73	2	1	2	1	2	1	2	1	2	1	2	1	2	1	2	1	2	1	2	1	2	1	2	1	2	1	2	1	2	1	2	1	2	1
74	1	2	2	1	2	1	2	1	2	1	2	1	2	1	2	1	2	1	2	1	2	1	2	1	2	1	2	1	2	1	2	1	2	1
75	2	1	2	1	2	1	2	1	2	1	2	1	2	1	2	1	2	1	2	1	2	1	2	1	2	1	2	1	2	1	2	1	2	1
76	1	2	1	2	1	2	1	2	1	2	1	2	1	2	1	2	1	2	1	2	1	2	1	2	1	2	1	2	1	2	1	2	1	2
77	1	2	2	1	2	1	2	1	2	1	2	1	2	1	2	1	2	1	2	1	2	1	2	1	2	1	2	1	2	1	2	1	2	1
78	2	1	2	1	2	1	2	1	2	1	2	1	2	1	2	1	2	1	2	1	2	1	2	1	2	1	2	1	2	1	2	1	2	1
79	1	2	2	1	2	1	2	1	2	1	2	1	2	1	2	1	2	1	2	1	2	1	2	1	2	1	2	1	2	1	2	1	2	1
80	2	1	2	1	2	1	2	1	2	1	2	1	2	1	2	1	2	1	2	1	2	1	2	1	2	1	2	1	2	1	2	1	2	2
81	2	1	1	2	1	2	1	2	1	2	1	2	1	2	1	2	1	2	1	2	1	2	1	2	1	2	1	2	1	2	1	2	1	1
82	1	2	2	1	2	1	2	1	2	1	2	1	2	1	2	1	2	1	2	1	2	1	2	1	2	1	2	1	2	1	2	1	2	2
83	2	1	2	1	2	1	2	1	2	1	2	1	2	1	2	1	2	1	2	1	2	1	2	1	2	1	2	1	2	1	2	1	2	2
84	1	2	2	1	2	1	2	1	2	1	2	1	2	1	2	1	2	1	2	1	2	1	2	1	2	1	2	1	2	1	2	1	2	1
85	1	2	1	2	1	2	1	2	1	2	1	2	1	2	1	2	1	2	1	2	1	2	1	2	1	2	1	2	1	2	1	2	1	2
86	2	1	2	1	2	1	2	1	2	1	2	1	2	1	2	1	2	1	2	1	2	1	2	1	2	1	2	1	2	1	2	1	2	2
87	1	2	1	2	1	2	1	2	1	2	1	2	1	2	1	2	1	2	1	2	1	2	1	2	1	2	1	2	1	2	2	1	2	1

(continued)

88	89	90	91	92	93	94	95	96	97	98	99	100	101	102	103	104	105	106	107	108	109	110	111	112
2	2	1	1	2	1	2	2	1	1	2	2	1	2	1	1	2	2	1	1	2	1	2	2	1
1	1	2	2	1	2	1	1	2	2	1	1	2	1	2	2	1	1	2	2	1	2	1	1	2
2	2	1	1	2	1	2	2	1	1	2	1	1	2	1	2	2	1	1	2	2	1	2	1	1
1	1	2	2	1	2	1	1	2	1	2	2	1	2	1	1	2	2	1	1	2	1	2	2	1
1	1	2	2	1	2	1	1	2	1	2	2	1	2	1	1	2	2	1	1	2	1	2	2	1
2	2	1	1	2	1	2	2	1	2	1	1	2	1	2	2	1	1	2	2	1	2	1	1	2
1	1	2	2	1	2	1	1	2	1	2	1	1	2	1	2	2	1	1	2	1	2	1	1	2
2	2	1	1	2	1	2	2	1	1	2	2	1	2	1	1	2	2	1	1	2	1	2	2	1
2	1	2	2	1	2	1	1	2	1	2	2	1	2	1	1	2	1	2	2	1	2	1	1	2
1	2	1	1	2	1	2	2	1	1	2	1	1	2	1	2	2	1	1	2	1	2	2	1	2
2	1	2	2	1	2	1	1	2	2	1	1	2	1	2	2	1	1	2	1	2	1	2	2	1
1	2	1	1	2	1	2	2	1	1	2	2	1	2	1	1	2	1	2	2	1	2	1	1	2
1	2	1	1	2	1	2	2	1	1	2	2	1	2	1	1	2	1	2	2	1	2	1	1	2
2	1	2	2	1	2	1	1	2	2	1	1	2	1	2	2	1	1	2	1	2	1	2	2	1
1	2	1	1	2	1	2	2	1	1	2	2	1	2	1	1	2	1	2	2	1	2	2	1	1
2	1	2	2	1	2	1	1	2	1	2	2	1	2	1	1	2	1	2	2	1	1	2	1	2
1	2	1	1	2	1	2	2	1	1	2	1	1	2	1	2	2	1	1	2	1	2	2	1	2
2	1	2	2	1	2	1	1	2	1	2	2	1	2	1	1	2	1	2	2	1	1	2	1	2
2	1	2	2	1	2	1	1	2	1	2	2	1	2	1	1	2	1	2	2	1	1	2	1	2
1	2	1	1	2	1	2	2	1	1	2	2	1	2	1	1	2	1	2	2	1	2	1	1	2
2	1	2	2	1	2	1	1	2	1	2	2	1	2	1	1	2	1	2	2	1	1	2	1	2
1	2	1	1	2	2	1	1	2	1	2	2	1	1	2	1	2	2	1	1	2	2	1	1	2
1	1	2	2	1	1	2	2	1	1	2	2	1	2	1	1	2	2	1	1	2	2	1	1	2
2	2	1	1	2	2	1	1	2	2	1	1	2	1	2	2	1	1	2	2	1	2	2	1	1
1	1	2	2	1	1	2	2	1	1	2	1	1	2	1	1	2	2	1	1	2	2	1	1	2
2	2	1	1	2	2	1	1	2	1	1	2	1	1	2	1	1	2	2	1	1	2	2	1	1
2	2	1	1	2	2	1	1	2	1	2	2	1	1	2	1	1	2	2	1	1	2	2	1	1
1	1	2	2	1	1	2	2	1	1	2	1	1	2	2	1	1	2	2	1	1	2	2	1	2
2	2	1	1	2	1	1	2	2	1	1	2	1	1	2	1	1	2	2	1	1	2	1	1	2
1	1	2	2	1	1	2	2	1	1	2	2	1	1	2	1	1	2	2	1	1	2	2	1	2
2	1	2	1	2	1	1	2	1	2	1	2	1	2	1	2	1	2	1	2	2	1	2	1	2

L$_{128}$(2^{127}) Orthogonal Array (*continued*)

Run/Expt. no.	94	95	96	97	98	99	100	101	102	103	104	105	106	107	108	109	110	111	112	113	114	115	116	117	118	119	120	121	122	123	124	125	126	127
113	1	2	1	2	2	1	2	1	1	2	1	2	2	1	2	1	1	2	1	2	2	1	2	1	1	2	1	2	2	1	2	1	1	2
114	2	1	2	1	1	2	1	2	2	1	2	1	1	2	1	2	2	1	2	1	1	2	1	2	2	1	2	1	1	2	1	2	2	1
115	1	2	2	1	1	2	2	1	2	1	1	2	1	2	2	1	2	1	1	2	1	2	2	1	2	1	1	2	1	2	2	1	2	1
116	2	1	1	2	2	1	1	2	1	2	2	1	2	1	1	2	1	2	2	1	2	1	1	2	1	2	2	1	2	1	1	2	1	2
117	2	1	1	2	2	1	1	2	1	2	1	2	2	1	2	1	1	2	2	1	2	1	1	2	2	1	1	2	1	2	1	2	1	2
118	1	2	2	1	1	2	2	1	2	1	2	1	1	2	1	2	2	1	1	2	1	2	2	1	1	2	2	1	2	1	2	1	2	1
119	2	1	1	2	2	1	1	2	1	2	1	2	2	1	2	1	1	2	2	1	2	1	1	2	2	1	1	2	1	2	1	2	1	2
120	1	2	2	1	1	2	2	1	2	1	2	1	1	2	1	2	2	1	1	2	1	2	2	1	1	2	2	1	2	1	2	1	2	1
121	2	1	1	2	2	1	1	2	1	2	2	1	2	1	1	2	1	2	2	1	2	1	1	2	1	2	2	1	2	1	1	2	1	2
122	1	2	2	1	1	2	2	1	2	1	1	2	1	2	2	1	2	1	1	2	1	2	2	1	2	1	1	2	1	2	2	1	2	1
123	2	1	1	2	2	1	1	2	1	2	2	1	2	1	1	2	1	2	2	1	1	2	1	2	2	1	2	1	1	2	1	2	2	1
124	1	2	2	1	1	2	2	1	2	1	1	2	1	2	2	1	2	1	1	2	2	1	2	1	1	2	1	2	2	1	2	1	1	2
125	1	2	2	1	1	2	2	1	1	2	2	1	2	1	1	2	2	1	1	2	2	1	2	1	1	2	1	2	2	1	2	1	1	2
126	2	1	1	2	2	1	1	2	2	1	1	2	1	2	2	1	1	2	2	1	1	2	1	2	2	1	2	1	1	2	1	2	2	1
127	1	2	2	1	1	2	2	1	1	2	2	1	2	1	1	2	2	1	1	2	2	1	2	1	1	2	1	2	2	1	2	1	1	2
128	2	1	1	2	2	1	1	2	2	1	1	2	1	2	2	1	1	2	2	1	1	2	1	2	2	1	2	1	1	2	1	2	2	1

Three-Level Orthogonal Arrays

No.	1	2	3	4
1	1	1	1	1
2	1	2	2	2
3	1	3	3	3
4	2	1	2	3
5	2	2	3	1
6	2	3	1	2
7	3	1	3	2
8	3	2	1	3
9	3	3	2	1

$L_{18}(2^1 \times 3^7)$ Orthogonal Array

No.	1	2	3	4	5	6	7	8
1	1	1	1	1	1	1	1	1
2	1	1	2	2	2	2	2	2
3	1	1	3	3	3	3	3	3
4	1	2	1	1	2	2	3	3
5	1	2	2	2	3	3	1	1
6	1	2	3	3	1	1	2	2
7	1	3	1	2	1	3	2	3
8	1	3	2	3	2	1	3	1
9	1	3	3	1	3	2	1	2
10	2	1	1	3	3	2	2	1
11	2	1	2	1	1	3	3	2
12	2	1	3	2	2	1	1	3
13	2	2	1	2	3	1	3	2
14	2	2	2	3	1	2	1	3
15	2	2	3	1	2	3	2	1
16	2	3	1	3	2	3	1	2
17	2	3	2	1	3	1	2	3
18	2	3	3	2	1	2	3	1

A special orthogonal array where interactions are distributed to all columns, more or less uniformly.

Conclusions regarding main effects are more robust against confounding of interactions.

$L_{27}(3^{13})$ Orthogonal Array

No.	1	2	3	4	5	6	7	8	9	10	11	12	13
1	1	1	1	1	1	1	1	1	1	1	1	1	1
2	1	1	1	1	2	2	2	2	2	2	2	2	2
3	1	1	1	1	3	3	3	3	3	3	3	3	3
4	1	2	2	2	1	1	1	2	2	2	3	3	3
5	1	2	2	2	2	2	2	3	3	3	1	1	1
6	1	2	2	2	3	3	3	1	1	1	2	2	2
7	1	3	3	3	1	1	1	3	3	3	2	2	2
8	1	3	3	3	2	2	2	1	1	1	3	3	3
9	1	3	3	3	3	3	3	2	2	2	1	1	1
10	2	1	2	3	1	2	3	1	2	3	1	2	3
11	2	1	2	3	2	3	1	2	3	1	2	3	1
12	2	1	2	3	3	1	2	3	1	2	3	1	2
13	2	2	3	1	1	2	3	2	3	1	3	1	2
14	2	2	3	1	2	3	1	3	1	2	1	2	3
15	2	2	3	1	3	1	2	1	2	3	2	3	1
16	2	3	1	2	1	2	3	3	1	2	2	3	1
17	2	3	1	2	2	3	1	1	2	3	3	1	2
18	2	3	1	2	3	1	2	2	3	1	1	2	3
19	3	1	3	2	1	3	2	1	3	2	1	3	2
20	3	1	3	2	2	1	3	2	1	3	2	1	3
21	3	1	3	2	3	2	1	3	2	1	3	2	1
22	3	2	1	3	1	3	2	2	1	3	3	2	1
23	3	2	1	3	2	1	3	3	2	1	1	3	2
24	3	2	1	3	3	2	1	1	3	2	2	1	3
25	3	3	2	1	1	3	2	3	2	1	2	1	3
26	3	3	2	1	2	1	3	1	3	2	3	2	1
27	3	3	2	1	3	2	1	2	1	3	1	3	2

L$_{36}$(2^{11} × 3^{12}) Orthogonal Array

No.	1	2	3	4	5	6	7	8	9	10	11	12	13	14	15	16	17	18	19	20	21	22	23
1	1	1	1	1	1	1	1	1	1	1	1	1	1	1	1	1	1	1	1	1	1	1	1
2	1	1	1	1	1	1	1	1	1	1	1	2	2	2	2	2	2	2	2	2	2	2	2
3	1	1	1	1	1	1	1	1	1	1	1	3	3	3	3	3	3	3	3	3	3	3	3
4	1	1	1	1	1	2	2	2	2	2	2	1	1	1	1	2	2	2	2	3	3	3	3
5	1	1	1	1	1	2	2	2	2	2	2	2	2	2	2	3	3	3	3	1	1	1	1
6	1	1	1	1	1	2	2	2	2	2	2	3	3	3	3	1	1	1	1	2	2	2	2
7	1	1	2	2	2	1	1	1	2	2	2	1	1	2	3	1	2	3	3	1	2	2	3
8	1	1	2	2	2	1	1	1	2	2	2	2	2	3	1	2	3	1	1	2	3	3	1
9	1	1	2	2	2	1	1	1	2	2	2	3	3	1	2	3	1	2	2	3	1	1	2
10	1	2	1	2	2	1	2	2	1	1	2	1	1	3	2	1	3	2	3	2	1	3	2
11	1	2	1	2	2	1	2	2	1	1	2	2	2	1	3	2	1	3	1	3	2	1	3
12	1	2	1	2	2	1	2	2	1	1	2	3	3	2	1	3	2	1	2	1	3	2	1
13	1	2	2	1	2	2	1	2	1	2	1	1	2	3	1	3	2	1	3	3	2	1	2
14	1	2	2	1	2	2	1	2	1	2	1	2	3	1	2	1	3	2	1	1	3	2	3
15	1	2	2	1	2	2	1	2	1	2	1	3	1	2	3	2	1	3	2	2	1	3	1
16	1	2	2	2	1	2	2	1	2	1	1	1	2	3	2	1	1	3	2	3	3	2	1
17	1	2	2	2	1	2	2	1	2	1	1	2	3	1	3	2	2	1	3	1	1	3	2
18	1	2	2	2	1	2	2	1	2	1	1	3	1	2	1	3	3	2	1	2	2	1	3
19	2	1	2	2	1	1	2	2	1	2	1	1	2	1	3	3	3	1	2	2	1	2	3
20	2	1	2	2	1	1	2	2	1	2	1	2	3	2	1	1	1	2	3	3	2	3	1
21	2	1	2	2	1	1	2	2	1	2	1	3	1	3	2	2	2	3	1	1	3	1	2
22	2	1	2	1	2	2	2	1	1	1	2	1	2	2	3	3	1	2	1	1	3	3	2
23	2	1	2	1	2	2	2	1	1	1	2	2	3	3	1	1	2	3	2	2	1	1	3
24	2	1	2	1	2	2	2	1	1	1	2	3	1	1	2	2	3	1	3	3	2	2	1
25	2	1	1	2	2	2	1	2	2	1	1	1	3	2	1	2	3	3	1	3	1	2	2
26	2	1	1	2	2	2	1	2	2	1	1	2	1	3	2	3	1	1	2	1	2	3	3
27	2	1	1	2	2	2	1	2	2	1	1	3	2	1	3	1	2	2	3	2	3	1	1
28	2	2	2	1	1	1	1	2	2	1	2	1	3	2	2	2	1	1	3	2	3	1	3
29	2	2	2	1	1	1	1	2	2	1	2	2	1	3	3	3	2	2	1	3	1	2	1
30	2	2	2	1	1	1	1	2	2	1	2	3	2	1	1	1	3	3	2	1	2	3	2
31	2	2	1	2	1	2	1	1	1	2	2	1	3	3	3	2	3	2	2	1	2	1	1
32	2	2	1	2	1	2	1	1	1	2	2	2	1	1	1	3	1	3	3	2	3	2	2
33	2	2	1	2	1	2	1	1	1	2	2	3	2	2	2	1	2	1	1	3	1	3	3
34	2	2	1	1	2	1	2	1	2	2	1	1	3	1	2	3	2	3	1	2	2	3	1
35	2	2	1	1	2	1	2	1	2	2	1	2	1	2	3	1	3	1	2	3	3	1	2
36	2	2	1	1	2	1	2	1	2	2	1	3	2	3	1	2	1	2	3	1	1	2	3

Index of Terms and Symbols

α	Statistical level of significance.
ANOVA	Analysis of variance.
β **(beta)**	Estimate of the slope.
Basel II	Basel II is the second of the Basel Accords, which are recommendations on banking laws and regulations.
BIDV	Business impacting decision variable.
C	correlation matrix
C⁻¹	Inverse of correlation matrix.
CDE	Critical data element.
COPDQ	Cost of poor data quality
DAIC	Define, Assess, Improve, and Control.
dB units	Decibel units.
DFSS	Design for Six Sigma.
DMADV	Define, Measure, Analyze, Design, and Verify.
DMAIC	Define, Measure, Analyze, Improve, and Control.
DQ	Data quality.
DQ score	A composite data quality score based on several dimensions. It can be calculated at the CDE level, at the business function level, or at the enterprise level.
DQOM	Data quality operating model.
DQPC	Data quality practices center.
D²	Mahalanobis distance
FMEA	Failure mode effect analysis.
IR	Issues resolution.

$L_a(b^c)$ representation of OA

Where	L denotes Latin square design
	a = number of experimental runs
	b = number of levels of each factor
	c = number of columns in the array
K	Number of variables.
OA	Orthogonal array.
M	Input signal.
MD	Mahalanobis distance.
MS	Mahalanobis space or reference group.
MTS	Mahalanobis-Taguchi Strategy.
ODS	Operational data source.
PQ	Process quality.
QLF	Quality loss function.
r	Sum of squares due to the input signal.
RWA	Risk-weighted assets.
S_β	Sum of squares due to slope.
Scaled MD	Scaled Mahalanobis distance.
S_e or SSE	Error sum of squares.
SME	Subject-matter expert.
S/N ratio	Signal-to-noise ratio.
σ or s or s.d.	Standard deviation.
SPC	Statistical process control.
S_T	Total sum of squares.
V_e	Error variance.
V(X)	Variance of X.
X_i	Original variables.
Z_i	Standardized variables.

References

REFERENCED RESOURCES

Albright, S. C., W. L. Winston, and C. J. Zappe. 2009. *Data Analysis and Decision Making.* Revised 3rd ed. Mason, OH: South-Western Cengage Learning.

Batini, C., and M. Scannapieco. 2006. Data Quality: Concepts, Methodologies and Techniques. Berlin: Springer.

Chiang, F., and M. J. Renee. 2008. "Discovering Data Quality Rules." *Proceedings of the 34th International Conference on Very Large Data Bases.* Auckland, New Zealand.

Deming, W. E. 1960., *Sample Design in Business Research.* New York: John Wiley & Sons.

———. 1993. *The New Economics: For Industry, Government and Education.* Cambridge, MA: MIT Press.

Duhigg, Charles. 2012. *The Power of Habit: Why We Do What We Do in Life and Business.* New York: Random House.

Gartner, Inc. 2012. *Big Data Strategy Components: IT Essentials.* Stamford, CT: Gartner, Inc.

Harrington, James. 2013. *The Five Pillars of Organizational Excellence.* Quality Digest. www.qualitydigest.com/aug06/articles/05_article.shtml.

Haug, Anders, Frederik Zachariassen, and Dennis van Liempd. 2011. "The Costs of Poor Data Quality." *Journal of Industrial Engineering and Management* 4(2):168–193.

Herzog, T. N., F. J. Scheuren, and W. E. Winkler. 2007. *Data Quality and Record Linkage Techniques.* New York: Springer.

Institute of International Finance (IIF) and McKinsey & Company. 2011. *Risk IT and Operations: Strengthening Capabilities Manual.* Johnson, Richard A., and Dean W. Wichern. 1992. *Applied Multivariate Statistical Analysis.* Englewood Cliffs, NJ: Prentice Hall.

Jugulum, Rajesh and Samuel, Philip (2008). *Design for Lean Six Sigma: A Holistic Approach to Design and Innovation*, New York: John Wiley & Sons.

Juran, Joseph M., and A. Blanton Godfrey. 1999. *Juran's Quality Handbook.* New York: McGraw-Hill.

Maydanchik, Arkady. 2007. *Data Quality Assessment.* Bradley Beach, NJ: Technics Publications.

McFadden, Fred R. 1993. "Six-Sigma Quality Programs."*Quality Progress* 26(6):37–42.

Montgomery, Douglas C., and Elizabeth A. Peck. 1982. *Introduction to Linear Regression Analysis.* New York: John Wiley & Sons.

Rao, C. R. 1973. *Linear Statistical Inference and Its Applications.* New York: John Wiley & Sons.

Redman, T. C. 1998. "The Impact of Poor Data Quality on the Typical Enterprise." *Communications of ACM* 41(2):191–204.

Shanks, G., and P. Darke. 1998. "Understanding Data Quality in a Data Warehouse." *The Australian Computer Journal* 30:122–128.

Taguchi, Genichi. 1986. *Introduction to Quality Engineering.* Tokyo: Asian Productivity Organization.

———. 1987. *System of Experimental Design.* Vols. 1 and 2. White Plains, NY: ASI and Quality Resources.

Taguchi, Genichi, and Rajesh Jugulum. 1999. "Role of S/N Ratios in Multivariate Diagnosis." *Journal of Japanese Quality Engineering Society* 7(6):63–69.

Taguchi, Genichi, and Rajesh Jugulum. 2002 *The Mahalanobis-Taguchi Strategy: A Pattern Technology.* Hoboken: John Wiley & Sons.

Tan, P.-N., M. Steinbach, and V. Kumar. 2005. *Introduction to Data Mining.* Reading, MA: Addison-Wesley.

Wang, R. Y., and D. M. Strong. 1996. "Beyond Accuracy: What Data Quality Means to Data Consumers." *Journal of Management Information Systems* 12(4): 5–33.

FURTHER RESOURCES

Anderson T. W. 1984. *An Introduction to Multivariate Statistical Analysis.* 2nd ed. New York: John Wiley & Sons.

Blake, R., and P. Mangiameli. 2011. "The Effects and Interactions of Data Quality and Problem Complexity on Classification." *Journal of Data and Information Quality,* 2(2):1–28.

Box, G. E. P. 1999. "Statistics as a Catalyst to Learning by the Scientific Method Part II—A Discussion." *Journal of Quality Technology* 31(1):16–29.

Brown, William C. 1991. *Matrices and Vector Spaces*. New York: Marcel Dekker, Inc.

Clausing, Don. 1994. *Total Quality Development: A Step-by-Step Guide to World-Class Concurrent Engineering*. New York: ASME Press.

Cong, G., W. Fan, F. Geerts, X. Jia, and S. Ma. 2007. "Improving Data Quality: Consistency and Accuracy." *Proceedings of the 33rd International Conference on Very Large Data Bases*. Vienna, Austria.

Creveling, C. M., J. L. Slutsky, and D. Antis, Jr. 2002. *Design for Six Sigma in Technology and Product Development*. Upper Saddle River, NJ: Prentice Hall.

Dasgupta, Somesh. 1993. "The Evolution of the D^2-Statistic of Mahalanobis." *Sankhya* 55:442–459.

Davenport, Thomas H., and Jeanne G. Harris. 2007. *Competing on Analytics: The New Science of Winning*. Boston: Harvard Business School Publishing.

English, L. 1999. *Improving Data Warehouse and Business Information Quality*. New York: John Wiley & Sons.

English, Larry P. 2009. *Information Quality Applied: Best Practices for Improving Business Information, Processes, and Systems*. Hoboken: John Wiley & Sons.

Grant, Eugene L., and Richard S. Leavenworth. 1996. *Statistical Quality Control*. New York: McGraw-Hill.

Hohn, Franz E. 1967. *Elementary Matrix Algebra*. New York: Macmillan.

Huang, K., T. Lee, and R. Y. Wang. 1999. *Quality Information and Knowledge*. Englewood Cliffs, NJ: Prentice Hall.

Jugulum, Rajesh. 2000. "New Dimensions in Multivariate Diagnosis to Facilitate Decision Making Process," Ph.D. Diss., Wayne State University.

Jugulum, Rajesh, Suneeta Ijari, and Madan Mohan Chakravarthy. 1996. "Six Sigma Quality Programs—Indian Case Examples." *Japanese Union of Scientists and Engineers (JUSE) Conference Proceedings*, Japan.

Jugulum, Rajesh, Shin Taguchi, and Kai Yang. 1999. "New Developments in Multivariate Diagnosis: A Comparison between Two Methods." *Journal of Japanese Quality Engineering Society* 7(5):62–72.

Kim, W. 2002. "On Three Major Holes in Data Warehousing Today." *Journal of Objective Technology* 1(4):39–47.

Kim, W., and B. Choi. 2003. "Towards Quantifying Data Quality Costs." *Journal of Objective Technology* 2(4):69–76.

Leitnaker, Mary G., Richard D. Sanders, and Cheryl Hild. 1996. *The Power of Statistical Thinking: Improving Industrial Processes.* Reading, MA: Addison-Wesley.

Madnick, S., R. Y. Wang, Y. W. Lee, and H. Zhu. 2009. "Overview and Framework for Data and Information Quality Research." *Journal of Data and Information Quality* 1(1):1–22.

Madnick, S., and H. Zhu. 2006. "Improving Data Quality through Effective Use of Data Semantics." *Data and Knowledge Engineering* 59(2): 460–475.

Mahalanobis, P. C. 1936. "On the Generalized Distance in Statistics." *Proceedings, National Institute of Science of India* 2: 49–55.

Montgomery, Douglas C. 1996. *Introduction to Statistical Quality Control.* New York: John Wiley & Sons.

Morrison, Donald F. 1967. *Multivariate Statistical Methods.* New York: McGraw-Hill.

———. 1990. *Multivariate Statistical Methods.* 3rd ed. McGraw-Hill Series in Probability and Statistics. New York: McGraw-Hill.

Park, Sung H. 1996. Robust Design and Analysis for Quality Engineering. London: Chapman & Hall.

Phadke, Madhav S. 1989. *Quality Engineering Using Robust Design.* Englewood Cliffs, NJ: Prentice Hall.

Phadke, M. S., and Genichi Taguchi. 1987. "Selection of Quality Characteristics and S/N Ratios for Robust Design." *Conference Record,* GLOBE-COM 87, IEEE Communication Society, Tokyo, Japan, 1002–1007.

Rao, C. R. 1997. *Statistics and Truth: Putting Chance to Work.* Singapore: World Scientific Publishing Co.

Redman, T. C. 1996. *Data Quality for the Information Age.* Boston: Artech House.

Siegel, Eric, and Thomas H. Davenport. 2013. *Predictive Analytics: The Power to Predict Who Will Click, Buy, Lie, or Die.* Hoboken: John Wiley & Sons.

Suh, N. P. 2001. *Axiomatic Design: Advances and Applications.* New York: Oxford University Press.

———. 2005. *Complexity: Theory and Applications.* New York: Oxford University Press.

Taguchi, Genichi. 1988. "The Development of Quality Engineering." *The ASI Journal* 1(1):5–29.

Taguchi, Genichi. 1993. *Taguchi on Robust Technology Development*. New York: ASME Press.

Taguchi, Genichi, and Rajesh Jugulum. 2000. "New Trends in Multivariate Diagnosis." *Sankhya, Indian Journal of Statistics,* Series B, Part 2:233–248.

Taguchi, Genichi, and Rajesh Jugulum. 2000. "Taguchi Methods for Software Testing." *Proceedings of JUSE Software Quality Conference I,* Japan.

Taguchi, G., R. Jugulum, and S. Taguchi. 2004. *Computer Based Robust Engineering: Essentials for DFSS*. Milwaukee, WI: ASQ Quality Press.

Taguchi, Genichi, and Jikken Kiekakuho. (1976–77). *Design of Experiments*. Vols. I and II. Tokyo: Maruzen Co.

Taguchi, Genichi, and Yuin Wu. 1985. *Introduction to Off-Line Quality Control*. Central Japan Quality Control Association, Tokyo, Japan.

Talburt, J. 2011. *Entity Resolution and Information Quality*. Burlington, MA: Morgan Kaufmann (Elsevier).

Tracy, N. D., J. C. Young, and R. L. .Mason. 1992. "Multivariate Control Charts for Individual Observations." *Journal of Quality Technology* 24:88–95.

Wu, C. F. J., and M. Hamada. 2000. *Experiments: Planning, Analysis, and Parameter Design Optimization*. New York: John Wiley & Sons.

Yang, Kai, and Basem S. EI-Haik. 2003. *Design for Six Sigma: A Roadmap for Product Development*. New York: McGraw-Hill.

Index